THE DUCK STAMP STORY

ART • CONSERVATION • HISTORY

*Detailed information
on the value and rarity
of every federal duck stamp*

Eric Jay Dolin

ERIC JAY DOLIN
BOB DUMAINE

Published by

krause
publications
The World's Largest Hobby & Collectibles Publisher

Please, call us for our free catalog. To place an order or receive our
free catalog, call 800-258-0929. For editorial comment and further
information, use our regular business telephone at (715) 445-2214.

Library of Congress Catalog Number: 99-67653
ISBN: 0-87341-814-X

Printed in Canada

Dedication

For Jennifer, Lily, and Harrison

EJD

For Rita, Libby, Michelle, my dog Lucy, and those wonderful ducks

BD

Contents

Foreword

When the authors of *The Duck Stamp Story* approached me about penning a foreword for this book, I was deeply honored to oblige. As the reader is about to discover, *The Duck Stamp Story* is the wonderfully told tale of the public's love for wildlife conservation. Since its inception in 1934, the Federal Duck Stamp Program has raised more than $500 million for conservation, with 98 cents out of every dollar going toward the purchase of more than 5 million acres of prime waterfowl habitat — that is an area twice the size of Yellowstone National Park (and then some). This efficient and popular federal program has even spun-off a youthful counterpart — the Junior Duck Stamp Program, a conservation education program for schoolchildren that combines art and biology. The Duck Stamp Program deserves to have its story told, and the authors have done a marvelous job of bringing the world of duck stamps to life.

The pages that follow tell the remarkable story of these incredible stamps, and the book is a fitting tribute to all the artists who create them . . . to the judges who decide the winning designs . . . to the talented professionals of the Bureau of Engraving and Printing who etch the plates . . . and to everyone — hunters, stamp collectors, wildlife lovers — who purchase duck stamps. Thanks to them, the future of waterfowl is taking wing.

The habitat acquired through the sale of duck stamps and related merchandise (including this book) have helped us expand and thereby strengthen the National Wildlife Refuge System, the only network of lands in the world dedicated to the conservation of fish and wildlife. Wildlife Refuges are places for waterfowl and hundreds of other species to rest, feed, and just plain live. By helping us preserve these places, the Duck Stamp Program has rallied a diverse group of people and involved them in wildlife conservation.

As we've come to learn at the Fish and Wildlife Service, duck stamps are not just for the birds. Hunters aged 16 or older are required to purchase them to hunt waterfowl, but others, such as bird watchers and hikers, buy them because they are passes for free entry into any of our more than 500 National Wildlife Refuges. Stamp collectors, conservationists, art lovers, and public service professionals like this Director of the U.S. Fish and Wildlife Service are also buying duck stamps.

Last July 1, at the First Day of Sale Event, I was extremely excited about having been chosen to be the very first buyer of the 1999-2000 duck stamp (graced with Jim Hautman's rendition of a pair of greater scaup), the one that would take us into the new millennium. Nothing could have kept me away that day . . . except impending motherhood. Realizing I would be unable to attend, I made sure Deputy Director John Rogers would go in my stead, and I made him promise to buy me that stamp.

What is it about duck stamps that inspire such passion? People have been known to fly from coast to coast to attend First Day of Sale events and duck stamp contests. For me, it appeals to many aspects of my life: as a conservationist, a bird watcher, a lover of wildlife photography, a biologist, and a civil servant. For duck stamp aficionados, the reasons are no doubt numerous and varied, but the attraction to the stamp comes from one simple truth: There is no better way to contribute to wildlife conservation than buying a duck stamp.

Jamie Rappaport Clark
Director, United States Fish and Wildlife Service

Foreword

Few conservation initiatives can claim as much success, and as much colorful history, as the Federal Duck Stamp Program. This bright idea was one of the first major wildlife conservation efforts in North America. And over the past six decades the program has evolved into much more.

The founding principle is still there — money raised from duck stamp sales is used to acquire and protect valuable wetlands and other habitats. But much of the program's success has come from its role in helping to establish a strong conservation ethic among outdoor enthusiasts.

The 1934 inaugural stamp gave waterfowl hunters and others one of the first systematic ways to contribute to the future health of wild populations of ducks, geese, and other species. And this spawned additional efforts by private groups like Ducks Unlimited to restore our continent's vanishing wildlife habitat. Fueled by a deep belief in the importance of giving back to our wild resources, supporters of these efforts have restored and protected millions of acres of valuable habitat in every corner of the continent.

It's entirely appropriate that North America's hunters and anglers should be at the forefront of such efforts. And it's also appropriate that some of North America's best wildlife art should be used as a very visible symbol of the Duck Stamp Program and its benefits to wildlife. The simple beauty of nature and its creatures is what draws many of us to the out-of-doors, and these miniature recreations of that beauty have made the Duck Stamp Program wildly popular with lovers of nature and lovers of art.

Much of that art can be found between the covers of this book, along with an exhaustive history of the program, its achievements, and the people who made it all possible. And, in keeping with the spirit of the Duck Stamp Program and all of the other conservation endeavors it has spawned, a portion of the proceeds from this book will be used in the continuing effort to provide places for wildlife.

A. Bronson Alcott, a 19th century educator and social reformer, wrote: "That is a good book which is opened with expectations and closed with profit." This volume should meet the expectations of even the most critical scholar of conservation and philately. Furthermore, by contributing to conservation it promises profits not only to the reader, but also to the continent's wild creatures and wild places.

As we enter the 21st Century, habitat projects funded through the Duck Stamp Program and others it has inspired will be all the more important and all the more urgent. More than half of North America's original wetlands — some of the most productive ecosystems on Earth — have been lost. And we continue to lose hundreds of thousands of additional wetland acres every year. As human populations continue to increase and place more and more demands on our fragile natural resources, we'll depend even more on sportsmen and others to help us find ways to use the land wisely, providing benefits for wildlife and for people as well.

Don Young
Executive Vice President,
Ducks Unlimited

Acknowledgments

Writing this book was a pleasure mainly because of the people who gave their time, knowledge, and assistance. We are extremely thankful to the following individuals and organizations for all they have done. The book is better for their contributions. Any errors are our own.

Robert C. Lesino, Program Manager for the Federal Duck Stamp Program, deserves special thanks because he introduced the two authors and supported the book from its inception. The assistance of his staff at the U.S. Fish and Wildlife Service Duck Stamp Office was invaluable. They include: Terry Bell, Lita Edwards, Anita Noguera (now with the Public Affairs Office at the Service), and Margaret Wendy. Mrs. Jeanette Cantrell Rudy's generous permission to use images from her collection of federal duck stamps enabled us to depict many rare and unusual stamps, and we thank her for that as well as the stories she shared with us. She is also to be congratulated for providing the money and materials necessary to establish a world-class, permanent exhibit at the Smithsonian Institution's National Postal Museum — "Artistic License: The Duck Stamp Story." It is a must-see for anyone interested in the program. The assistance of Jim O'Donnell, of the National Postal Museum, was invaluable in pulling together images from Mrs. Rudy's collection, as well as providing other key photos. We are also very appreciative of the support of James H. Bruns, Director of the museum. Christopher "Kip" D. Koss, grandson of J.N. "Ding" Darling and trustee of the J.N. "Ding" Darling Foundation, offered us important insights into his grandfather's life and graciously gave us permission to reproduce some of "Ding's" cartoons. William B. Webster, and the staff at his company, Wild Wings, provided great information and images for the book.

We would also like to thank the following who are listed in relation to the organizations for which they work: Leonard Buckley (retired), Gary Chaconas, Claudia Dickens, Larry Felix, Jerry L. Hudson Sr., Neil McGarry, and Cecelia Wertheimer of the Bureau of Engraving and Printing; Pete Lesher and Lindsley Hand of the Chesapeake Bay Maritime Museum; Mark Stumme of Drake University; Tracy Hirz and Bruce Mountain at the Iowa Natural Heritage Foundation; Arlene Mott, Montgomery County Public Libraries; Alan C. Villaverde and Maureen Brigid Gonzales of The Peabody Orlando; Elizabeth Jackson, Anne Post Roy (and her volunteers), Janet A. Tennyson and LaVonda Walton of the U.S. Fish and Wildlife Service; Robert McCown of the University of Iowa. Other individuals whose time, encouragement, and support helped make the book better include: Gary "Radar" Burghoff, David H. Curtis, Jack H. Elrod, Gene German, Dorothy Hautman, Karen Hollingsworth, Russell A. Fink, Dr. Christine Leche', Mark Meany, David McBride, Dr. Ian McTaggert-Cowen, R.D. Miner, George Reiger, Howard Richoux, Lowell Thompson, Joe and Donna Tonelli, David R. Torre, and E.J.S. Van Dam.

Winning federal duck stamp artists who graciously contributed their time, knowledge, and materials include: Arthur Anderson, Neal Anderson, Edward J. Bierly, Wilhelm Goebel, Adam Grimm, Jim, Joe, and Bob Hautman, Nancy Howe, Ron Jenkins, David Maass, Alderson Magee, Bruce Miller, Edward A. Morris, Martin R. Murk, Richard Plasschaert, Maynard Reece, John Ruthven, Phil Scholer, Daniel Smith, Stanley Stearns, Robert Steiner, and John S. Wilson.

The first person at Krause to express interest in this book was Wayne Youngblood and we thank him for passing our proposal to a very supportive acquisitions editor, Mary Jo Kewley. Kevin Michalowski, our editor, and the rest of the staff at Krause did a great job transforming the manuscript into a book.

Bob would like to give very special thanks to Rita Wahrer, who graciously provided needed support and understanding, and for her countless hours spent on scanning photos and helping gather data. Several employees of Sam Houston Duck Company were helpful, especially Pam Johnson, Libby Wahrer, and Michelle Dumaine, Bob's daughter. Finally, a sincere thanks to co-author Eric Jay Dolin for his patience, guidance, professionalism, and friendship throughout this project.

Eric would like to thank his parents, Ruth and Stanley Dolin, for always encouraging his writing and curiosity. Eric would also like to express his deep appreciation for Bob Dumaine, whose encyclopedic knowledge of duck stamps, devotion to the Federal Duck Stamp Program, and desire to create a comprehensive book made him the perfect co-author. More than anyone else, it was Eric's wife, Jennifer, daughter, Lily, and son, Harrison, who lived through the writing of this book. Their good humor and support were invaluable.

Eric Jay Dolin and Bob Dumaine,
January 1, 2000

Introduction

Flying north in the spring and south in the fall, each year migratory waterfowl repeat one of nature's most breathtaking journeys of birth and renewal. For the past sixty-seven years a stamp has helped the birds make the flight. Sales of the federal duck stamp, topping half a billion dollars, have enabled the United States Fish and Wildlife Service (U.S. F&WS) to purchase more than 5 million acres of National Wildlife Refuge (NWR) lands, critical habitat that migratory waterfowl and other species depend on for their survival. The duck stamp story is one of vision, dogged persistence, commitment, and beauty which conservationists, hunters, bird watchers, stamp collectors, and art lovers all can appreciate. Most importantly, the duck stamp story is about great results. The Federal Duck Stamp Program is one of the most successful conservation efforts ever devised. It is a true national treasure.

The program began in 1934 with the passage of the Migratory Bird Hunting Stamp Act. From that point forward, all migratory waterfowl hunters 16 and older have been required to purchase a duck stamp to legally hunt. Since then, sixty-seven federal duck stamps have been issued, each with a different design of migratory waterfowl species on its face. The term "duck stamp" is a misnomer because the program covers all migratory waterfowl, not just ducks. This is reflected on the stamps, some of which show geese and swans. Nevertheless, the stamps are commonly referred to as duck stamps and that is the convention used here.

The seeds of the federal duck stamp program were sown well before 1934. From the 1600s through the 1800s, the pressures of population growth, development, and hunting, particularly market hunting, combined to place many migratory waterfowl populations in a precarious position. By the end of the 19th century it was clear that action to reverse these declines was necessary, not just at the state level where it had already begun, but at the federal level, too. In the early decades of the 20th century, a variety of laws designed to protect migratory waterfowl were enacted. Still, by 1919, it was clear this was not enough. That year, the idea of a hunting stamp for migratory waterfowl made its first appearance on the national scene. Over the next fifteen years an incredibly diverse cast of characters conducted a lively and at times heated public debate on the merits of various bills that would create a "duck" stamp and preserve migratory waterfowl habitat. These deliberations resulted in the 1934 law and, as a testament to the foresight of the law's designers, the basic outlines of the Federal Duck Stamp Program have remained largely intact.

Being so successful, it is not surprising that the Federal Duck Stamp Program has spawned many imitators. At one time or another, all fifty states have run their own duck stamp programs. Local and tribal governments, as well as various private organizations have also issued duck stamps. The concept has spread beyond the United States' borders, to the point where eighteen foreign countries now boast duck stamp programs of their own.

The Federal Duck Stamp Program, like the migrations of waterfowl, follows an annual cycle. In the fall the art contest is held and the design that will appear on the next year's duck stamp is chosen. Hundreds of artists from around the country vie for the honor of being crowned winner and the level of competition is high. The winning artist and his or her design goes on a "victory tour" at waterfowl festivals,

Above Image: Mallards exploding off the water at Wheeler NWR, Alabama. Credit: John and Karen Hollingsworth.

Adam Grimm's beautiful oil painting of a mottled duck stretching in the sunlight after a preening session will grace the 2000 federal duck stamp. Grimm, 21, is the youngest winner ever of the Federal Duck Stamp Contest. He placed fourth in the 1996 Junior Federal Duck Stamp Contest. Credit: Adam Grimm.

stamp shows, and other events, spreading the word about the program. At the same time, the Bureau of Engraving and Printing (BEP) is busy at work translating the winning painting into a miniature work of art — the duck stamp. The Bureau's work is complete by early summer and the new duck stamp is officially issued for sale, usually on July 1. Then the cycle begins anew.

Duck stamp sales are not the only way the federal duck stamp program makes money to purchase critical habitat. Manufacturers of all types of products, including refrigerator magnets, computer mouse pads, and calendars are licensed by the U.S. F&WS's Duck Stamp Office to reproduce the image of the duck stamp on the items they sell. Part of the proceeds for such sales go to the U.S. F&WS to buy refuge lands. While the duck stamp image is the property of the U.S. F&WS, the artwork is not. The artists retain the rights to their art and can earn a considerable amount of money selling prints of their winning designs to collectors.

The Federal Duck Stamp Program spans many years and touches many lives. But mostly, it's for the ducks.

Conservation

Snow geese in wetland at Bosque Del Apache NWR, New Mexico. Credit: Karen Hollingsworth and the U.S. Fish and Wildlife Service.

FROM ABUNDANCE TO SCARCITY

When the first Europeans settled on the eastern shores of North America the abundance of wildlife astounded them. Beavers, wild turkeys, deer, waterfowl and other game seemed to have numbers without end. The situation was all the more amazing since the bounty of wildlife on the heavily populated European continent paled in comparison. In *New England's Prospect*, written in 1634, William Wood noted that "If I should tell you how some have killed a hundred geese in a week, fifty ducks at a shot, forty teals at another, it may be counted impossible though nothing more certain." Prodigious quantities of fish caused some settlers to claim that one could walk across streams on their backs without getting wet. Thomas Morton, who landed in Boston Harbor in 1624, called his surroundings "nature's Master-peece..." and concluded that "If this land not be rich, then is the whole world poore [sic]." Of all the species that inspired awe, none surpassed the passenger pigeon, whose annual migrations blanketed the sky. John Josselyn wrote in 1673 that "I have seen a flight of pidgeons in the spring, ... for four or five miles that to my thinking had neither beginning nor ending, length or breadth, and so thick I could see no sun."

While there was no arguing about the truly impressive numbers of wildlife in the New World, some colonists felt it necessary to temper the accounts sent back over the Atlantic lest potential immigrants harbor unrealistic expectations. Writing in 1628, Christopher Levett stated, "I will not tell you ... that the deer come when they are called, or stand still and look on a man until he shoot him, not knowing man from beast; ... [nor] that the fowls will present themselves to you with spits through them." Nevertheless, nature's abundance created the opportunity to provide for daily needs and to establish stronger trade ties domestically and with Europe through the sale of meat, fur, and feathers. With a seemingly inexhaustible supply of wildlife at their disposal, settlers hunted with zeal. Although the individual hunter seeking sustenance had an impact on wildlife populations, it was the market hunter who traded in wildlife for a living who took the greatest toll. Goose and swan feathers were in great demand in Europe where they were used to stuff quilting and feather beds, and the market hunters fed that demand. Morton, one of the first market hunters, said that he often "... had one thousand Geese before the muzzle of ... [his] gun." In the colonies, residents of growing cities and towns added to the demand for the game market hunters provided.

Subsistence and market hunting were not the only pressures bearing down on wildlife populations in the 17th century. In 1621, Edward Winslow of the Massachusetts Colony advised new immigrants and sportsmen to come prepared for excellent waterfowling near Plymouth. "Let your piece [musket] be long in the barrel and fear not the weight of it, for most of our shooting is done from stands." According to George Reiger, in his excellent book *Wings of Dawn*, the first duck hunt in America recorded in writing took place in the fall of 1686, when Baron Lahontan, Lord Lieutenant of the French Colony in Newfoundland, was at the north end of Lake Champlain in the company of Indian guides. Lahontan described the scene this way.

> ... thirty or forty of the savages that are very expert in shooting and hunting and perfectly well equipped with the proper places for finding waterfowl, ... [the] water huts are made of branches and leaves of trees, and contain three or four men.
>
> For a decoy, they have the skins of geese ... and ducks, dry'd and stuff'd with hay. The two feet being made fast with two nails to a small piece of a light plank, which floats around the hut. This place being frequented by wonderful numbers of geese, ducks, bustards, teals, and an infinity of other fowl unknown to Europeans; when these fowls see the stuff'd skins swimming

with the head erect, as if they were alive, they repair to the same place, and so give the savages the opportunity of shooting'em, either flying or upon the water; after which the savages get into their canoes and gather 'em up.

Adding to the impact of subsistence, market, and sport hunters on game birds was the fact that all of these groups operated without any legal restrictions on take. Bag limits and closed seasons were nonexistent. Still, hunting was affected by natural, technological, and commercial limitations. Migratory birds were only present at certain times of year and the widely-used flintlock rifle was inaccurate, highly susceptible to misfiring, and slow to reload. Making the first shot the most important and likely the only one before the birds had flown out of range. The lack of refrigeration, combined with the need to transport food unspoiled to consumers further limited the amount of game that could be profitably taken.

The expanding population of the colonies placed pressures on wildlife by building on or plowing under habitat. This was most likely of marginal impact during most of the 1600s and on through much of the next century when the settler's imprint on the land was small. In 1700 there were only 250,000 non-Indians in the colonies. It is unclear how much of a deleterious impact all of these pressures had on gamebirds during the first two centuries of colonization. There were no bird censuses taken and information is anecdotal and widely scattered. Yet, that

there were such negative impacts there can be no doubt, for it was during this time that gamebird protection first became an issue. For example, in 1708 certain counties in central New York instituted the first closed-season on birds, protecting the heath hen, ruffed grouse, quail, and turkey. Two years later, Massachusetts prohibited the use of camouflaged canoes or sailboats in the pursuit of waterfowl. It is not until the 19th century, however, that the taking of gamebirds and the need for government control became increasingly apparent.

All of the pressures on gamebirds in 1600s and 1700s were present in the 1800s, only more so. The population of the newly minted United States grew at a rapid rate, jumping from 4 million in 1790 to 63 million in 1890. This growth and the associated development impinged on prime gamebird habitat. The United States occupied land that coincided with the eastern flyway used by waterfowl and other birds on their annual migration northward and southward. The introduction of the railroad in the early 1800s spurred the creation of new cities and towns that spread throughout the country and onto other lands that were also in the paths of the historic flyways of migratory waterfowl.

With more mouths to feed, both subsistence and market hunters kept busy. Ducks, geese, quail and other gamebirds could be found on the menus of fancy restaurants and on the dinner tables of homes throughout the land. Great numbers of waterfowl were also slaughtered to satiate the demand for

Trumpeter swans at Malheur NWR in Oregon. Credit: Ray Erickson and the U.S. Fish and Wildlife Service.

*Dr. Harry Walsh holding two punt guns. These enormous guns could kill scores of birds with a single shot.
Credit: Harry Walsh Collection, Chesapeake Bay Maritime Museum.*

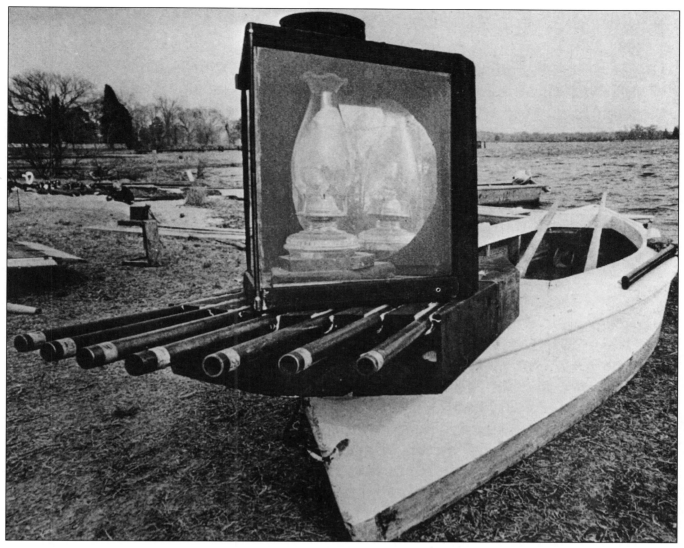

Skiff equipped with battery gun and gunning light. Credit: Harry Walsh Collection, Chesapeake Bay Maritime Museum.

woman's apparel. In one example, the Governor and Company of Adventures into Hudson's Bay, latter known as the Hudson's Bay Company, handled 17,671 swan skins between 1853 and 1877, the majority of which came from the trumpeter swan, North America's largest waterfowl. A market hunter, recounting his glory days, told a story that could certainly be repeated with different particulars many times over by his peers: "In 1858 I began to shoot for the market. I sold 2,300 ducks to one man in Janesville from September 15 to November 1 of that year. I used a muzzle-loading gun at that time. In 1872 I furnished the Sherman House, Chicago, with several hundred canvasbacks at fifty cents each." In the 1870s, It was not unusual for gunners on the Chesapeake Bay to kill upwards of 15,000 ducks in a single day.

Technological advances aided market hunters in their deadly trade. Improved refrigeration and the introduction of railroads meant game could travel farther, faster and in better condition, thereby increasing the size of the market and the demand for product. Around 1820, the flintlock began being replaced by muzzle-loading percussion guns, which were more reliable and accurate. Some of these guns were double-barreled allowing the hunter to get off two shots, quickly, one after the other. At about the same time, the punt gun was developed. More cannon, than gun, this new entrant into the war on gamebirds could throw a pound of shot per firing. Punt guns were used primarily at night, mounted or propped on a shallow-draft boat, which would be rowed into position near a group of birds feeding or resting on the top of the water. When the gunner got within eighty or so yards of the quarry, the powder was ignited and a mighty explosion sent the shot into the mass of stunned and helpless birds. It was not uncommon for a single shot to kill or severely injure scores of geese or ducks. Similar in impact, but different in design, was the so-called "battery," a

This 1850 wood engraving appeared in the Illustrated London News on December 4 of that year. While sink boxes were effective for hunting, they were susceptible to swamping in rough weather. An errant discharge of a hunter's gun could quickly send the boat to the bottom and/or seriously injure the hunter. Credit: Library of Congress.

Postcard printed around the turn of nineteenth century, showing Jesse Poplar in action in a sink box, on Chesapeake Bay, near Havre de Grace, Maryland. He was one of the best-known wing shots and market hunters of the day. An article appearing in the November 1, 1893 edition of the Baltimore Sun recounts one of his outings when he killed 5,000 ducks in a single day, taking most of the birds from a sink box. He and his partner, who manned the pickup boat, split $150 for their efforts, a considerable sum at that time. Credit: Harry Walsh Collection, Chesapeake Bay Maritime Museum.

grouping of gun barrels in a row mounted on the bows of small watercraft, sometimes accompanied by a gunning light. Although many punt guns and batteries did their work with great efficiency, some, especially the less professional ones, malfunctioned thereby reducing the population of market hunters, one or two at a time.

The sink-box was another addition to market hunter's arsenal that made its appearance around 1820. As the name implies, the hull of this small boat with a box-like compartment was submerged to the point where the top was even with the waterline. It was kept from sinking by two large wooden doors that spread out to either side of the box, serving as floatation devices. The doors would be weighted down to compensate exactly for the weight of a hunter as well as one or more loaded guns lying at his side. Painted to blend in with its surroundings, the sink-box would be moved into position near or above vegetation preferred by the targeted waterfowl. So as not to scare the birds, the hunter would lay flat in the well of the sink-box. When the birds, often lured by decoys, landed near the sink-box, the hunter would bolt upright and fire until they flew out of range. A nearby boat would then collect the dead and injured. Like the punt gun, sink-boxes were not particularly safe. Rough weather could swamp the craft, appropriately "sinking" it to the bottom, or cause one of the loaded guns to shift position, discharge and blow a hole in the hull leading to the same result. Worse, if the hunter's foot were in the way it could be blown off.

Adding to the technologies available to the market hunter was a new technique for attracting waterfowl. The mid-1800s saw the first use of live decoys, a ploy said to have originated in Massachusetts in 1840 with a group of cobblers. Looking for a way to make extra money, these men built a camouflaged shack along a pond where they took their tools and made shoes while waiting for geese to land. When a flock arrived they put down their tools and took up their guns. Rather than selling their slightly wounded geese, they tethered them to the shack and developed a captive flock that, in turn, lured other geese to land, whereupon the shooting commenced again. Combining their wages from shoemaking with the sale of the birds, it is safe to say that these cobblers' children did not go shoeless, especially when the sale of a single goose could rival a day's wages. From this curious beginning, the use of live duck and goose decoys became widespread, particularly in market hunting circles, for the balance of the 19th century and into the beginning of the next.

On a different plane from the market hunters were the sportsmen who sought game for recreation and personal consumption. During the 1600s and 1700s, sportsmen often sold surplus game and market hunters found sport in their work, blurring the distinctions between the two groups, but the divide became clearer in the 1800s. This was particularly true from the perspective of sportsmen who by the turn of the 20th century viewed market hunting and market hunters with disgust. Perhaps the best encapsulation of this view was offered in 1906 by former President Grover Cleveland, an avid duck hunter:

> There are those whose only claim to a place among duck hunters is based on the fact that they shoot ducks for the market. No duck is safe from their pursuit in any place, either by day or night. Not a particle of sportsmanlike spirit enters into this pursuit, and the idea never enters their minds that a duck has any rights that a hunter is bound to respect. The killing they do amounts to bald assassination - to murder for the sake of money. All fair-minded men must agree that duck hunters of this sort should be segregated from all others and placed in a section by themselves. They are the market shooters.

There are exceptions to every rule and not all sportsmen respected the "rights" of ducks. As one contemporary observer noted,

> ... unfortunately, there are men among the legion included under the title of sportsmen, as distinguished from market-gunners, who have never learned the virtue of moderation. They are never satisfied; they cannot kill enough... . The market-gunner has a poor business, but he has at least a tangible excuse for killing all he can. For the 'game-hog' there is no extenuation, unless we credit him with a weak mind.

The rise in market hunting not only often placed market hunters and sportsmen directly at odds when pursuing the same game, but the relentless nature of the market hunters' pursuit made already skittish birds more so. This frustrated sportsmen because it made it difficult to lure birds to decoys. An outcome of the growing acrimony between market and sport hunters was the creation of hunting clubs, privately financed preserves where wealthy sportsmen, often attended by servants, could hunt waterfowl without the disruption of market hunters and then repair to impressive lodges to relax, eat and recount the day's activities. The first was the Caroll's Island Club, just north of Baltimore, Maryland, established in 1832. It was soon joined by others around the country. Despite the clear distinctions between market hunters and true sportsmen, the latter, whose numbers grew steadily during the 1800s, must still share some, albeit a much smaller amount of the responsibility for placing migratory waterfowl populations under increasing pressure.

Towards the end of the 1800s, the plight of migra-

WILD DUCK SHOOTING.
ON THE WING.

A Currier & Ives print showing hunters patiently waiting for a good shot. Credit: Library of Congress.

tory waterfowl became more acute. The Labrador Duck, also called the "pied" or "sand-shoal" duck, rare at the beginning of the century became officially extinct on December 12, 1875, when the last specimen was shot on Long Island, New York. Other species were in serious decline. Near the top of this list was the beautiful wood duck, or "woodie." Ranging up and down the eastern seaboard, the woodie's habitat was among the most threatened by the expansion of cities and towns and the increase in market hunting. Once again, the march of technology helped fuel the decline. In the 1870s, breech-loading guns replaced the less accurate muzzle-loaders, and towards the end of the century the widespread use of repeating shotguns made the killing of birds more effective and efficient still. Market hunters, taking full advantage of the new technologies and the intense demand for waterfowl, prowled the countryside recording huge kills. One such hunter, on a single camping trip, bagged and delivered nearly 2,000 assorted birds to market. On a single morning along the Mississippi, the same hunter shot 122 wood ducks before 9 a.m. The serious state of affairs was captured by Clarence M. Weed and Ned Dearborn in their seminal book *Birds in Their*

Relation to Man, published in 1903:

> For years professional hunters slaughtered, dealers handled, and gluttons gobbled without reason or restraint. There could be but one result: wild fowl have become scarce. Gunners no longer return at night with more birds than they can carry; not seldom they come in empty-handed. But the millionaire makes up the shortage by paying higher prices. When a pair of canvas-backs [sic] bring a five-dollar note there is still money in shooting ducks.

Hunting was not solely to blame for this predicament. Deforestation, drainage of prime nesting and feeding areas to make way for farming and population growth, and a rise in the number of natural predators all contributed to the decline in waterfowl. As one observer at the time wrote, "[s]hooting alone has not brought the sport to its low ebb, broadly of course, the decline has come as a result of man's throwing to the four winds, the balance of nature." Migratory waterfowl were not the only animals threatened by the actions of man. The massive slaughter and near extinction of the buffalo fueled a lucrative trade in animal parts and became a symbol of waste and destruction. In 1867 it was estimated that 13 million buffalo roamed the plains; by 1883 their numbers had plummeted to 200. Another animal whose plight dramatically worsened throughout the 1900s was the passenger pigeon. At the turn of century there were estimated to be 5 billion of these birds in North America. The sightings of flocks miles long and deep, darkening the sky, were still common occurrences. In 1813, John James Audubon,

the great painter and naturalist, traveling in Kentucky claimed to have observed a flight of more than a billion birds. But pigeons, easy to kill and tasty, were pursued relentlessly by market hunters, and to a lesser extent, by sport hunters. Many millions of dead birds were shipped by rail to eager consumers. There is also evidence that passenger pigeon populations suffered from another form of hunting that was neither for sport nor the market. But "hunting" is certainly the wrong word for the

Joseph Whittington Lincoln (1859-1938) is generally recognized as one of America's greatest decoy carvers. He used a hatchet to chop the bodies of his decoys from white cedar logs. He then whittled the heads by hand, and painted each bird, setting them out to dry at his workshop in Accord, Massachusetts. The wood duck decoy (lower right) was intended to be a working decoy and was made for Lincoln's close friend, Chester Spear. But Spear liked it so much he put it on his mantle, a move for which later owners of the decoy can give thanks. The decoy sold at auction in 1996 for $165,000. Credit: From the collection of Joe and Donna Tonelli.

Successful market hunters artistically displaying their take around 1900. Credit: Library of Congress.

actions of colonists like these upstate New York villagers, depicted in James Fenimore Cooper's fictional book, *The Pioneers*. Mass hysteria seems more appropriate.

The reports of the firearms became rapid, whole volleys rising from the plain, as flocks of more than ordinary numbers [passenger pigeons] darted over the opening [of a highway], shadowing the field like a cloud; and then the light smoke of a single piece would issue from among the leafless bushes on the mountain, as death was hurled on the retreat of affrighted birds, who were rising from a volley, in a vain effort to escape. Arrows, and missils [sic] of every kind, were in the midst of the flocks; and so numerous were the birds, and so low did they take their flight, that even long poles, in the hands of those on the sides of the mountain, were used to strike them to the earth... . None pretended to collect the game, which lay scattered over the fields in such profusion as to cover the very ground with the fluttering victims.

How often such attacks took place, there is no record. That they took place, there is little doubt. The impact of the dogged pursuit of passenger pigeons became readily apparent toward the century's end when masses of pigeons no longer blanketed the sky. Calls for protecting this species in the late 1880s had little effect, and in 1914, Martha, the last passenger pigeon died in a Cincinnati Zoo.

While pigeons were killed for their meat, other birds came under attack because of their beauty and the millinery demands of the day. The fashionable woman of the Victorian era often wore hats festooned with the brightly colored plumes of birds such as snowy egrets, roseate spoonbills, the scarlet ibis, and the Great White Heron. Some went so far as to have landscaped scenes atop their heads, replete with stuffed birds strutting about. A Chicago reporter, observing this trend at the century's end, wrote, "it will be no surprise to me to see life-sized turkeys or even ... farmyard hens, on fashionable bonnets before I die." At that time roughly 5 million birds were being killed annually for fashion's sake. One hunter set a record by killing 141,000 birds in a single season. An ornithologist strolling through the streets of New York surveyed 700 women's hats and found 542 of them to be displaying parts of various birds. Worse, most of the birds used for millinery purposes were taken during the breeding seasons when plumes were at their most beautiful. Since the plume was often all the hunter was after, the rest of the bird was left behind to rot.

As the numbers of migratory waterfowl, buffalo, passenger pigeons, plume birds, and other species declined over the course of the 19th century, public concern for wildlife grew. One of the early voices for wildlife protection was Audubon's. His massive tomes, *Birds in America* (1827-1838) and *Viviparous Quadrupeds of North America* (created with his sons between 1831 and 1839), illustrated the impressive range and beauty of the natural kingdom to a broader audience. He was highly critical of the hunt-

SHOOTING WILD PIGEONS IN IOWA.

Even as late as the 1850s, when this wood engraving was made, there were still great numbers of passenger pigeons. These Iowa farmers were shooting the pigeons to protect their crops. The accompanying text reads, in part, "[t]he farmers of many of the western counties were much troubled with pigeons in the spring; in fact the hordes became a perfect scourge." Credit: Library of Congress.

Fashionable women with a penetrating gaze and bird plumage upon her hat. Credit: National Audubon Society.

John James Audubon is most famous for his drawings of birds and wildlife. These wood ducks and Canada geese are two of his most beautiful renditions of migratory waterfowl. Credit: Library of Congress.

ing practices that were common for the day. Witnessing a buffalo hunt in 1843, Audubon stated, "this cannot last. Even now there is a perceptible difference in the size of the herds. Before many years the buffalo, like the great auk, will have disappeared."

Other influential people raised their voices in defense of wildlife and nature. Transcendentalist philosophers, such as Henry David Thoreau and Ralph Waldo Emerson, extolled the virtues of living in harmony with the natural world. John Muir, gave voice to the "preservationist" movement, arguing that humankind's intrusion and impact on nature should be kept to a bare minimum. "Conservationists" such as Gifford Pinchot also wanted to protect wildlife and wildlands but viewed the relationship between man and nature in more utilitarian terms, advocating multiple use of natural resources and achieving the greatest good for the greatest number of people. George Bird Grinnell, the famous editor of *Forest and Stream* (later to become *Field & Stream*), in an 1894 editorial focused his attention on the need to halt the depredations of the market hunter.

The game supply which makes possible the general indulgence in field sports is of incalculable advantage to individuals and the nation; but a game supply which makes possible the traffic in game as a luxury has no such importance. If this is granted, public policy demands that the traffic in game be abolished... We suggest this declaration, the sale of game should be forbidden at all seasons, as a plank in the platform of that vast body of men scattered in hosts over the country ... interested in preserving the game of the continent...

Calls for action led to the creation of organizations devoted to protection of wildlife, such as the American Ornithologists Union (1883), the Audubon Society (1886), The Boone and Crockett Club (1887), and the Sierra Club (1892). It became more common for magazines and newspapers to educate their readers on the worsening situation. Perhaps the most influential of these was *Forest and Stream*, the bulk of whose readers were the very sportsmen who could most clearly see the results of widespread wildlife decline.

One of the magazine's correspondents sent back this report in 1884 from the Platte River in Nebraska. "The gunners have so increased in the last three years that the weary goose, coming down from the North, or in from the fields to rest and slake its thirst, can hardly find a place out of the range of some one's gun. Blinds line the [sand] bars in the stream for 100 miles so thickly as to preclude all chance of a fair bag."

By 1880 all states had passed legislation protecting various species of wildlife. In 1870, California took the novel step of setting aside land to create a sanctuary for birds in what is now known as Lake Merritt in downtown Oakland. At this time, the Federal government took its first steps to protect the nation's natural heritage. The United States Bureau of Fisheries and the Division of Economic Ornithology and Mammalogy were created in 1871 and 1886, respectively. Ancestors of the modern-day U.S. F&WS, these agencies undertook programs aimed at insuring the integrity of wildlife populations. Yellowstone, the first National Park, was created in 1872, and was followed by Yosemite and Sequoia national parks in 1890. And in 1892, President Benjamin Harrison established the first federal sanctuary for wildlife, "the Afognak Forest and Fish-Culture Reserve," located on Kodiak Island in Alaska, which some claim was the nation's first true wildlife refuge.

The 1800s were also a time of changes that held out hope for halting and perhaps reversing the declining numbers of waterfowl species. States, in increasing numbers, passed laws restricting the hunting of such birds. In 1838, New York instituted the first law against the use of multiple guns [batteries] on waterfowl and in 1846 Rhode Island enacted the first restrictions on the spring shooting of birds, including the black and wood duck. While both of these laws became so unpopular that they were later repealed, other states eventually took up the "closed season" banner. In 1872, spurred on by sportsmen concerned about their quarry, Maryland provided "rest days" for redhead ducks and canvasbacks, when they were not to be hunted. Three years later, Arkansas became the first state to outlaw the market hunting of geese and ducks.

Although the protection of waterfowl was still the province of the states, the rumblings of concern at the federal level were beginning to be heard. On October 22, 1891, W. M. Elder, Secretary of the Chatham Fish and Game Protective Association, penned a letter to President Benjamin Harrison asking him to support local efforts to protect gamebirds.

With the knowledge of your great interest in field sports, I take the liberty of addressing you on a subject which is of vital importance to the propagation and protection of game birds. We

On April 15, 1852, Henry David Thoreau wrote in his journal: "How indispensable our one or two flocks of [Canada] geese in spring and autumn. What would be a spring in which that sound was not heard? Coming to unlock the fetters of northern rivers. Those animal steamers of the air." Credit: Robert Shallenberger and the U.S. Fish and Wildlife Service.

are using our strength towards the abolishment of spring wildfowl and snipe shooting and also of shooting woodcock in the summer. As a sportsman, you can readily perceive the short-sighted policy of killing and disturbing birds on their way to breeding haunts, the result of which has been to steadily diminish the class of game mentioned, and you will at once recognize the great benefit which would surely follow united action on the part of the different states.

To bring this question of a close[d] season during the spring and early summer to a successful settlement, it should be placed prominently before the sportsmen of the country and by them taken to their respective legislatures. We know the problem is a difficult one and it may take years to accomplish the results we are seeking, but I feel that we are acting rightly in asking your approval and cooperation. Your recommendation of the change would have great influence and be most effective in crystallizing the efforts of the game societies of the country.

Harrison replied:

I have your letter of the 22d, in which you discuss the necessity of a closed season for migratory game birds. I do not doubt that the adoption of legislation by the States, prohibiting the shooting of these classes of game birds, would greatly tend to increase their numbers, and I have sometimes thought that it was essential to the preservation of some of these species.

Whether Mr. Elder was emboldened or disheartened by Harrison's letter, this correspondence is extremely important on several levels. It clearly shows the locus of control and action on waterfowl issues still residing at the state and local level in the late 1800s. It is also the first known instance of official Presidential concern for and understanding of the plight of migratory waterfowl. Finally, it serves to foreshadow the future and critical role of the federal government in the protection of such species.

Above: President Benjamin Harrison Credit: Library of Congress.

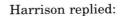

Right: A letter from President Harrison to W. M. Elder, expressing concern about the preservation of migratory waterfowl. Credit: Sam Houston Duck Company.

THE FEDERAL GOVERNMENT STEPS IN

However reluctant the federal government was to impinge on state and local prerogatives to manage wildlife, it overcame its trepidation at the turn of the 19th century with the passage of the Lacey Act in 1900, named after its sponsor, Representative John F. Lacey (R-IA). The law had two main purposes — to supplement and enforce state wildlife protection laws and to prohibit the importation of species perceived to be injurious to agricultural and horticultural interests. It was the first of these purposes that legislators felt was the most important and that had the most direct bearing on migratory waterfowl. The Lacey Act made it illegal to transport birds killed in violation of state laws across state boundaries and levied significant fines on those caught breaking the law.

Not too long after the Lacey Act's passage another event took place which was of pivotal importance to the future of waterfowl protection. On September 13, 1901, while hiking down Mt. Marcy, the highest peak in the Adirondacks, Vice President Theodore Roosevelt was informed that President William McKinley lay dying, the victim of an assassin's bullet. Roosevelt hastened back to Washington to take the reigns of government. Many preservationists as well as conservationists viewed Roosevelt's ascension to the Presidency with great optimism. His concern for nature and wildlife was well known. A veritable force of nature himself, Roosevelt aggressively embraced the out of doors and the rugged life. So great was his immersion in natural history that during his first years at Harvard University he thought of going into that profession, only to settle on politics and law a bit later, apparently shifting course to please his college beaux and future wife. He was an avid hunter and became one of the founders of Boone and Crockett Club, originally a select group of 100 well-off and well-connected men who had each killed at least three species of North American big game "in fair chase." A sportsman in every sense of the word,

Roosevelt greatly respected the game he pursued. By the turn of the century he began voicing concerns about the depletion of wildlife. "When I hear of the destruction of a species," he penned in a letter, "I feel just as if all the works of some great writer had perished."

Roosevelt had the utmost respect for Muir and his preservation philosophy, yet when it came to man's relation to nature, the new President eschewed preservation in favor of conservation. He sought to balance human and nature's needs, benefiting both and he certainly lived up to his moniker as the "Conservation President." One of the best examples of his direct approach to wildlife protection was the creation of the Pelican Island NWR in Florida. This small, federally owned island was an important rookery for brown pelicans which influential ornithologists and birders had been arguing needed protection from the ravages of market hunting. Roosevelt first considered selling the land to the Audubon Society so they could turn it into a bird sanctuary, but avoided this path because of concerns about the legality of selling federal land. Roosevelt then asked one of his assistants, "is there any law that will prevent me from declaring Pelican Island a federal bird reservation." Upon hearing that there was not, Roosevelt said, "very well, then I so declare it." On March 14, 1903, Roosevelt issued an executive order setting aside Pelican Island "as a preserve and breeding ground for native birds."

Most chroniclers see Roosevelt as the father of the National Wildlife Refuge System (NWRS), while a small minority claim it is President Harrison who should get the honor with his set aside of Afognak Island in 1892. Even if you grant paternity to Harrison, there is no debating that it was Roosevelt who got the NWRS on its feet. By the end of his second term, Roosevelt had created 52 wildlife refuges. Through his actions he made it clear that the federal government had the right and the responsibility to take action to conserve wildlands and wild-

Theodore Roosevelt, the "Conservation President," in a photograph taken shortly after leaving office. He once said, "[t]he Nation behaves well if it treats the natural resources as assets which it must turn over to the next generation increased and not impaired in value." Credit: Library of Congress.

Theodore Roosevelt and John Muir on Glacier Point, Yosemite Valley, California (1906). Credit: Library of Congress.

life, including migratory waterfowl. In so doing, he established a pattern of federal leadership on this issue that would have incalculable benefits in the years to come. Taking its cue from Roosevelt, Congress got into the act in 1905, by authorizing the President to establish a bison refuge in the Oklahoma Territory. Four years later, Congress for the first time authorized, and President William Howard Taft approved the use of federal funds to protect wildlife through the purchase of land, which led to the creation of the National Bison Range, now part of the refuge system. States, too, put aside land

for refuges, with Indiana becoming the second one to do so, in 1903, thirty-three years after California had led the way with the establishment of the Lake Merritt sanctuary. Pennsylvania (1905), Alabama (1907), Massachusetts (1908), Idaho (1909), and Louisiana (1911) soon followed suit.

The establishment of refuges benefited migratory waterfowl and was a much-needed shot in the arm for those who had been fighting for habitat and species protection. Unfortunately, the benefits hoped for from the implementation of the Lacey Act were more illusory. Highly commendable in theory, in practice the Lacey Act was not very successful. Many states had weak wildlife protection laws. Even where strong laws were on the books, a lack of state enforcement often restricted federal efforts. The work of "citizen-enforcers," members of conservation organizations who prowled markets looking for violations, while noteworthy was hardly enough to make up for enforcement from above. Despite these shortcomings, the Lacey Act was not a complete failure. In many instances it helped to curb illegal trade in game. Due to its relative lack of success the Lacey Act also highlighted the need for stronger government involvement in this area. Organizations and individuals concerned about the plight of migratory waterfowl and other birds redoubled their efforts to strengthen state laws and to push the federal government into a more active role as the protector of those species.

In 1904, Congressman George Shiras (R-PA) introduced "A Bill to Protect Migratory Birds of the United States," that would move the federal government from the periphery of migratory bird management to center stage. The bill highlighted the inadequacies of the Lacey Act and then proposed a novel idea: "Be it enacted in Congress assembled, That all wild geese, and wild swans, brant, wild ducks, snipe, plover, woodcock, rail, wild pigeons, and all other migratory game birds which do not remain permanently the entire year within the borders of any State or Territory shall hereafter be deemed to be within the custody and protection of the Government of the United States."

The bill went on to direct the Department of Agriculture to establish closed seasons throughout the country to protect the birds when they were at their most vulnerable. More of a trial balloon than a serious attempt to create a new law, Shiras hoped that the premise of the bill, that the federal government assume the role of protecting these species, would stir a national debate. It certainly did. Relying on the Constitution's sweeping Interstate Commerce Clause, Congressman Shiras's proposal to extend the federal reach in this manner stirred the anger of many constitutional scholars and state's rightists who were in firm opposition to this form of creeping federalism. Shiras's bill died with the end of the congressional session, but the idea it embraced did not.

Audubon Societies, the American Ornithologists Union, and other supporters of the increased protection of migratory waterfowl who were favorably disposed towards federal intervention lobbied, in favor of this new approach. *Field & Stream* weighed in with editorials pointing out how such federal intervention squared with the Constitution. In the ensuing years other bills, quite similar to Shiras's were introduced and voted down. In 1912, the Weeks-McClean bill, named after its sponsors,

Congressman John W. Weeks (R-MA) and George P. McClean (R-CT), became the focus of attention. Much more far-ranging that the earlier bills, it placed all migratory game and insectivorous birds as well as migratory songbirds under federal control and forbid the taking of them except as provided for by federal regulations.

A powerful array of supporters lined up behind it, including the aforementioned groups as well as the New York Zoological Society and the newly created American Game Protective Association (AGPA), the main goal of which was to promote wildlife restoration domestically and abroad. Henry Ford, famed automobile manufacturer and bird lover, also threw his weight behind the bill's passage and dispatched one of his top advertising men to Washington with orders to remain there until the bill was passed. Ford added to the pressure by asking the 600 Ford dealers to write to their congressman, urging passage.

Opposition to the bill was strong as well. State's rightists still chafed at the notion of federal intrusion under the guise of protecting interstate commerce. In March 1913, after months of lobbying on both sides, it appeared as if the Weeks-McLean bill would suffer the same fate as its predecessors. But then some of the bill's wilier supporters, opting to avoid controversy, attached the content of Weeks-McLean to a larger agricultural appropriations bill that passed both houses of Congress, landing on President Taft's desk during the waning hours of his Presidency. Taft, convinced that the Weeks-McLean bill was an unconstitutional infringement on state powers, signed the appropriations bill totally unaware that the text of Weeks-McLean was buried within. When later commended by a sportsmen friend for passing the nation's first migratory bird protection law, Taft bristled, stating that had he known that Weeks-McLean was included, he would have vetoed the entire appropriations bill. It would not be the last time that the cause of migratory bird protection benefited from congressional sleight of hand.

No sooner was the Weeks-McLean law in place than it came under serious attack, both in Congress where calls were made for its repeal and through the courts where litigation threatened to overturn it. The law's supporters, especially nervous that it would not withstand Constitutional scrutiny, immediately laid the groundwork for achieving the law's goals through alternative means. Leading this effort was Senator Elihu Root (R-NY), who supported the concept of having the federal government protect migratory waterfowl but believed that the approach offered by Weeks-McLean was unconstitutional. He preferred an approach based on the President's uncontested right to enter into international treaties. As a result, just prior to the passage of Weeks-McLean, Root introduced a resolution giving the President the power to enter into treaties with other countries for

the purpose of protecting migratory birds. Root's approach didn't garner much attention until Senator McLean took up the cause and introduced a similar resolution, which passed on July 7, 1913.

With Weeks-McLean on shaky ground, the Departments of State and Agriculture immediately began drafting a migratory bird treaty, but their efforts were delayed by the onset of World War I and the shifting priorities of a country at war. Nevertheless, progress on the treaty did not stop and on August 16, 1916, the Migratory Bird Treaty between the United States and Great Britain was signed in Canada, and two days later it was signed by President Woodrow Wilson. The treaty was intended to save "from indiscriminate slaughter and ... [to insure] the preservation of such migratory birds as are useful to man or harmless, ..." It established open and closed seasons for game birds, prohibited the hunting of insectivorous birds, and greatly restricted the taking of other non-game birds. It also repealed the Weeks-McLean law and singled out the wood duck and eider for special protection. It took nearly two more years for Congress to approve the treaty, and on July 3, 1918 it went into effect. The passage of the treaty was the last act for those who had actively opposed the Weeks-McLean law in the courts. In 1914, a federal court had ruled the law unconstitutional because it infringed on state rights.

As the appeals process dragged on, the law's opponents eagerly awaited the day when their case would be heard by the Supreme Court, but that day never came. With the treaty in place and the Weeks-McLean law repealed, the question of the law's legality became moot and the case was dropped.

Creating regulations for the new treaty went to the Biological Survey, a division within the Department of Agriculture. The Survey, in turn, eliminated spring and market hunting, restricted the Fall hunting season to three and a half months, and established daily bag limits of ten geese and twenty-five ducks per hunter. A turnaround for bird populations appeared to be in sight.

Just as the Weeks-McLean law before it, the treaty came under immediate attack from state's rightists, market hunters who saw it restricting their livelihood, and some large duck hunting clubs in the Midwest who were opposed to federal incursions into their realms. While the Presidential power to enter into treaties rested on solid constitutional grounds, there was still some doubt as to whether that power extended to migratory waterfowl. The only body that could definitively answer that question was the Supreme Court and it wasn't long before they were given the opportunity to do so.

In the spring of 1919, Frank McAllister, Attorney General of Missouri, and four of his hunting buddies

Blue-winged teal pair at Horicon NWR, Wisconsin. Credit: John and Karen Hollingsworth.

went out for a shoot. That such spring shooting was illegal under the Migratory Bird Treaty didn't concern them and by 10 a.m. they had bagged seventy-six ducks and one goose. Their excitement didn't last long. Someone had tipped off U.S. Game Warden, Ray Holland, and he arrested the group, each of whom immediately posted $1,000 bail and was released. This encounter soon ended up in court, becoming the heavily publicized case of *Missouri v. Holland*, in which Missouri sought to have the treaty overturned claiming that it usurped state's rights under the Constitution. The District Court for the Western District of Missouri sided with the federal government and Missouri appealed to the Supreme Court where, on April 19, 1920, the District Court's decision was affirmed. The treaty would be the law of the land. Writing for the court, Justice Oliver Wendell Holmes eloquently pointed out the weaknesses of the state's arguments:

> The state ... founds its claim of exclusive authority upon an assertion of title to migratory birds ... To put the claim of the state upon title is to lean upon a slender reed. Wild birds are not in the possession of anyone ... the whole foundation of the state's rights is the presence within their jurisdiction of birds that yesterday had not arrived, to-morrow [sic] may be in

another state, and in a week a thousand miles away... Here a national interest of very nearly the first magnitude is involved. It can be protected only by national action in concert with that of another power... But for the treaty and the statute, there soon might be no birds for any powers to deal with. We see nothing in the Constitution which compels the government to sit by while a food supply is cut off and the protectors of our forests and of our crops are destroyed. It is not sufficient to rely upon the states. The reliance is vain, ...

After this decision, McAllister and his four friends plead guilty to violating the treaty and paid their fines.

In the legislative arena the decade between 1910 and 1920 was a heady time for those who worked for the protection of migratory waterfowl. The Weeks-McLean Bill and, more importantly, the Migratory Bird Treaty Act signaled a fundamental shift in the terrain. With the addition of federal oversight and enforcement, the future looked brighter. Another positive sign was the increase in the number of refuges. The federal government added more land to this growing system of protected areas, mostly for colonial nesting birds. The ranks of states establishing their own refuges also continued to swell.

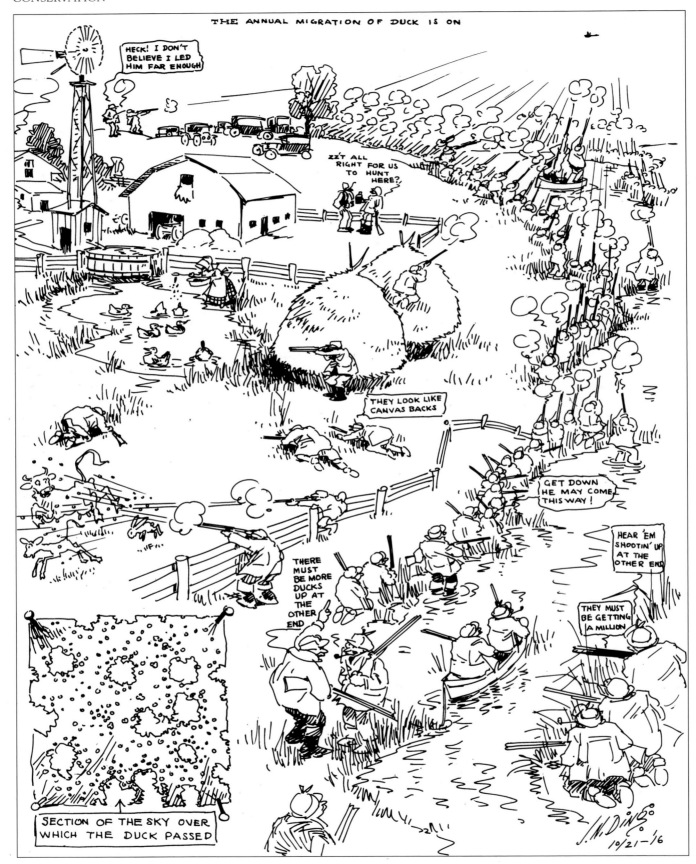

"Ding" Darling's "The Annual Migration of Duck is On" (October 21, 1916). Credit: the J.N. "Ding" Darling Foundation.

Despite the promise of this legislation and the addition of refuges, migratory waterfowl populations were still in trouble. On October 21, 1916, a cartoon appearing in the *New York Herald Tribune* brilliantly captured the concerns shared by many. Titled "The Annual Migration of Duck is On," the cartoon painted a simultaneously hilarious and deeply disturbing picture of the pressures facing migratory waterfowl. A raft of hunters all aiming for a lone duck overhead end up missing the duck but turning the sky into a tattered rag, with holes throughout, so great was their firepower. The artist was Jay Norwood Darling, affectionately known as "Ding," a moniker derived by combining the first initial of his last name with its last three letters. A well-known figure that would become one of the most influential political cartoonists of the century, and a two-time Pulitzer Prize winner, Darling was, as one of his peers recounted, "an extreme extrovert, awed by nobody, overflowing with self-confidence." He listed as hobbies, dairy farming, black bass fishing, rock gardening, Roquefort cheese, ornithology and duck shooting. Darling was also a dedicated conservationist. He believed to his core that a nation that squanders its natural resources is failing to wisely invest in its future. This cartoon was published on his 40th birthday and was his debut as a nationally syndicated political cartoonist. It was one of the first and the most influential in a long string of cartoons in which Ding would highlight the critical need for the

J.N. "Ding" Darling, 1876-1962. Credit: the J.N. "Ding" Darling Foundation.

increased protection of migratory waterfowl. His cartoons helped to galvanize public opinion in favor of such protection and in that capacity he was a powerful ally to those working at the state and federal levels on this issue. Later on, in the 1930s, Ding would lay down his pen for a short time to play an essential role in the passage and implementation of the Migratory Bird Hunting Stamp Act, which created the Federal Duck Stamp Program.

The Survey argued that more refuges were needed to insure healthy waterfowl populations. A report in 1917 stated that "[I]ncreased protected areas for breeding places for the migratory wild geese, ducks, cranes, swans, ... should be provided. Additional wildlife refuges along the paths of migration are needed in order to secure improved and equalized opportunities for shooting wild fowl for food and recreation ..."

Nevertheless, towards the end of the teens anecdotal information indicated that migratory populations were rebounding, with observers reporting larger migrations of birds. It is not clear what led to these changes, but a strong argument can be made that they were more the result of natural population fluctuations, state actions, and the reduction in hunting pressures during the war than of stepped up enforcement efforts at the federal level. In these early years, the budgets given to the Survey to implement the Migratory Bird Treaty Act were meager, often less than the amount single states spent on waterfowl regulation. Making matters worse, the liberal bag limits allowed under the Act often didn't offer enough protection to the birds and by 1920, eleven states imposed limits below the federal maximum. Larger populations, however, didn't mean healthy populations, and whatever increases there might have been were obscured by larger social and cultural changes that spelled trouble for waterfowl.

As World War I raged, the United States responded to food shortages among our allies with the stepped up production of wheat and other staples. This led to the draining of the wetlands waterfowl relied on during their annual migrations. After the war, America entered a period of peace and prosperity that led to the further transformation of the landscape. Not only were more farms needed to feed the burgeoning population, which had swelled from 76 million in 1900 to 106 million 1920, but those same people created a great demand for new construction of houses, office buildings, and roads. During the first part of the 20th century, 100 million acres of wetlands were drained to make way for these new developments, placing waterfowl in an increasingly precarious position. The return to normalcy after the war also led to an increase in the number of hunters. By the early 1920s, more than 4 million state hunting licenses were being issued annually, a dramatic increase over the one and a half

The earliest known example of art by "Ding" Darling, drawn when he was eight years old. "Jay," the artist, and his older brother "Frank," trail their parents. Credit: the J.N. "Ding" Darling Foundation.

million that were given out in 1911. Part of this increase was due to the combined effects of shortened workweeks and increased wealth. With more leisure time and the financial means to enjoy it, many turned to outdoor pursuits including hunting. And the hunters of the late teens and early twenties had advantages not shared by their predecessors. Gun designs had improved even further, giving the hunter an added edge. New roads and a dramatic increase in the number of privately owned cars, allowed hunters to venture farther afield in the pursuit of game and, inevitably into areas that formerly were somewhat protected by virtue of being so remote.

Those who cared about maintaining healthy populations of migratory waterfowl greeted these trends with alarm. Theories abounded on what action should be taken, but the debate soon focused on the idea of creating public shooting grounds and more refuges. The most active support for such measures came from Sportsmen and, in particular the AGPA. At first, AGPA called for public shooting grounds only. In May 1919, E. A. Quarles, the editor of the AGPA's *Bulletin* presented the organization's proposal to purchase lands where the public could hunt game. Motivating this position was the concern that as migratory waterfowl populations decreased, only the wealthy hunters with access to private hunting clubs would be able to pursue their passion. As Quarles noted:

[s]ome people believe that this country is on the verge of becoming Europeanized to the extent that in a very few years we will have not shooting except by land-owners or lessees on their private reserves. This is something which no patriotic American wants, because we believe that one of the keystones of our national

prosperity is the free shooting which our citizens have enjoyed. There is no question but that free shooting over large sections of the country is seriously endangered and that in some places it has disappeared.

The editorial reprinted a resolution recently adopted by AGPA, calling for state fish and game departments to take up this issue and find ways to acquire lands where public shooting could take place. Two months later, John B. Burnham, President of the AGPA, elaborated upon this proposal, pointing out that not only public shooting grounds were needed, but also refuges, or "reserves" where shooting was not allowed:

If the young men of the next generation are to enjoy from the country's wild life anything like the benefits derived by the present outdoor man, we must be the one to shoulder the burden and see that our thoughtlessness or selfishness

does not allow us to squander that which we hold in trust.

Public shooting grounds must be established for the rank and file of the gunners who cannot afford to belong to exclusive clubs. This is the duty of the state, but sportsmen must take the initiative. In many places land of little value from a commercial standpoint furnishes the best hunting territory. Why shouldn't such tracts be set aside as public recreation grounds for all time to come? ... With the public shooting grounds must come more reserves where the birds should have absolute protection, for as the country becomes more settled, shooting would become impossible without them...

One issue left unanswered was how the purchase of such lands would be accomplished. Shortly after this editorial appeared, however, the proposal for public shooting grounds took a turn in the federal direction and an idea for funding was born.

Fulvous whistling ducks at Blackwater NWR, Maryland. Credit: John and Karen Hollingsworth.

COULD A STAMP HELP?

For some time, Ray Holland, of *Missouri v. Holland* fame, and his boss, George A. Lawyer, Chief U.S. Game Warden, had talked about the need to set aside refuges for migratory waterfowl, but they were unsure how to finance this effort. Shortly after Holland left federal service to become editor of the *Bulletin of the AGPA*, his old boss came across a news release from Dr. E.W. Nelson, Chief of the Survey, in which Dr. Nelson advocated the need for protecting wetlands. This gave Lawyer an idea. What if the federal government required hunters to purchase hunting stamps, through the post office, and used the proceeds to purchase land? This would have the dual benefit of generating a revenue stream while not creating another burdensome bureaucracy. Lawyer wrote to Holland, "why not sell [hunting stamps] as the government is selling war savings stamps?" Lawyer even went so far as to sketch out a possible design for the new hunting stamp. His idea

for a hunting stamp did not come out of thin air. For many years states had been requiring hunters and fisherman to purchase licenses. In 1909, California became the first state to issue paper licenses featuring designs. Lawyer's sketch for a federal hunting license came right on the heels of his trip to California, during which he purchased a $10, 1919-1920 non-resident hunting license. There is little doubt that Lawyer was influenced by this and other state licenses in sketching his own design for a federal issue.

The idea of a federal hunting stamp took hold and the AGPA, along with other organizations, began pushing it into the national consciousness. In the July 1920 issue of the *Bulletin*, Holland wrote:

> [I]s a Federal hunting license practical? Is it desirable? It has been suggested that gunners who hunt migratory game birds be required to

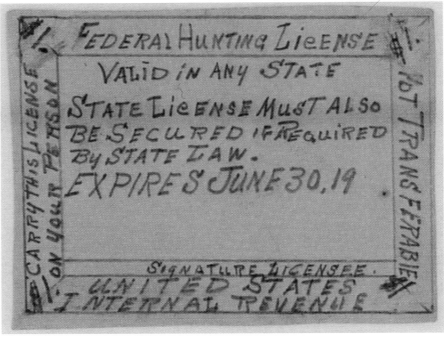

George Lawyer's proposed design for the first federal hunting license, drawn in 1919. Credit: David R. Torre Collection.

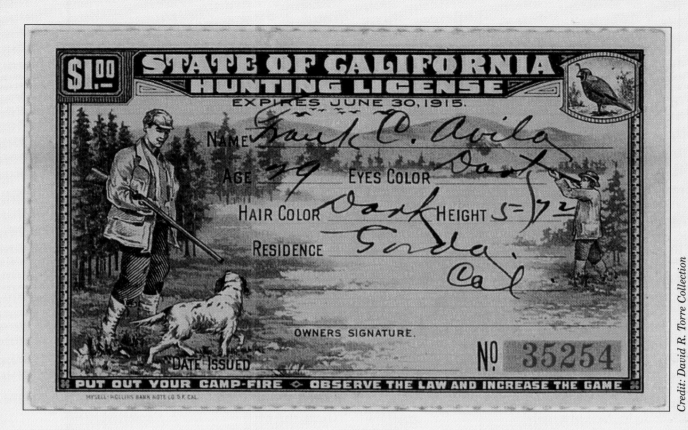

Credit: David R. Torre Collection

An example of the beautifully illustrated 1914-15 California resident hunting license (Above), and George Lawyer's 1919-20 California non-resident hunting license (Below).

Credit: David R. Torre Collection

take out a Federal hunting license for that privilege. This Association believes the idea is a good one and thinks that the necessary legislation to put the proposed plan into effect should be passed at the earliest possible moment... The funds to put this entire programme into effect could easily be secured through a Federal hunting license for migratory birds.

The editorial went on to outline a proposal recently offered by A.S. Houghton, of the AGPA, at the organization's Sixth Annual Game Conference. Houghton's proposal was to provide for a license in the form of a stamp to be sold at Post Offices, costing fifty cents, which migratory bird hunters would be required to affix to their state hunting licenses. The stamp would be cancelled by writing the name of the purchaser and the date of purchase across its front. In states where a license wasn't required, an identification card would be furnished. The funds thereby generated would be used "only for the purpose of securing refuges, feeding grounds, and public shooting grounds for migratory birds and for enforcing the Federal laws protecting these species." In April 1921, Frederic C. Walcott, former Fish and Game Commissioner for Connecticut, penned an article titled "The Necessity of Free Shooting Grounds," which also appeared in the *Bulletin*. One of the most interesting items in the article was a drawing provided by Belmore Browne which further refined Lawyer's earlier sketch of a possible hunting stamp. It showed a Canada Goose in flight and perhaps the most remarkable thing about it was how closely it paralleled the design of future federal duck stamps.

On May 2nd and 5th of that year, Senator Harry S. New (R-IN) and Congressman Dan R. Anthony (R-KS), introduced identical bills "providing for establishing shooting grounds for the public, ... game refuges and breeding grounds, for protecting migratory birds, and requiring a Federal license to hunt them." The license, in the form of a stamp, would cost $1 and be purchased at Post Offices throughout the country. Forty-five percent of the proceeds would go towards the purchase or rental of public shooting grounds and adjacent migratory bird refuges, the latter of which would be off-limits to hunting. It would be up to the Secretary of Agriculture to regulate hunting on these lands. A Migratory Bird Refuge Commission, consisting of the Secretary, Attorney General, Postmaster General, and two members each from the Senate and House, would be entrusted with the responsibility of selecting the lands to be purchased or rented.

An impressively broad list of organizations, in addition to the AGPA, supported the bill. Among these were the National Association of Audubon Societies, the Boone and Crockett Club, the Department of Agriculture, the Camp Fire Club of America, and the International Association of Game, Fish and Conservation Commissioners. There were opponents as well. State's rights advocates decried the bills' reach. According to Congressman Finis Garrett (D-TN), "they [supporters of the bill] fail to realize the precedent that is fixed here. They fail to appreciate the fact that this is but enhancing federal power, taking another step towards adding to the restlessness and discontent of the average citizen with the Federal Government."

Others argued that the bill was an unconstitutional use of federal power, refusing to accept the fact that the Supreme Court had already clearly stated that the federal government does have the right to regulate migratory waterfowl. Congressman

Belmore Browne's suggestion for the design of a federal hunting license, as it appeared in the April 1921 issue of the Bulletin of the American Game Protective Association.

Franklin Mondell (R-WY), taking this line, despaired for the nation. "I believe the measure, if so far-reaching in its consequences, would be so tremendously harmful in the long run to my country and to its people, that I can not bring myself to support it or any part of it." Opposition also came from some wealthy duck hunting clubs who feared that the federal hand would reach down and take their private reserves to allow for public access. Still others opposed the law because they opposed the shooting grounds provision and would rather have the government set aside refuges inviolate than offer what they perceived to be as merely additional opportunities for hunters to deplete waterfowl populations.

The bill passed the Senate, but fell short in the House by 10 votes, with Congressman Mondell leading the opposition. Coming so close, sponsors of the bill introduced it again in 1924 during the 68th Congress. More supporters fell in line, including the editorial pages of *The New York Times* and *The Saturday Evening Post*, The American Association for the Advancement of Science, the Izaak Walton League, the National Federation of Women's Clubs, the American Forestry Association, as well as a host of other groups. Hopes ran high and the House moved first, easily passing the bill 211-69. The Senate, however, adjourned before considering it. The supporters rallied again next term and introduced essentially the same bill once more. The expectation for passage was so great that some states began identifying lands that could be purchased under the soon to be enacted law.

Darling's cartoon, "Why Drain Our Lakes to Make More Farms When We Are Already Suffering From Over Production of Farm Products?" (August 14, 1923). Credit J.N. "Ding" Darling Foundation.

This time the opposition became more fierce and effective. Dr. William T. Hornaday, Director of the Bronx Zoo, who had opposed earlier bills led the charge. Hornaday was a fiery, iconoclastic character who had long been a major and irascible voice for wildlife protection. At the outset of his career he was an avid hunter who had collected an impressive number of trophies on various trips around the world. In the early 1900s his cause was not the extermination of hunting, but the extermination of market hunters. By the time he published the very popular book, *Our Vanishing Wild Life*, in 1913, his philosophy had fundamentally changed. In the book he wrote, "I have been a hunter myself but times have changed, and we must change also." Predicting that numerous species, including some migratory waterfowl, would be extinct if we didn't take decisive action, he advocated extreme restrictions on hunting. His strident, damn-the-enemy approach, and relative lack of civility in pursuing his crusade made him numerous enemies. Yet he remained a formidable force whose pen and voice still had a big impact on public opinion. When the public shooting grounds bill was introduced for the third time, Hornaday pounced on it.

His attack was two-pronged. First he tried to discredit the bill itself and its supporters. The public shooting grounds provision was, to him, the equivalent of creating "slaughter pens" making it more convenient for hunters to kill migratory waterfowl. Supporters of the bill were called "game hogs," "butchers," and "the armies of destruction." Worse were the broadsides Hornaday launched against what he believed were the real backers of the bill - the gun and ammunition companies. Through magazine and newspaper editorials, Hornaday argued that "the sportsmen are led by the men and organizations *interested in killing* - with profits, salaries and emoluments at stake. The *only* money available for our much vaunted 'protection' is the blood money derived from the annual sale of licenses to kill game!! [original emphasis]" The second prong of Hornaday's attack was to urge Congress to establish fixed hunting seasons and bag limits far below those currently being implemented by the Bureau of Biological Survey.

Hornaday's exhortations helped to sway public opinion against the bill. Combined with the continued opposition of state's rightists, hunting clubs, and other assorted groups, the bill seemed destined for defeat once again. But the coup de grace came in the spring of 1926, when Senator Fiorella La Guardia (D-NY), a supporter of Hornaday, read some earlier correspondence between Burnham, President of AGPA, and gun and ammunition manufacturers. The letters seemed to indicate that the motivation behind the efforts of these two groups to pass the public shooting grounds bill was less to help the sportsmen than to increase the profits of the manufacturers who stood to benefit from increased sales. Elaborating on this relationship and echoing Hornaday's claims, La Guardia stated "[t]hese lobbyists know that the sole purpose of this bill is not to conserve birds but to slaughter birds and to create a better market for cartridges, powder, and guns." The fact that the manufacturers provided the vast majority of the AGPA's funding didn't make things look any better. While undoubtedly many members of the AGPA supported the bill out of concern both for the sport and the viability of the migratory waterfowl, these letters cast a black cloud over the debate and served as a lightning rod for the opposition. One casualty of this fight was Burnham, who resigned in the summer of 1926. His departure, however, had no effect on the outcome of the debate. On the Senate side, the opposition kept the bill from even being considered. In the House, Congressman Anthony, one of bill's main supporters, was sidelined with injuries sustained in a car accident and was unable to provide the leadership necessary to the bill to the floor. Once again, the bill failed.

As the legislative battle raged on, the status of waterfowl worsened. Dr. Nelson, writing in the mid-1920s, feared for the future lest action be taken soon. "The danger to the perpetualism of the stock of wild-

Senator Peter Norbeck (D-SD) played a critical role in creating the Federal Duck Stamp Program. Credit: United States Senate Historical Office.

fowl is so great and so imminent ... that there is the most vital need for all conservationists and lovers of wildlife to sink petty differences of opinions as to the details and unite in constructive work to insure the future of our migratory game birds." An opportunity to unite behind a single approach was at hand.

In the waning days of the 69th Congress, a new player emerged on the scene. Senator Peter Norbeck (D-SD), highly respected by his peers and keenly interested in the issue of wildlife protection, decided that it was worth trying one more time to pass legislation to protect migratory waterfowl. Norbeck's bill was quite similar to those that had failed before, but it was clear that he had learned some lessons from past legislative battles. While not using the politically charged term "public shooting grounds," the bill nevertheless allowed for them, but with a twist. Its main purpose was to provide refuges where migratory waterfowl could feed and breed, thereby helping to ensure healthy populations. However, if the Secretary of Agriculture found that "a sufficient surplus of said birds exists, so that public hunting of migratory game birds on certain of said areas [refuges] or parts thereof would not endanger the future supply of birds," then he could open part or all of specific refuges to public hunting. The $1 stamp provision was the same, and sixty percent of the proceeds were to go towards the purchase of land, with the remainder to be used for implementing the treaty, printing the stamps and other administrative needs.

The battle over Norbeck's bill was both familiar and heated. Semantics did not win over those opposed to "public shooting grounds." They argued that any possibility of public hunting on the refuges should be stricken from the bill; the need was for "inviolate" refuges. According to Senator John Blaine (R-WI), "[t]his is not a conservation measure. This is a measure that promotes vandalism of our wild life. It is a measure that is sailing under false colors; ..." There was still strong opposition to the extension of federal power into areas better left to the states. Again, Blaine weighed in. "The time was when ... Uncle Sam's legislation ... [was] held in high regard, but never in the history of America has there been such disregard for law. Why? Simply because Congresses have been engaged in a veritable diarrhea of legislation, until no man knows what the law is... The States are being deprived of their self-government, ..." A number of Senators argued against "taxing" hunters and instead taking money from the Treasury. Senator Claude Swanson (D-VA) succinctly captured the philosophy of this argument. "... I do not think it is right to tax the people of the

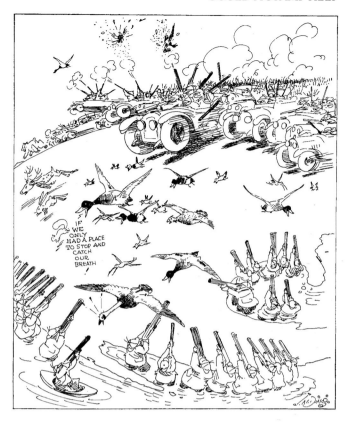

Darling's cartoon, "Wanted: More And Better Game Refuges" (April 30, 1928). Credit: the J.N. "Ding" Darling Foundation.

various states by requiring licenses of them and making them pay the Federal government for the privilege of shooting ... If a national interest is to be subserved, if the purpose is to aid the entire nation, and to protect birds everywhere, the money ought to come out of the Treasury."

In the face of concerted opposition to various provisions of the bill, Norbeck reluctantly chose compromise over confrontation. One by one, the controversial provisions were stripped away. First to go was that which would have allowed for public hunting. All refuges would be "inviolate." Upon hearing of this change, Hornaday wrote to Norbeck, urging him on. "Your wise and generous amendment ... has completely transformed ... [the bill] into a safe, sane, and far-reaching agency for a general increase in waterfowl ... No true sportsmen or game defender can fail to support your bill as amended... .I hope you will stand as firm as the Rock of Gibralter for the Federal license fee ..." With former opponents now in his camp, Norbeck tried to save the stamp. He argued strenuously that relying on appropriations from Congress rather than a license fee would doom the law to failure because little if any appropriations would be forthcoming. He was not convincing enough. Believing that passage of a neutered law was better than no law at all, Norbeck stripped away

Darling's cartoon, "Why It Seems About Time To Begin Talk About Conservation" (November 16, 1928). Credit: the J.N. "Ding" Darling Foundation.

the licensing fee provision altogether. Funding would have to come from Treasury. With all the roadblocks cleared, former enemies of the bill offered their support. The Senate bill passed, as did a similar one in the House, sponsored by Congressmen Andersen. On February 18, 1929 President Hoover signed the Migratory Bird Conservation Act.

The creation of the Act was no cause for celebration. Although supporters were encouraged that a law was in place, they were equally concerned that it would have a limited impact. Few felt the federal government would come through with adequate funding, and without such funding the Act was a paper tiger. Many sportsmen viewed the loss of the public shooting grounds feature with dismay. Holland, reflecting on the situation years after, claimed that "... the bill [with the shooting grounds provision] was defeated by a group of long-haired boys who called themselves conservationists... Later, the bill was hamstrung, quartered and drawn ..." to guarantee passage.

If there was any hope of funding, events overwhelmed it. In the late 1920s, the bull market on Wall Street was surging ahead, outstripping expectations at every turn. As the buying frenzy inflated stock values to new heights, the actual health of American business began to decline. The gulf between speculative hope and fiscal reality reached an apogee in October 1929. Once it became apparent that the stock market was a house of cards, it came crashing down with a frightful violence. The "Roaring Twenties" ended and the Great Depression began. A country reeling from a financial meltdown had little interest in the relatively insignificant cause of migratory waterfowl protection. Human survival took precedence. The promise of funding for the purchase of refuges almost completely evaporated along with the market. While some money was made available to purchase refuges during this period, it was minimal.

But something much worse for the ducks than the lack of money was about to occur. During the spring and summer of 1930, the skies over much of the eastern United States dried up. The drought that ensued set all-time records for lows in precipitation in twelve states. Then in 1931, the band of drought moved westward, settling on the Great Plains. By mid-decade it was onto the Southern Plains. Vast areas in Kansas, Colorado, New Mexico, Oklahoma, and Texas, bore the brunt of the drought. Year after year of low precipitation and intense heat wreaked havoc with the land. Decades of transforming the plains into farmland, roads, towns and cities had rendered it defenseless against the ravages of nature. With so much land denuded of its natural vegetation, stripped of its dense sod, the parched soil was lofted into the sky by dry winds, creating great dust storms that blew across the region, turning day into night. According to historian Donald Worster, the Dust Bowl occurred "because the expansionary energy of the United States had finally encountered a volatile, marginal land, destroying the delicate ecological balance that had evolved there."

This was a devastating time for migratory waterfowl. The resting, nesting, and feeding areas they relied on literally disappeared into thin air. Vast lakes were transformed into small ponds, and small ponds and swamplands turned into cracked mud. Where water did remain, other problems arose. As evaporation increased, high concentrations of alkaline salts made the remaining water a deadly brew. Stagnant, fetid bodies of water, with masses of dying and decaying vegetation provided a breeding ground for "duck sickness" or avian botulism. Waterfowl were dying in large numbers. Even the populous mallard was in dire straits. Dr. T. Gilbert Pearson of the National Association of Audubon Societies, commented that "[w]ild water-fowl [sic] in this coun-

Arthur Rothstein's powerful image of a farmer and sons walking in the face of a dust storm in Cimarron County, Oklahoma (1936). The dust bowl years had a devastating impact on migratory waterfowl. Credit: Library of Congress.

try have recently passed through two very adverse breeding seasons and their numbers are less today then during the life time of any one present." During the early thirties, hunters often looked to the sky in vain in search of birds. According to Darling, in 1934, hunters nationwide let forth with a "melancholy chorus of wails: 'the ducks are gone!' This was not the first year of frightening shortages - it was just the worst!"

The dire situation re-invigorated the debate over what should be done to save waterfowl. Some advocated killing crows, others wanted to raise ducklings and release them to the wild, while still others felt blame rested with the Biological Survey and their supposed mismanagement of the resource. Reflecting on this, Darling commented that "the sportsmen's fraternity was as full of misinformation as a Soviet broadcast, and it quarreled over as many theories for salvation of the ducks as religionists over formulas for getting into heaven." From other quarters there were calls for either a ban on hunting or dramatic reductions in bag limits. Despite all these differences of opinion, there was one thing upon which all could agree - waterfowl needed more refuges to survive and thrive.

The importance of refuges was underscored by scientists who were in the midst of creating a new field of study called wildlife management.

Darling's cartoon, "Why Call Them Sportsmen?" (March 26, 1932). Credit: the J.N. "Ding" Darling Foundation.

Aldo Leopold, often called the "father of wildlife management" in North America, was the best known of this new cadre of scientists. He had a special fondness for migratory waterfowl, having begun hunting when still a boy in Iowa. He believed that preserving habitat was critical to the survival of these species. In 1930, a policy committee he chaired came out with a detailed report on game management. One chapter focused on migratory waterfowl and one of its main conclusions argued for the establishment of a continental system of refuges.

The Migratory Bird Conservation Act already had imbedded within it the basic mechanism enabling the federal government to purchase refuges. What was lacking was money. Two ideas were proposed for generating funds. The AGPA resuscitated the approach they had been advocating for years and they launched a nationwide campaign for the passage of a duck stamp bill, using the slogan "Ducks for a Dollar." More Game Birds for America, which later became Ducks Unlimited (DU), supported a one-cent tax on shotgun shells to raise revenue. The latter idea quickly faded from view in the face of arguments that it would be unfair to tax all game hunters to benefit those who hunted waterfowl. The duck stamp approach took center stage. A bill incorporating this provision was offered during the waning days of the Hoover administration but was never brought to a vote. When Franklin Delano Roosevelt entered the White House in 1933, he faced a dizzying array of problems to address in a country that had been torn apart by the Depression and the ravages of the Dust Bowl. Thanks to the insistent demands of scientists and sportsmen, one issue he couldn't duck was what to do about the ducks.

"THE BEST FRIEND DUCKS EVER HAD"

At the end of 1933, President Roosevelt appointed a special "duck committee" to evaluate the situation and recommend a waterfowl restoration plan. Its members were Darling, Dr. John C. Merriam of the Smithsonian Institution, and Thomas H. Beck, editor-in-chief of *Collier's Weekly*, chairman of the Connecticut State Board of Fisheries and Game, President of More Game Birds for America and an outspoken critic of the Survey and its management of the waterfowl. Merriam was unable to accept the honor and was replaced by Aldo Leopold. Beck was named chairman, and from then on it was known as the Beck Committee. On its face the most curious addition to the committee was Darling, and many editorialists of the day decried this choice. What was a cartoonist doing giving advice to the President on this topic? To those who knew this man, the question was ridiculous. Darling, through his brilliant cartoons capturing the plight of waterfowl and his strenuous support of sound wild-

President Franklin Delano Roosevelt's signature in 1934 put the Federal Duck Stamp Program into place. Credit: Library of Congress.

life management in Iowa and throughout the nation, had sterling bona fides to be offering such advice. Some argued that Roosevelt's real reason for convening the committee in the first place was to appease sportsmen and others agitating for action without really doing anything - a means of reducing the political heat through indirection. If that was his goal, Roosevelt made a bad mistake. Neither this committee nor those fighting for change would go quietly into the night.

At the outset of the committee's deliberations there was considerable optimism. In announcing its creation a White House spokesman had promised $1 million to fund the committee's plan if it were approved. Press organizations around the country expected great things. *The Chicago Tribune* predicted that out of the committee would come a "gigantic national project to increase game birds in this country ... utilize 20 to 50 million acres ... [and] increase healthful recreation for million[s] of outdoor fans, ..." Darling, Leopold, and Beck dove into their work with enthusiasm, interviewing federal, state and local wildlife managers, soliciting management suggestions, and documenting lands suitable for potential purchase as refuges. Numerous individual and organizations proposed projects to the committee, lobbying so vigorously that Roosevelt warned the committee against "playing favorites." In a private letter to Darling, Leopold made clear the importance of the committee's work. "[W]e must not delude ourselves by seeing this job as merely a heaven-sent chance to buy some lands. It is, ... the chance to make or break federal leadership in wildlife conservation."

Five weeks after beginning their work, they took up the task of writing a report with policy recommendations, and all hell broke loose. "If there is a word in the English language expressing violent explosion, only louder and longer lasting, I'd like to use it now." Darling stated in a later article on this period. Beck, with a booming voice and imperious manner, insisted that the report state that the

Biological Survey was "incompetent and unscientific," and recommended that it be abolished. This position and the person that held it so incensed Leopold that he left for home. Darling tried to salvage things by preparing a compromise report but wasn't completely successful. In early February, the three submitted a joint report which focused only on recommended projects, while Beck submitted his own "policy report" to the President.

In the joint report were some serious recommendations, the most important of which were for the federal government to spend $25 million on wildlife restoration, to purchase 12 million acres of submarginal lands for wildlife protection, and to give another $25 million to the Public Works Administration to support efforts for restoring these lands. Administration officials attacked the plans, especially the large expenditures, as too ambitious. President Roosevelt himself had no reaction. His silence brought calls in the press to take a stand. The ostensible reason for the President's silence soon became apparent. At a press conference, a reporter asked what had happened to the Duck Committee report? Roosevelt had no answer and looked over at his press secretary for help to no avail. Later it was reported that the President had never read the report and that it was found sitting on a table near his bed, buried under other documents.

President Roosevelt then took a most unusual step, or at least so it seemed. He asked Darling, who had returned to Iowa after the Beck Committee disbanded, to come back to Washington and take over as head of the Survey. This took Darling by surprise. At first, he clearly did not want the job. "A singed cat," Darling later said, "was never more conscious of the dangers of fire than I was of the hazards in trying to get anything done in Washington." He was a staunch Republican and was unsure he wanted to "aid and abet" the opposition. He finally decided to go, leaving behind his six-figure income as a nationally syndicated cartoonist at the *Des Moines Register*. His motive was to put the Survey back on its feet and help the cause of wildlife protection, especially as it pertained to migratory waterfowl. It has been argued, though, that Darling's appointment had nothing to do with promoting wildlife protection. As an outspoken Republican, Darling had wielded his acid pen in the direction of Roosevelt many times. His cartoons often attacked the "New Deal" policies central to this new administration. To some, Roosevelt's decision to appoint Darling was just a wily means of shutting up one of his fiercest critics. If that was his goal, Roosevelt made another big mistake.

Darling was sworn in on March 10, 1934. Six days later President Roosevelt signed into law the Migratory Bird Hunting Stamp Act, a successor to the duck stamp bill that was introduced at the end of the Hoover administration. On the Senate side the fight for the bill was led by two Senators who had a longstanding interest in this issue: Senator Norbeck was the prime author of the Migratory Bird Conservation Act of 1929, and Senator Frederic Walcott (R-CT) was the very same person who back in 1921 penned the article on public shooting grounds which displayed Belmore Browne's rendition of what a duck stamp might look like. On the House side, Congressman Richard Kleberg (D-TX) led the fight. The new law, commonly referred to as the duck stamp act, required any person sixteen years or older hunting ducks, geese, swans or brant to have a $1 duck stamp and a valid state hunting license. During the first year of the program, the hunter was not required to sign his name across the stamp for it to be valid, but in all subsequent years that requirement was in effect. The stamp was distributed through U.S. Post Offices, and hunters were required to affix the stamp to either their state hunting licenses, if such a license were required, or to a certificate furnished by the postmaster for that purpose. Those light blue certificates were called Form 3333 and were intended for use only for the 1934 stamp, but for a variety of reasons sporadic usage of Form 3333 continued for some years after. Revenues generated went to a Migratory Bird Conservation Fund. Ninety-percent of that money was "available for the location, ascertainment, acquisition, administration, maintenance and development of suitable areas for inviolate migratory bird sanctuaries." The remaining ten-percent was for printing and distribution as well as enforcement of the act. After fifteen years of fighting and the combined efforts of many dedicated individuals, the duck stamp was a reality. And it came none too soon. By one estimate, 1934 marked an all-time low for migratory waterfowl populations - 27 million.

Despite the turmoil surrounding the Beck committee's report and the President's lack of inter-

The first federal duck stamp. Credit: U.S. Fish and Wildlife Service

Form 3333 with 1934 stamp affixed and "Division of Finance" cancel, from Houston, Texas. Credit: Jeanette Cantrell Rudy and the National Postal Museum, Smithsonian Institution (photo by Larry Gates).

est in its findings, it had a powerful impact on the legislative battle over the duck stamp act. During its deliberations, the committee had written to every state wildlife conservation group, Izaak Walton League chapter and gun club asking for support and advice on which lands should be purchased for refuge system. According to Darling, "[t]he response was magnetic." Not only was the committee swamped with suggestions, but it also had, perhaps unwittingly, energized a vast and powerful political force that was now keen on insuring that at least some of the committee's recommendations were implemented. Since the key to purchasing lands was money, this political force became an important factor in the successful passage of the duck stamp act. Victory, however, was not complete. Without money in hand to purchase refuges, nothing would change. While the Act promised a stream of future revenues, Darling desperately needed money soon to start the ball rolling before more lands were plowed under, cemented over, or dried out. Darling had accepted his new position only after Roosevelt had renewed his promise to find $1 million for the Survey to use in purchasing lands identified by the Beck Committee report. The President seemed willing to follow through and he invited Darling to "smoke a good cigarette" to seal their deal. In the ensuing months, whenever Darling would ask the President to make good on his promise, Roosevelt would write out an IOU for the $1 million that Darling was supposed to use in wrenching the money free from some part of the administration.

In the beginning, Darling took these IOUs or chits as they were called very seriously and thought they were like winning lottery tickets, all he had to do was cash one in with the right person in the administration. "No small boy with a new cowboy hat and Texas boots ever felt more like a big shot than I did walking out of the White House with my first ... [chit] signed with the familiar 'F.D.R.' in his own handwriting!" As he was shunted from one administration official to another, Darling became increasingly frustrated. Instead of providing money, the officials would regard the chit with gravity and then say, "sorry, I just don't have it." Darling began to feel as if he was caught in a game of "cat and mouse," or worse that he was the butt of one of the President's famous practical jokes. Nothing brought home this feeling more than a particular interaction with Harry Hopkins, head of the Works Progress Administration, the Civil Works Administration, and the Federal Emergency Relief Administration, who had under his control billions of dollars in aid. After a number of meetings with Darling, Hopkins finally relented, saying he would have the money ready the next morning at 9 o'clock, sharp. When Darling perused the paper that day before heading off to the meeting, he saw a headline that read "Harry Hopkins Sails for Europe." He had left at midnight the night before and when Darling visited his office, Hopkins assistant said he knew nothing of the money and that he wasn't interested in Darling's explanation of Hopkin's promise.

If Darling was anything, he was persistent. Frustrated by the White House, he went to Capitol Hill and enlisted the support of Senator Norbeck who agreed to ask for a unanimous consent for a Senate Resolution giving the Survey $1 million out of the previous year's unexpended federal relief funds to be used to purchase refuges. He got that and more in what Darling called "one of the funniest incidents of the whole restoration procedure." Norbeck was approaching the end of an illustrious career in the Senate where he was much beloved by his peers, all of whom were well aware that he was dying of cancer. In early June 1935, on the final day of the debate over the Omnibus Bill for the Biological Survey, Norbeck asked Carl D. Shoemaker, Secretary of the Special Senate Committee on Wildlife, to come by his office. Norbeck wanted to attach a rider to the bill requesting the money he and Darling had discussed. Shoemaker wrote up the appropriate language and at Norbeck's request raised the ante from $1 million to $6 million. Norbeck read the language and then asked Shoemaker to follow him to the Senate floor. On the walk over, Norbeck was extremely uncomfortable. He had recently had all of his teeth extracted and his dentures were giving him great pain, so he took them out and placed them in his vest pocket. As Norbeck strode into the chamber, the Omnibus Bill was being called for a vote. Norbeck, waving the amendment in his hand, rushed to give it to the clerk. The presiding Senator, Bennett Champ Clark asked the clerk to read it out loud, which he did in a quick manner that was hard to decipher. Clark then asked Norbeck to read the amendment as well. With his dentures in Norbeck was hard to understand because of his thick Scandinavian accent. With his dentures in his vest pocket he was virtually incomprehensible.

Shoemaker observed that his words sounded like "glut, glut, oogle, glut ..." Out of respect for the man who had fought so hard, so long for migratory water-fowl, his fellow Senators passed the rider unanimously even though nobody knew exactly what it contained. That afternoon, Norbeck successfully steered the appropriations bill through the Senate-House conference committee, whereupon the bill was carried by messenger over to the White House for the President's signature. Time was of the essence because Roosevelt was heading off for a Caribbean fishing trip the next morning. Darling had told the President to keep an eye out for the bill and when he saw it on his desk before just before leaving he signed it after giving it only a cursory glance. The President then went on vacation, blissfully unaware he had just given Darling's Survey $6 million. The waterfowl restoration program was finally flush.

On July 26, 1935 After getting the $6 million, Darling sent the President an illustrated letter asking him to reinstate a $4 million appropriation

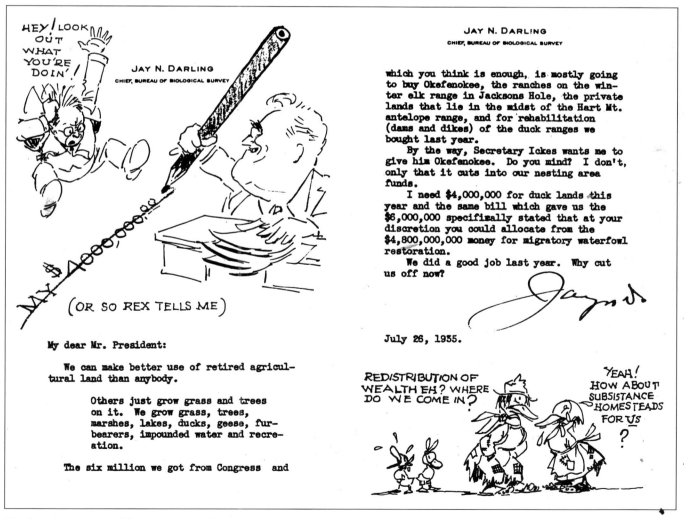

Darling's animated letter urging Roosevelt to free up more money for migratory waterfowl and the purchase of national wildlife refuges. Credit: the J.N. "Ding" Darling Foundation.

THE WHITE HOUSE
WASHINGTON

July 29, 1935.

Dear Jay:-

As I was saying to the Acting Director
of the Budget the other day - "this fellow Darling
is the only man in history who got an appropriation
through Congress, passed the Budget and signed by
the President without anybody realizing that the
Treasury had been raided."

You hold an all-time record. In addition
to the six million dollars ($6,000,000) you got,
the Federal Courts say that the United States
Government has a perfect constitutional right to
condemn millions of acres for the welfare, health
and happiness of ducks, geese, sandpipers, owls
and wrens, but has no constitutional right to
condemn a few old tenaments in the slums for the
health and happiness of the little boys and girls
who will be our citizens of the next generation!

Nevertheless, more power to your arm!
Go ahead with the six million dollars ($6,000,000)
and talk with me about a month hence in regard
to additional lands, if I have any more money left.

As ever yours,

Franklin D Roosevelt

Honorable J. N. Darling,
Bureau of Biological Survey,
South Building,
Washington, D. C.

President Roosevelt's response to Darling, indicating his admiration for Darling's determination and success in finding funds. Credit: the J.N. "Ding" Darling Foundation.

which Rex Tugwell, Deputy Secretary of Agriculture, had told Darling the President was going to disapprove. In the letter, Darling implored "we can make better use of retired agricultural land than anybody... I need $4,000,000 for duck lands this year. ... we did a good job last year. Why cut us off now?" Roosevelt's reply showed his grudging respect for Darling's tenacity in the pursuit of funds as well as the President's sense of humor.

As I was saying to the Acting Director of the Budget the other day - 'this fellow Darling is the only man in history who got an appropriation through Congress, past the Budget and signed by the President without anybody realizing that the Treasury had been raided.

You hold an all-time record... Nevertheless, more power to your arm! Go ahead with the six million ... and talk to me about a month hence in regard to additional lands, if I have any more money left.

With money and tremendous drive, Darling transformed the demoralized Biological Survey into a self-respecting organization proud of its work. Duck stamp revenues, combined with Norbeck's $6 million and other appropriations, enabled many of the ambitious land acquisition and improvement projects which had been shelved for years to move forward. Although he had no prior administrative experience, Darling proved quite adept at energizing the troops and making bureaucratic decisions. He also surrounded himself with motivated and skilled staff, including J. Clark Salyer II, Clarence Cottam, and Ira N. Gabrielson, who later took over the reins of the Survey when Darling left. Salyer is often referred to as the 'father of the refuge system' for his tireless efforts, crisscrossing the country in search of suitable lands to

buy. Salyer feared flying and, indeed, there is no record of him ever having left the ground during his travels. Instead, he would drive upwards of 700 miles in a day if that was what was needed to look at a potential purchase site or seal a deal. During his nearly thirty-year tenure, Salyer directed the addition of 600,000 acres and fifty refuges to the burgeoning refuge system. Darling credits many individuals as being critical during those first few years after the Duck Stamp Act's passage, but of Salyer, Darling would later say, he "was the salvation of the Duck Restoration Program of 1934-1936. He did most of the work for which I was given credit and awarded medals."

In addition to overseeing the purchase of key refuges and other lands, Darling took more direct steps to halt the decline in migratory waterfowl populations. In 1935, the open season was reduced to thirty days, bag limits for duck and geese were slashed to ten and four, respectively, magazine shotguns holding more than three shots, bait and live decoys were outlawed. When asked to defend his actions, Darling said, "[t]he regulations will stay as long as they are needed to bring back the ducks, and if tougher restrictions are needed, we will find some tougher regulations."

Darling played a particularly unique role in the creation of the first duck stamp in 1934. With the bill in place, a duck stamp was needed. The BEP, however, required a design to work with before creating the stamp. Darling was asked to sketch out some ideas of what he thought a stamp might look like. "There was no one else available to make a design," Darling later recalled. So he made six sketches on six cardboard stiffeners that laundries use to keep shirts wrinkle-free. The reason for the unusual "medium" had to do with haste and availability of materials. He had to get the sketches done quickly and the cardboard stiffeners were easily accessible. Darling often

Original drawing by "Ding" Darling for the first duck stamp, titled "Mallards dropping in." Credit: Jeanette Cantrell Rudy and the National Postal Museum, Smithsonian Institution (photo by Larry Gates).

worked late and he needed to be prepared for unexpected nighttime social or political engagements. He kept a supply of fresh shirts on hand in his office for this purpose, each one of which came with cardboard backing. Colonel Sheldon, the Bureau's Chief of Public Relations, rushed Darling's sketches to the BEP. Three days later Darling asked what the printers had done with the sketches, whereupon he was told they had selected one and the engravers had already started production. Darling, who thought his sketches were ideas for the BEP to elaborate upon, not drawings to be duplicated on the stamp, was very

upset. "I could have murdered Colonel Sheldon and all the Bureau of Engraving personnel," he later recalled, "and every time I look at that proof design of the first duck stamp I still want to do it." Darling was concerned that the quickly drawn design of a mallard hen and drake landing in a marsh would reduce the artistic merit of the first stamp and hurt sales. He needn't have worried. The stamp was a success and 635,001 of them sold.

Approaching 60, Darling stepped down as head of the Survey in late 1935 to return to his first passion - political cartooning. He accomplished a great deal

Darling's cartoon, "Lest You Forget" (November 9, 1936). Credit: the J.N. "Ding" Darling Foundation.

in his relatively short tenure and felt he left at the right time. Darling commented "what is it about the Washington atmosphere that makes a man, after brief exposure, unable to tell the truth? It's lucky that my stay was short." With characteristic humility, Darling downplayed the importance of his tenure at the Bureau. "Any other well-informed individual, freed from the fear of losing his job with the government, could have done equally well and probably better than I did." He was not only humble, but wrong. Darling's political skill and tenacity played a major role in garnering from federal coffers more than $20 million to further Survey programs, especially those relating to waterfowl. This money went towards the purchase of nearly half a million acres of refuges and restoration areas. Darling also was instrumental in getting the President to set aside more than 3 million acres of public land through executive orders. This, combined with his earlier efforts on behalf of waterfowl, is the reason Darling clearly earned his honorary title, "the best friend ducks ever had."

On the topic of President Roosevelt, Darling stated, "I am completely oblivious to anyone's slant on FDR's contribution to the Duck Restoration Program, but so far as I'm concerned he blocked me, and consciously too, in every effort to finance the program which he himself had asked me to carry out." A fanciful explanation for why Roosevelt seemed opposed to Darling's efforts is that a goose once threatened his life. The President was fond of telling a story about a particular hunt he was on before moving to the White House. It was a clear sky and two geese flew overhead towards some decoys. Roosevelt took aim, firing at the lead goose and hit it. As he swung around to shoot the other, the first goose fell on his shoulder, knocking him forcibly back into the blind. Had it fallen a few inches over the President told listeners, it might have killed him. It is unlikely, however, that the President harbored a grudge against waterfowl. He was certainly concerned about their plight. An interesting memo from the President to the Secretary of Agriculture, penned on May 24, 1934, shows as much. In it, he wrote, "I hope that in addition to the million dollars already allocated, we can get from land purchase, relief, etc., another five millions [sic]. By the way, the Congressman say the million dollars which I allocated has got lost somewhere. Will you conduct a search party?" The $1 million he refers to is, of course, the same million for which Darling searched high and low to no avail. Perhaps a more charitable way of characterizing Roosevelt's behavior is to say he was sympathetic to the cause of waterfowl protection, but this was not foremost on his mind during his first term and for whatever reason he did not push the issue. During his second term, Roosevelt was more inclined to help wildlife and took many

A pair of the 1938 stamp, singed by President Roosevelt. Credit: Sam Houston Duck Company.

actions which specifically helped waterfowl, including recommending that all federal lands be closed to duck hunting, refusing to extend the hunting season in the face of some unusual weather conditions, halting operations on an artillery range in Utah to protect a small population of trumpeter swans, and proclaiming a National Wildlife Week.

For the rest of his life, Darling was extremely active on behalf of wildlife in general, and migratory waterfowl in particular, both in his home state of Iowa and on the national scene. He was a founder of the National Wildlife Federation (NWF) and in 1942 was awarded the (Theodore) Roosevelt Medal for Conservation. Soon after he retired from cartooning, the Izaak Walton League passed a resolution requesting the Department of the Interior to place Darling's portrait on the 1950-51 duck stamp. In characteristic Darling style, he dashed off a letter to the Secretary of Interior imploring him, "please, oh please, Mr. Secretary DON'T. Since it is I who have been chosen for this innovation I want to be the first one to protest against it." The duck stamp was to depict waterfowl, not people. Speaking with a Reader's Digest editor in 1953, Darling offered his underlying rationale for devoting so much energy to the cause of waterfowl:

Of course you understand that I am not nearly so much interested in the preservation of migratory waterfowl as I am in the management of water resources and the crucial effects of such management upon human sustenance. Wild ducks and geese and teeter-assed shore birds are only the delicate indicators of the prognosis for human existence just as sure as God made little green apples.

Darling died on February 12, 1962, but his legacy endures. Shortly after his death, many of his friends created the J.N. "Ding" Darling Foundation. One of its first successes was to spearhead the move to have the Sanibel NWR on Darling's beloved Sanibel

Imperforate pair of the 1984 commemorative postage stamp honoring the fiftieth anniversary of the Migratory Bird Hunting Act. Credit: Sam Houston Duck Company.

Island, in Florida, renamed in his honor. In 1967 it was renamed the J.N. "Ding" Darling National Wildlife Refuge, which is today one of the most-visited refuges in the nation, with more than 800,000 people passing through its gates annually. The Foundation is dedicated to fostering the ideals and continuing the important work of Darling. All of the funds it raises go towards conservation efforts and conservation education projects ranging from the elementary level to graduate school. Another element of Darling's legacy is the "Ding" Darling Wildlife Society, a non-profit, friends-of-the-refuge organization created in 1982. The Society is an integral part of the refuge, raising money to fund important projects not covered by the federal budget, including educational programs, publishing free maps and information pamphlets, and a "Ding"

Darling Birthday and federal duck stamp celebration during National Wildlife Refuge Week in October of each year.

While Darling's face never graced a duck stamp, he received two philatelic honors in addition to designing the first federal duck stamp. The first one came in 1984, when the USPS celebrated the 50th anniversary of the Migratory Bird Hunting Act by issuing a commemorative reprint of Darling's 1934 duck stamp design. Then, in 1999, Palau issued a commemorative pane of sixteen stamps, honoring "Environmental Heroes of the 20th century." Right there alongside Rachel Carson, Jacques Cousteau, and Aldo Leopold, is Darling himself. He is pictured with a broad grin and a copy of the first duck stamp in the background.

SIXTY-SEVEN AND GOING STRONG

In 1939, the Biological Survey was transferred into the Department of the Interior, and a year later it was merged with the Bureau of Fisheries to become the United States Fish and Wildlife Service (U.S. F&WS). Today the Federal Duck Stamp Program is run out of the U.S. F&WS's Duck Stamp Office. In the words of James Bruns, Director of the National Postal Museum, "the Federal Duck Stamp Program represents the American government at its best." Few would disagree. During the sixty-seven years of its existence, the program has played a crucial and very effective role in the restoration of migratory waterfowl populations. If Lawyer, Holland, Houghton, Burnham, Norbeck, Salyer, Darling or any of the others whose work and inspiration helped to create and sustain this program could come back and see it now, they would be immensely proud and for good reason.

The program has been extremely stable, especially when one considers the unpredictable changes often visited on government programs. Some of the significant changes relate to price, wording, format, hunting, and the use of duck stamp revenue. To keep pace with the rising costs of land and the need to expand the impact of the program, duck stamp prices have risen to the current price of $15 with the following stops along the way: $2 (1949), $3 (1959), $5 (1972), $7.50 (1979), $10 (1987), $12.50 (1989), and $15 (1991). There have been wording changes on both the front and the back of the stamp over the years.

Beginning with the 1946 stamp, a back inscription was printed directly on the paper of the stamp, then gummed. The message read that "it is unlawful to hunt waterfowl unless you sign your name in ink across the face of the stamp." Starting with the 1954 issue the message was placed on top of the gum and has been that way ever since. The reasons for the change were simple — economy of cost, and reducing the susceptibility to fraud such as re-gumming the stamp, which could deceive collectors. While the gumming process has stayed the same, the message itself has gone through ten iterations since 1959.

The major change to the front of the stamp came in 1977. Prior to that time, the words "Migratory Bird Hunting Stamp" were printed on the face, but with the 1977 stamp and ever since the wording has read "Migratory Bird Hunting and Conservation Stamp," a change that more truly reflects the broad scope of the duck stamp program and was intended to encourage other users of refuges to purchase the stamps, i.e. photographers and birdwatchers. From 1934 through 1997, the basic duck stamp format was that of a gummed stamp which would have to be wetted to affix to a license. In 1998, the U.S. F&WS launched the self-adhesive federal duck stamp single on a three-year trial basis. The format change responds to requests from commercial stamp distributors, including supermarket chains, and their consignees for

U.S. Fish and Wildlife Service logo. Credit: U.S. Fish and Wildlife Service.

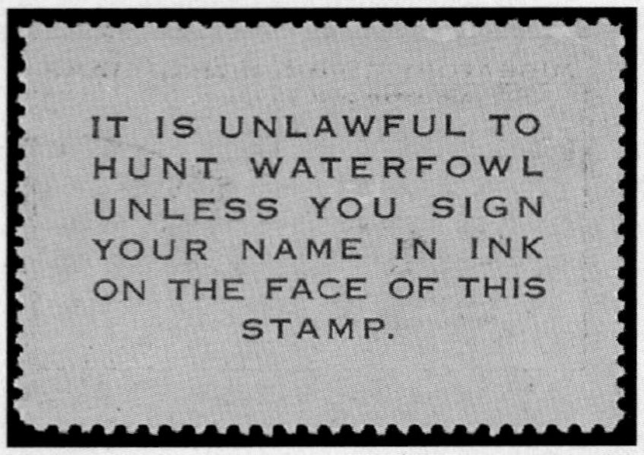

Type 1 1946-53 (Issues 13-20)
Message printed directly on stamp
paper, under gum. (1934-45 issues
are without reverse printing)

Type 1a 1954-58 (Issues 21-25)
Same message applied on top of gum.

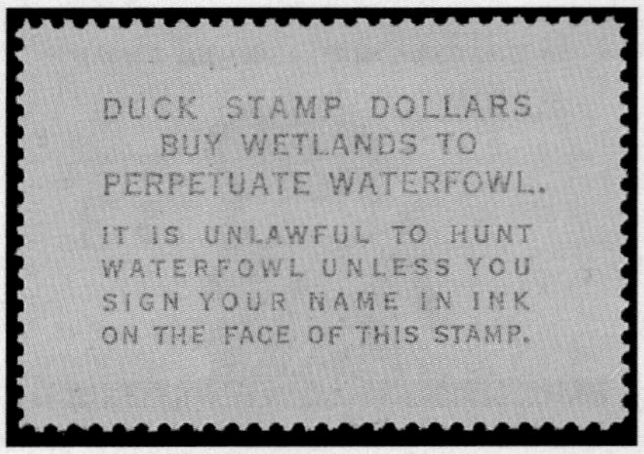

Type 2 1959-60 (Issues 26-27)

Type 2a 1959 (Issue 26)
Inverted on 1959 issue.

Type 3 1961-67 (Issues 28-34)

Type 4 1968-69 (Issues 35-36)

Type 5 1970-86 (Issues 37-53)

Type 6 1987-89 (Issues 54-56)

Type 7 1990 (Issue 57)

Type 8 1991-92 (Issues 58-59)

Type 9 1993 (Issue 60)

Type 10 1994-96 (Issues 61-63)

Type 11 1997- (Issue 64-)

*The message on the back of the federal duck stamp has gone through eleven iterations. Credit - Sam Houston
Duck Company.*

Front of the 1998 self-adhesive federal duck stamp. Credit: U.S. Fish and Wildlife Service.

a single stamp format that would be easy to handle and which could comfortably fit in a cash register (a 1997 change in the law allowed other establishments and facilities to sell duck stamps, besides the USPS and the U.S. F&WS). The self-adhesive stamp looks exactly the same as the gummed version on the front, including perforations, and has the same dimensions. It has no wording on the back, but the sheetlet on which it comes has plenty of space, on the front and back to convey pertinent information to purchasers.

Other legislative changes pertain to hunting. As originally envisioned under the duck stamp act, refuges were to be "inviolate" sanctuaries where migratory waterfowl could rest and feed without the pressures of hunting. This practice held until 1949, when Congress raised the stamp price to $2 and authorized the secretary of the U.S. F&WS to set aside up to twenty-five percent of any lands purchased with duck stamp revenues for use as wild-life management areas where hunting of resident and migratory game birds was allowed. In 1958 this provision was expanded to cover forty percent of the land. Then, in 1966, the National Wildlife Refuge System Administration Act authorized the secretary to permit hunting on any refuge lands as long as such activity was determined to be compatible with the primary purposes for which the refuge was established.

The practice of spending duck stamp funds has also changed over time. Under the original law, much of the duck stamp revenue could be used for activities other than the purchase of refuges, such as stamp production, the enforcement of waterfowl regulations, and the development and maintenance of refuge lands. Some years the funds shunted to these other activities approached eighty percent. This rankled hunters and conservationists who

wanted the funds used to expand the refuge system, not to go towards administration, maintenance or enforcement. An amendment to the duck stamp act in 1958, made effective in 1960, remedied this. Since that time, all the duck stamp revenues, minus the costs associated with the sale of the stamps through USPS, have been earmarked for the purchase of land. In practice, this means that roughly ninety-eight cents out of every dollar spent on a duck stamp is used to acquire critical habitat. In 1958, the duck stamp act was also amended to authorize the use of funds to acquire small wetland potholes as Waterfowl Protection Areas (WPAs). These potholes, while often small in size, contain critical wetlands and grasslands for waterfowl and other wildlife.

Duck stamps are not only for hunters. As Darling stated in July 1934, "[n]o one ... is under any obligation to kill a duck just because he owns a federal hunting stamp, nor is there any rule to prevent a man who wants to help restore the migratory waterfowl from purchasing several of these duck-saving stamps." In later years, the U.S. F&WS came out with public appeals to stamp collectors and wildlife enthusiasts to pitch in by purchasing stamps. In 1960, the U.S. F&WS began a short-lived campaign to sell duck stamps to "conservation minded persons," and was helped in this endeavor by the NWF, which provided a 5-inch x 7-inch certificate of appreciation to the purchaser. More recently, on October 19, 1998, President Bill Clinton signed "The Migratory Bird Hunting and Conservation Stamp Promotion Act." It authorizes the Secretary of Interior to utilize up to $1 million a year from the sales of duck stamps, for five consecutive years, to promote additional stamp sales through a variety of means, including advertising. According to Robert C. Lesino, Program Manager of the Federal Duck Stamp Program, the basic goal of the act is to double sales and make the federal duck stamp a "household name." As the number of hunters continues to wane, getting other groups, such as stamp collectors, birders, and non-hunters interested in conservation more interested in purchasing stamps is a good investment in the program's future.

With all of these changes, one thing remains constant. The Federal Duck Stamp Program is phenomenally successful. Sales of the stamp have netted more than $500 million and enabled the U.S. F&WS to purchase more than 5 million acres of habitat. If you have ever visited a national wildlife refuge, chances are that part or all of it was purchased with duck stamp revenue. Every person who has purchased a duck stamp should share in the pride of this accomplishment. The WPAs are a particularly important part of the refuge system. The U.S. F&WS has used duck funds to acquire more than 2 million acres of WPAs from 28,000 landowners in eight north-central states (Idaho and Maine also each have a single WPA). Although WPAs cover less than two percent of the land in the prairie pothole region of the U.S., they are responsible for producing nearly twenty-three percent of the area's waterfowl.

That is why WPAs are often referred to as "duck factories." As a recent U.S. F&WS publication stated, "if wetlands in this vast Prairie Pothole Region were not saved from drainage, hundreds of species of migratory birds would literally have gone down the drain."

To appreciate the full impact of the duck stamp program one must step back and look at the NWRS in its entirety. As the world's largest network of public lands set aside exclusively for the conservation of fish, wildlife and plants, the NWRS is truly one of this country's great natural treasures. The broad scope of the System is reflected in its mission statement, which says that its goal "is to administer a national network of lands and waters for the conservation, management, and where appropriate, restoration of fish, wildlife, and plant resources and their habitats within the United States for the benefit of present and future generations of Americans."

There are over 500 NWRs, spanning the fifty states and several U.S. territories. They range in size from the .6-acre Mille Lac NWR in Minnesota to the Arctic NWR, which sprawls over 19.2 million acres. While the vast majority of refuges are in the

lower forty-eight states, Hawaii and U.S. territories, eighty-five percent of refuge land is in Alaska. Every conceivable type of habitat falls within the boundaries of one or more of the NWRs - mangrove swamps, grasslands, tundra, wind-swept mountain peaks, desert, coral reefs, hardwood forests, coastal marshes. NWRs provide important habitat for more than 700 bird species, 220 mammal species, 250 reptiles and amphibian species, and more than 200 species of fish. Forty-six percent of the nation's endangered and threatened species can be found within their borders. All told, the refuge system contains more than 93 million acres of land and water, close to four percent of the surface area of the U.S, making it larger than the National Park System. Ninety-eight percent of refuge land is open to the public, and anyone can use a federal duck stamp to gain free admission. Each year roughly 38 million people visit NWRs to pursue a great variety of activities, including observing and photographing, hunting, fishing, and participating in educational programs.

The NWRS plays an absolutely critical role in maintaining healthy populations of migratory waterfowl. For example, in 1935 the Darling-Salyer team

A trusty companion on the hunt. Credit: John Sarvis and the U.S. Fish and Wildlife Service.

Beauty of the hunt. Credit: Pat Hogan and the U.S. Fish and Wildlife Service.

America's National Wildlife Refuge System

The blue goose is the logo for the National Wildlife Refuge System and was designed by Darling. Credit: U.S. Fish and Wildlife Service.

More than migratory waterfowl benefit from duck stamp dollars, like this American crocodile at the J.N. "Ding" Darling NWR, Florida, and these two red fox pups at the Agassiz NWR, Minnesota. Credit for crocodile shot: David Gilliam and the U.S. Fish and Wildlife Service; Credit for fox pups: John and Karen Hollingsworth and the U.S. Fish and Wildlife Service.

Waterfowl at sunset on wetland at the Lacassine NWR, Lousiana. Credit: John and Karen Hollingsworth.

Nene Geese at Kilauea NWR, Hawaii. Credit: John and Karen Hollingsworth and the U.S. Fish and Wildlife Service.

Canada geese and fall cypress at Cypress Creek NWR, Illinois. Credit: John and Karen Hollingsworth and the U.S. Fish and Wildlife Service.

John Heinz NWR at Tinicum, Pennsylvania. This is one of the more urban refuges. Philadelphia can be seen in the distance. Credit: John and Karen Hollingsworth and the U.S. Fish and Wildlife Service.

The foreboding Aghileen Pinnacles at Izembek NWR, Alaska.   Credit: John Sarvis and the U.S. Fish and Wildlife Service.

created the Red Rock Lakes NWR in Montana in order to save the last seventy-three trumpeter swans known to exist in the wild. Today, more than 16,000 of these grand birds are found in the upper Midwest, Alaska, and Montana. Of the more than 500 NWRs, 425 have active migratory bird management programs.

With so much variety there is no such thing as a "typical" NWR. They all have unique characteristics, sights and sounds. A tour through the Blackwater NWR, located just south of Cambridge, Maryland, offers a glimpse of the wonders one can find in a refuge. Blackwater was established in 1933 specifically for migratory waterfowl. Prior to that much of its land supported a fur farm, with muskrats being the primary "crop." There was also logging and other agricultural uses. Walking through its 17,121 acres one can still see the evidence of these activities in the form of drainage furrows and ditches as well as relatively young stands of trees. A key stopping off point

on the Atlantic Flyway, Blackwater hosts roughly 33,000 geese and more than 15,000 ducks during the fall migration. Commonly seen species include mallards, black ducks, blue-winged teal, green-winged teal, wigeon, and pintails. The refuge is also home to great blue herons, towhees, woodcocks, red fox, nutria, Asian sika deer and otters. Protecting endangered species, such as the Delmarva fox squirrel, is a key goal of the refuge and special efforts are taken to restore and maintain the habitat necessary for their survival. The rhythm and population of the marsh changes with the seasons. On a winter's walk you could find bald and golden eagles and swans and ducks that are wintering in the refuge. Come spring and you might spy young eaglets and watch the return of migrants such as blue- and green-winged teal. In the summer unsteady goslings take their first tentative trips into the air while the marsh and woodland flowers are in full bloom. During the autumn months, waterfowl numbers are on the rise

Sunrise at Blackwater NWR, Maryland. Credit: Robert Shallenberger and the U.S. Fish and Wildlife Service.

Jack H. Elrod, a noted conservationist and creator of the Mark Trail comic strip, drew this cartoon in 1989 to draw more attention to the Federal Duck Stamp Program. The cartoon also appeared as part of a souvenir card for the World Stamp Expo in 1989. Elrod was a judge for the 1991 duck stamp art contest. Credit: Jack H. Elrod.

and the trees put on a dazzling and fiery show of color as the leaves turn. Like all refuges, Blackwater has the ability to offer each visitor a unique natural show.

The federal government isn't the only entity working hard to preserve critical habitat and come to the aid of migratory waterfowl. Following the federal lead, all fifty states have instituted their own waterfowl hunting stamp programs; although never did all fifty do so at the same time. Several states have issued voluntary-purchase duck stamps, not required for hunting. The proceeds from the sales of these various state ducks have purchased refuges and sanctuaries. Tribal governments, too, have issued waterfowl stamps, and most of the generated revenues go into "conservation pools" which distribute the money as needed. Non-government organizations have also been extremely effective. Foremost among these groups is DU, the world's largest wetlands and conservation group, with over 700,000 members. DU's mission is to "fulfill the annual life cycle needs of North American waterfowl by protecting, enhancing, restoring and managing important wetlands and

associated uplands." Since its inception in 1937, DU has generated more that $1.3 billion that has helped to conserve nearly 9 million acres spread over all fifty states, Canada, and parts of Mexico. DU's engineering experts and biologists are involved in a great range of projects intended to support the groups' mission. These include restoring grasslands and watersheds, replanting forests, and working with private landowners to ensure that lands under their control are more wildlife friendly. DU amplifies the impact of its work by partnering with a variety of organizations, including the U.S. F&WS.

From the dismal days of the 1930s, migratory bird populations have made a dramatic comeback. During the 1990s, fall migrations of ducks were, on average, very strong. The 1999 fall flight index, published by the U.S. F&WS, predicted a total of 105 million ducks flying south in Autumn, a substantial increase over the previous year's index of 84 million, and considerably higher than the record of 92 million set in 1997. The population of breeding ducks has also remained at high levels, with 1999 recording 43.8 million breeders in key nesting areas, the highest level since the

Breeding Waterfowl and Habitat Survey began in 1955. While there are other factors, such as weather conditions, which contribute to this turnaround there is no doubt that the combined effects of setting aside critical habitat as well as improving the management of species has had a major impact on the improved health of migratory waterfowl populations nationwide in the decades since the "dirty thirties." Without the efforts of the federal, state, and tribal governments, as well as private groups like DU, many species of migratory waterfowl would be in critical, perhaps terminal, shape and duck hunting would likely be a relic of times gone by.

Healthier populations translate into better and increased hunting opportunities. There are roughly 300 hunting and 300 fishing programs offered within the refuge system. Nevertheless, the battle is far from won. While overall populations of ducks are in good shape, certain species are still struggling. Also there is a great variability in species counts as one moves from region to region and from year to year. The wealth of migratory waterfowl is not evenly divided geographically or temporally. There will continue to be good and bad times. Hence, there is a critical need for more refuges, improved waterfowl management, and continued responsible hunting practices on the part of sportsmen. The Federal Duck Stamp Program will continue to play an integral role in insuring that never again will anyone look to sky and wail "the ducks are gone!"

IMITATION IS THE SINCEREST FORM OF FLATTERY

The Federal Duck Stamp Program's success in preserving critical natural habitat has spawned many imitators at the state, tribal, federal, and international level. In the United States there have been more than 1,500 different types of non-federal duck stamps issued since the 1930s. Referring to state, local, and tribal duck stamps as such is a misnomer. The vast majority of these stamps are actually waterfowl stamps covering not just ducks, but also a great variety of gamebirds. For example, only two states, Nevada and California have issued true "duck" stamps. Nevertheless, the common "duck" designation is used here, interchangeably with waterfowl stamps.

State duck stamps are the most diverse from virtually any perspective. The dizzying profusion of formats, issues, purposes, styles, prices, species, etc., makes state duck stamp collecting challenging and exciting. Ohio was the first state to issue a duck stamp to raise funds for the protection of waterfowl. In 1937, Ohio and Pennsylvania entered into an agreement that allowed Ohio residents to pay an extra fee for the privilege of hunting waterfowl on Pymatuning Lake, a large man-made reservoir that straddles the border between the two states, but which was controlled by Pennsylvania. The following year, Ohio began issuing Pymatuning Lake Waterfowl Stamps and continued to do so annually until 1945, when the agreement was repealed and the lake opened to licensed hunters from either state without an extra charge. Because these stamps have only text on their face and no artwork, they are usually referred to as non-pictorial waterfowl or duck stamps. Recent research by David R. Torre, the leading expert on non-pictorial waterfowl stamps, suggests that there might have been an undated Lake Pymatuning Waterfowl Stamp issued in late 1937. No matter the year of issue, these stamps are exceedingly rare, with as few as 100 stamps being sold annually.

Following Ohio's lead, many states created non-pictorial duck stamps in subsequent decades. One of

The much-coveted, 1938 Pymatuning hunting license stamp. While there is some evidence that an undated Pymatuning license stamp was issued to cover part of the waterfowl season in 1937, most people believe the 1938 issue to be the first of this series, which ended in 1945. For over forty years, this 1938 stamp was not only the only copy for that year known, but also the only copy of any Pymatuning stamp known. According to David R. Torre, this is "as legendary of a rare stamp as any we get in the waterfowl hobby."

The first state-pictorial stamp. Credit: Sam Houston Duck Company.

the most interesting facets of collecting these stamps is their condition. With no eye-catching design on the front to lure collectors, these stamps were true workhorses, produced and sold for one purpose - to enable the purchaser to hunt waterfowl. That is why, in many cases, all known examples are used, ones that have been removed from licenses - no mint copies exist. It was not until 1971 that California issued the first state-issued pictorial duck stamp, and since then many other states have followed suit, further expanding the reach and variety of state duck stamp collecting.

All states, at one time or another, have used duck stamps to raise funds for conservation, but there has never been a single year in which every state has issued a stamp. Many states take after the national program in that the design is selected through a public competition and the price of the stamp and its expiration date appear on the face. A significant number of states commission artists to come up with a design. In recent years, the number of states with stamps has fluctuated between the low forties and fifty. Reasons cited by states for dropping their programs are heightened costs of production and diminishing revenue. A growing trend is for states to issue electronic, point-of-sale hunting licenses instead of the more traditional printed stamps. In some instances, these "electronic" states still retain printed stamps which can be voluntarily purchased but are not required for hunting. One thing is certain, the number of duck stamp-issuing states will rise and fall as state legislatures and allied organizations continue to reevaluate their commitment to these programs.

Not long after Ohio paved the way with state-level duck stamps, local governments got into the act. In 1941, Marion County, Kansas became the first of these to issue a local waterfowl stamp. Two years later, Marion County achieved another distinction by issuing the world's first stamp with the words "DUCK STAMP" on its face. Marion County continued issuing waterfowl stamps up through 1973, making it the longest consecutively issued waterfowl stamp series of any state or local government. This series of stamps has produced some of the most interesting and sought-after gems in the hobby of duck stamp collecting. In 1969, a typesetting error created a number of stamps that misspelled "Duck" as "Dusk," apparently giving the holder the right to hunt for twilight or perhaps a little known species of waterfowl. The 1949 "Waner" license, which has affixed to it the Marion County duck and fishing stamps issued that year (the only recorded examples of both issues), as well as a Kansas Quail stamp and the 1948 federal duck stamp, is generally regarded as the most important license in fish and game philately.

In addition to state and local governments, Indian tribes have also issue waterfowl stamps. Indian reservations are established by treaty, and they are considered the land of "sovereign" Indian Nations. In 1959,

A selection of excellent state duck stamps - Iowa 1985, Minnesota 1991, New Hampshire 1997, and North Carolina 1994. Credit: Sam Houston Duck Company.

the Rosebud Sioux Tribe in South Dakota became the first tribal government to issue waterfowl stamps. Other tribes have added stamps of their own, including the Cheyenne River Sioux, Crow, Crow Creek Sioux, Lower Brule, Oglala Sioux, Jicarilla Apache, and the Confederated Salish and Kootenai Tribes. Some tribes issue separate waterfowl hunting stamps, while others issue general hunting stamps or combined hunting and fishing stamps. Hunters are required to purchase a tribal stamp before hunting on the reservations. There are instances where the stamp sold to tribe members differs from those sold to non-members.

Defining which state stamps are true duck stamps is a pursuit that is not for the faint of heart. Consider the following permutations that face the would-be cataloguer. Each stamp in Massachusetts' long-running Waterfowl Stamp program depicts a decoy, and some of them do not even represent migratory waterfowl species. Texas, Utah, and other states have issued waterfowl stamps that are not valid for hunting, their purchase is purely voluntary. In 1994, New Mexico issued an $80 jumbo Wetlands Benefactor stamp, roughly 2 inches x 3 inches, to raise funds for wetlands conservation. Some states, including Idaho and Mississippi have issued stamps showing a photograph of waterfowl rather than an image based on a painting. Nevada's 1991 duck stamp pictures a white-faced ibis, which should be red-faced since it is neither a gamebird nor a commonly recognized species of migratory waterfowl. New Hampshire's 1987 Governor's Edition waterfowl stamps were not sold by the state, but by a private organization. Are all these duck stamps variations on a theme, or are some of them so far afield from the duck stamp concept that they should be considered something else entirely? The State Revenue Society became so concerned about the confusion arising from the great variety of state issues that in 1998 they published in their newsletter

The "Waner" License, issued to Marion County Park and Lake Supervisor, John Waner, is generally regarded as the most important license in fish and game philately. Credit: David R. Torre Collection.

1989 Crow Creek Sioux Tribe resident waterfowl stamp. Credit: David R. Torre Collection.

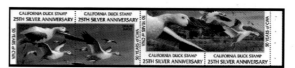

California's 1995 stamp, voted the "Most Abusive and Confusing" by Bob Dumaine, due to the cost to collectors ($42) and the juxtaposed, cluttered design. The actual stamp measures 8 3/8" long. Credit: Sam Houston Duck Company.

an article with the title "When is a State Duck Stamp not a Revenue Stamp?" offering readers a list of criteria that they could apply. While such a list might be a helpful guide, beauty is still in the eye of the beholder. Where you fall on the scale, from purist to those with a laissez-fare attitude, will determine how you classify state duck stamps. Perhaps the best advice for the wary is the oldest - if it looks like a duck, walks like a duck, and quacks like a duck, it's a duck!

One of this book's authors, Bob Dumaine, annually writes a light-hearted review of the best and the worst of the state issues in his Duck Stamps column for *Linn's Stamp News*. Although you can quibble with his selections, they are always interesting and sometimes hilarious. Dumaine admits to not having any artistic talent, and his comments and suggestions are his opinions from his daily, repetitive handling of the stamps. Dumaine says, "Some of these characteristics just jump out at you, and while all the artwork is good, some stretch the imagination. Remember, movie critics cannot act, but are free to give opinions in the same vein as my observations are offered." He hopes that by offering a tongue-in-cheek look at some of the artwork, it will spur the artists to create what he considers a better quality and more salable stamp. The honors for the all-time ugliest duckling of duck stamps goes to the 1978 California issue, where, through a bureaucratic mix-up, the artist's work was only traced onto the stamp face, instead of reproduced fully in color. California's 25th Anniversary issue, a strip of four, meant to be a block of four, gained his chilling award of "the most abusive and confusing" stamps of 1995. Since all four stamps have a different design, a collector needs all four to maintain a complete collection. At $10.50 per stamp, that amounts to a nifty $42 per collector. Worse yet, the design was modified to fit a booklet of four format, resulting in a juxtaposed design. Massachusetts garnered two tackiest color stamp awards for the "best" fuschia stamp in 1994, and again in 1997 for their neon-yellow stamp. Washington's 1994 stamp won that year's award for the most ducks on one stamp, with about seventy-five ducks and decoys wedged into the image, none of which are very clear. Oklahoma's 1990 stamp and Delaware's 1991 stamp merit Dumaine's bookend awards. Both were painted by the same artist, and are too close for comfort. Dumaine recalls the agent of Delaware calling him in to report the winning design. When he saw the image, he called the state agent and told her he was not

Massachusetts' 1994 and 1997 state stamps garnered the "Tackiest Color" awards for their fushia and neon yellow designs. Credit: Sam Houston Duck Company.

Washington's 1994 stamp weighs in with roughly 75 ducks, winning the "Most Ducks on One Stamp" award. Credit: Sam Houston Duck Company.

The same artist, Ron Louque, as is apparent, painted Oklahoma's 1990 stamp and Delaware's 1991 stamp. He did a similar design, featuring two mergansers, on Pennsylvania's 1989 stamp. Credit: Sam Houston Duck Company.

California's 1978 stamp, voted "All Time Ugliest" state stamp. A bureaucratic mix-up caused only the outline of the design to appear on the stamp. Credit: Sam Houston Duck Company.

The 1983 Federal Duck Stamp and the 1993 Minnesota state duck stamp were both done by artist Phil Scholer, and look quite similar in design. Credit for the federal stamp: U.S. Fish and Wildlife Service; Credit for the state stamp: Sam Houston Duck Company.

The 1998 Junior Duck Stamp. Credit: U.S. Fish and Wildlife Service.

Ryan Kirby's winning artwork of wood ducks that appeared on the 1999 Junior Duck Stamp. Credit: U.S. Fish and Wildlife Service.

surprised it won, since it had won the Oklahoma contest the year before. He recalls the agent saying "Oh no!" The same artist did a similar design, but featuring two mergansers, on Pennsylvania's 1989 stamp, proving if you've got a good thing, stick with it. A duplicate award goes to the artist for the 1993 Minnesota stamp which mimics his winning 1983 federal design. Except for changing the species from blue-winged teal to pintails, the images smack of duplication, probably due to the same photo shot being used as a model. Dumaine points out that most of the state designs have terrific artwork, and artists are strained to come up with a new design each year. So what's his all-time personal choice for the best state duck stamp? Dumaine says, "it's the one that hasn't been issued yet. However, Arkansas, Delaware, Minnesota, and South Carolina consistently have maintained beautiful and accurate stamps over the years, as well as a smart and non-abusive program to collectors. In addition to a few others, almost any from these states would qualify as my favorite."

In 1989, the Federal Duck Stamp Program expanded to include a Junior Duck Stamp Conservation and Design Program. The goal of this contest is to teach students about conservation through the arts. The program, which began as a collaboration between the U.S. F&WS and the National Fish and Wildlife Foundation, now is run by the Duck Stamp Office. Combining curricular materials focusing on conservation with an art contest, the Junior Duck Stamp Program has taught thousands of students nationwide about this country's waterfowl and the need to protect them.

Each year the "best of show" winner from each state's junior competition advances to the nationwide contest in Washington, D.C. As in the federal competition, a panel of experts in waterfowl, art, and philately judges the student entries. The first-, second-, and third-place finishers, along with their art teachers, receive a three-day trip to Washington where they attend the Federal Duck Stamp Competition and are honored at a formal reception. The first place painting is made into a stamp and the winning artist is awarded a $2,500 scholarship. Junior duck stamps can be purchased through the Duck Stamp Office and many duck stamp dealers. The revenue from the sales of these stamps supports conservation efforts in the states. Like its adult counterpart, the Federal Junior Duck Stamp Program allows for merchandising of both the stamp image itself, as well as the artwork.

The Federal Junior Duck Stamp program gained additional prominence in 1999 when Tennessee decided to place on its duck stamp artwork by Bethany Carter, the winner of the state's junior duck stamp competition who went on to represent her state at the federal level. It is the first time a winning state junior artwork has been depicted on a state stamp. This was accomplished with the approval of the U.S. F&WS since the junior duck stamp design contest is federally funded and use of the images requires the service's approval. Perhaps other states will follow Tennessee's lead, especially since art costs are nil and the quality of the artwork often quite high.

The success of the federal duck stamp has not been lost on foreign governments, a number of which have come up with their own programs. As is the case with state issues, foreign "ducks" are a confusing group because of the various governmental differences. Many of these programs have elements that are comparable to the U.S. program, i.e., stamps are issued by the government, must be possessed while hunting, and the revenues go toward conservation of migratory waterfowl. A number of the "foreign government" duck stamps are not actually issued by the government and are therefore not official. Others, while issued by the government, are not required for hunting and seem more aimed at the philatelic market, as they come in a great variety of formats, including mini-sheets, souvenir sheets, singles, gutter pairs and plate blocks. Some that appear to be duck stamps are actually better termed conservation stamps since revenue is not dedicated to the cause of migratory waterfowl, but more generally to wildlife conservation. Once again, whether it is or isn't a foreign duck stamp is for you to decide.

Determining which foreign government was the first to issue a duck stamp is a bit tricky. It depends on how you define foreign government. As early as 1946, the Canadian Province of British Columbia issued a 50-cent duck stamp. The light green and black stamp also used the words "Duck Stamp," rather than the conventional "waterfowl" term. This same identification was used for the next year, a yellow and blue issue, which is far more common than the 1946 issue. For the 1948 through 1951 issues, the designation was modified to "Conservation Stamp." Both the 1946 and 1947 stamps were issued in booklet panes of four each, with 25 panes to a booklet. A great deal of mystery surrounds these issues, particularly regarding their use and purpose. Perhaps these stamps were the first duck hunting revenue stamps of a foreign country, although British Columbia is a Province of Canada, and a province is akin to a state of the United States, not a stand-alone foreign government. According to Dr. Ian McTaggart-Cowan, and avid hunter who was on the scene in 1946 and familiar with these stamps, the stamps were "semi-official," having been issued by the British Columbia Hunter and Anglers Association, with all of the proceeds going to the government for conservation. Funds so received were publicly accounted for in British Columbia's

annual report, attesting to the formal nature of the program. Dr. McTaggert-

The 1946 British Columbia Duck Stamp. Credit: E.S.J. Van Dam.

A selection of extremely attractive foreign duck stamps - Argentina 1994, Australia 1996, Iceland 1991, and Spain 1996. Credit: Sam Houston Duck Company.

Cowan said the stamps were not mandatory, but were sold wherever licenses were sold, and bought by many hunters. A recognized expert in the field, E.S.J. Van Dam of Toronto, Canada, stated he has seen these issues actually used on licenses, but that fact alone does not mean they were required for duck hunting. Van Dam publishes The Canadian Revenue Stamp Catalogue, which lists the 1946 stamp at $1,600, and the 1947 at $20, both in Canadian dollars. Van Dam said the difference in value was almost certainly the result of remnants of the 1947 issue being obtained by collectors, whereas remnants of the former issue were destroyed. He also acknowledged that the 1947 issue exists mainly without gum, a few with disturbed gum, and very few with full original gum. This curiosity leads to the conclusion these stamps were discarded, and fell into moist conditions, possibly outdoors, and later recovered. Van Dam lists the 1948 issue at $110, 1949 at $275, and the 1950-51, a decal, at $650, all in Canadian dollars. The 1946 issue is the crown jewel of non-U.S. duck stamps, and highly sought by collectors, regardless of its uncertain purpose. The City of Winnipeg, in Manitoba, also issued a Wildlife Conservation stamp during the early 1950s. This issue was sponsored by the Winnipeg Game and Fish Association, and is considered as "semi-official." Large quantities of this issue on the market in various perforation varieties. Van Dam lists this issue's value at $7.50 Canadian. Canada began issuing Wildlife Habitat Conservation stamps in 1985, and since that date were joined by conservation issues from Nova Scotia, New Brunswick, Newfoundland, Labrador, Ontario, Quebec, Alberta, British Columbia, Saskatchewan, Manitoba, the Yukon, and the Northwest Territories, all of Canada's provinces. The conversation stamp idea has very strong roots in this important waterfowl habitat country.

Other foreign governments issuing duck stamps include (the first year of issue is in parentheses): Australia (1989), Russia (1989); United Kingdom (1991); Iceland (1991); Costa Rica (1992); Venezuela

(1993); Mexico (1993), New Zealand (1994); Argentina (1994); Mexico (1994); Denmark (1995); Israel (1995); Spain (1996); Sweden (1996); Ireland (1997); Croatia (1997); and Italy (1998).

In addition to duck stamps issued by governments, there are a great variety of waterfowl stamps issued by private, mostly non-profit organizations, such as DU and the NWF. Many of these organizations donate their surplus funds to the conservation of ducks and wetlands. While not required for hunting, their membership is encouraged to purchase the stamps, and in some cases the stamps are mandated for specific hunting areas or trips. The images on the stamps are frequently outstanding designs by well-known wildlife artists. For example, Darling designed the first stamp issued by the NWF in 1938. This is very appropriate since he helped to found the group and was its first president. Other federal duck stamp artists to design NWF stamps are Edward J. Bierley, Albert Earl Gilbert, Wilhelm Goebel, Robert W. Hines, Francis Lee Jaques, Maynard Reece, and Walter A. Weber. Most of these private stamps have a value, the organization's name, and the date of issue on the face of the stamp. Occasionally, some groups have sold the stamps post-season at a discount. In such cases, the stamps usually sell for less than the stated face value, usually about one-half, depending on the issue. In other cases, stamps were sold framed with accompanying prints, such as some DU issues, so the value of the stamp standing alone can be quite high. If the societies that support other game, such as quail, turkey, deer and other wildlife were placed alongside those that focus on waterfowl, the list would run for many pages. The list below includes a few of the organizations that are basically waterfowl-related, which include retrievers and decoys, and have issued stamps at one time or another. The list was prepared using data from David H. Curtis and Howard Richoux. In February 1997, Richoux published the Fish, Game, Nature and Society Catalog, which details many society stamps and their estimated values. It is available on CD-ROM or as a hard copy catalog, from Howard Richoux, 6721 Shamrock Rd. Lincoln, NE 68506, email howard.lnk@ispi.net.

Left: The very first National Wildlife Federation stamp in 1938, was designed by Darling and is quite similar to the image that appeared on the first federal stamp. Credit: Sam Houston Duck Company.

Right: The National Retriever Club's 1982 stamp, reminiscent of the famous federal stamp of King Buck (1959). Credit: Sam Houston Duck Company.

Dates of stamp issues follow the name

Alabama Chapter Wildlife Federation (1983-1984)
Alaska Professional Hunters Association (1985/1987)
Alaska Fish & Wildlife Federation (1986)
American Museum of Wildlife Art (1982)
American Sporting Dog Heritage (1982-1983)
Audubon Society Wildlife Conservation (1985-Present)
Buzzard Council of America (1980-1983)
Chesapeake Bay Conservation/Izaak Walton (1984-1987)
Colorado- Conservation Stamp (1974-1979)
Ding Darling Foundation (1984)
Ducks Unlimited Stamp of the Year (1984-Present)
Georgia Chapter Wildlife Federation (1983)
Iowa Ducks Unlimited (1989)
Indiana Chapter Wildlife Federation (1982-1983)
International Wildlife Foundation (1981-1983)
Long Island Wetlands & Waterfowl League (1977-1983)
Louisiana Wildfowl Carvers & Collectors Guild (1984-1986)
Louisiana Chapter Wildlife Federation (1985-1988)
Marshland Fund (1982)
Maryland- Wildlife Conservation (1985-1989)
Massachusetts Wildlands Stamp (1993-Present)
Michigan Duck Hunters Association (1982-1986)
Michigan Ducks Unlimited Sponsor (1986-Present)
Minnesota Conservation Federation (1982-1988)
Minnesota Farmers, Landowners & Sportsmen (1981-1983)
Mississippi Chapter Wildlife Federation (1982-1984)
Mississippi Conservation Stamp (1975)
Montana- Bird Art (1980)
National Fishing & Wildlife Foundation (1987-Present)
National Retriever Club (1982-1984)
National Wildlife Federation Stamp of the Year (1984-1991)
Nebraska Chapter Wildlife Federation (1983)
Nevada Chapter Wildlife Federation (1983)
New Mexico Chapter Wildlife Federation (1985)
North American Decoy Collecting Club (1983-1985)
North American Waterfowl Management Plan (1989-1990)
Ohio Wildlife Conservation Stamp (?)
Ohio Chapter Wildlife Federation (1985)
Oklahoma Ducks Unlimited (1989)
Pennsylvania Federation of Sportsmen's Club (1981-1990)
South Carolina Waterfowl Association (1988-Present)
Susquehanna River Waterfowl Association (1992-1994)
TVA Land Between the Lakes Wildlife (1988)
Tennessee Conservation League (1982//1991)
Virginia Chapter Wildlife Federation (1987)
Ward Brothers Decoys (1983)
Washington State Sportsmen's Council (1956-1958)
Waterfowl (USA) Limited (1983-1987)
Waterfowl (USA) Limited Wood Duck (1984//1986)
Wildlife Legislative Fund of America (1985)
Wyoming Chapter Wildlife Federation (1982-1984)

Stamps & Stamp Collecting

One of the most popular of all federal duck stamps, 1959 "King Buck" Stamp. Credit: U.S. Fish and Wildlife Service.

RY BIRD HUNTING STAMP

VOID AFTER
JUNE 30, 1960

$3

RTMENT OF THE INTERIOR

OBJECT OF DESIRE

On the first day of sale for the very first federal duck stamp, August 22, 1934, Darling purchased twenty-five stamps, graced with his own design, all affixed to Form 3333 as required by law. An affidavit officially documenting this event was prepared which signifies that Darling bought the first stamp at 1:30 p.m. The affidavit also indicates that he immediately presented this stamp to William M. Mooney, Postmaster of Washington, D.C. Thus, Mooney became the "first" federal duck stamp collector in the world. Darling also gave one of the first stamps to President Roosevelt, and the others were distributed among his friends and colleagues. After this auspicious start, duck stamp collecting took off. Mr. Mooney and President Roosevelt have since been joined by a legion of devoted followers of the longest running, continuous series of stamps ever issued in the United States, which can boast some of the most beautiful stamps ever created.

Duck stamp collectors are not a homogeneous group. Some are strictly stamp collectors, who focus on mint or used specimens, or both. Others are hunters who either save their hunting stamp or purchase additional copies because they are pretty or to serve as mementos of the hunt. Still others purchase the stamps primarily to support conservation efforts or because they collect hunting licenses including those for waterfowl. If you add together all these different types of collectors, their ranks swell to between 300,000 and 400,000. The quantity of duck stamps available to collectors is quite limited. Only 635,001 of the first

duck stamp were sold and many of those were discarded or remain hidden away among personal family papers. While sales of duck stamps have fluctuated since 1934, the numbers are relatively small compared to all but the most limited of regular U.S. stamp issues. For example, 1,913,861 of the 1984 duck stamp, the 50th anniversary issue, were sold. In contrast, the U.S. Postal Service issued 123,575,000 of the 1984, 20-cent stamp commemorating the 50th anniversary of the duck stamp.

With so much demand for the stamps, and only a finite supply, it is little surprise that the market for

"J.N. "Ding" Darling (center) purchasing the first duck stamp from 3rd Assistant Postmaster General C.B. Eilenberger (right). Washington D.C. Postmaster W.M. Mooney looks on at left. The date of the purchase was August 22, 1934. · Credit: National Postal Museum, Smithsonian Institution.

duck stamps is strong and their value has risen considerably over the years. A collector who purchased each stamp the year it was issued would have paid a total of $349, face value, up through 1999. Today, a mint set of all these stamps would be worth between $3,000 and $9,000, depending on their condition. The pre-1940 stamps are particularly rare since the Migratory Bird Hunting Stamp Act originally required the destruction of all stamps that were not sold during the first year of issue. The rarest of these is the 1935 stamp, of which only 448,204 sold out of a total print run of 2,089,920. Although unsold stamps are still destroyed, the USPS and other select distributors currently sell each stamp for three years following its date of issue, giving collectors a little more time to add to their collection. (For a complete listing of duck stamp prices for all issues, please see the appendix titled Federal Duck Stamp Values on page 198.)

When one thinks of stamps, it is usually in the context of mailing letters or packages. This is not the case for duck stamps. Although they have a denomination on their face, duck stamps are not valid for postage. Instead, they are part of a varied and much-storied grouping called revenue stamps that are designed as a tax or fee on an activity. Money raised is used to support a particular government purpose. The first revenues in the American colonies were embossed imprints applied by the British government to general documents as well as playing cards and newspapers. These early revenue stamps symbolized one of the central conflicts between the colonists and their British rulers. The issue of taxation without representation ultimately fueled the American Revolution. The newly formed United States continued issuing embossed revenue stamps after the revolution, but with the new form of government they were now a form of taxation with representation, much more acceptable to the politically engaged populace. During the Civil War years, President Abraham Lincoln instituted a sweeping revenue-raising plan, part of which relied on the extensive use of revenue stamps which looked like postage stamps and were affixed to taxable items. Since that time, revenues have been applied to numerous products, including patent medicines, cosmetics, matches, potatoes, cigarettes, beer, wine, and narcotics, including opium, cocoa leaves and their derivatives. In the case of duck stamps, of course, the government purpose served is to purchase habitat to ensure the survival of waterfowl populations.

Although duck stamps are not to be used for postage, there is one very famous case where this rule was broken. It involved the so-called Graf Zeppelin cover. On September 19, 1934, G.W. Bartlett, of Glen Ridge, New Jersey, placed an envelope on board the SS Europa, bound for Southampton, England (evidenced by the duplex cancel on the stamp and a backstamp that was placed on the cover's reverse). It was addressed to him in care of some friends in Rio de Janeiro, Brazil. Such a lengthy trip required considerable postage and Mr. Bartlett obliged by sticking a single specimen of the first duck stamp on the cover. Whether Mr. Bartlett did this by design or by accident is lost to history, but given the particulars of the story it appears likely that he knew exactly what he was doing and wanted to see if he could get this most unusual and improper cover successfully through the mail.

After leaving New York, the cover landed in Southampton on September 23, where it was sent via catapult mail flight from the deck of the SS Europa to Berlin (cancellation on the lower-left corner of the cover). The cover arrived in Berlin on the same day and was immediately forwarded via air post to Freidrichshafen, Germany (cancellation near the cover's center). From there it was placed aboard the Graf Zeppelin, bound for Rio de Janeiro by way of Pernambuco, Brazil (cancellation in upper-left corner). From this destination, the cover was returned to Mr. Bartlett either by the addressee or through some other means.

During its circuitous route, the zeppelin flight commander, Hugo Eckner, signed the cover. This probably happened in Friedrichshafen or upon arrival in Brazil. Eckner's personal signature was difficult to acquire, so perhaps Bartlett had made some special arrangement or was a personal friend of the commander. The cover also bears a curious pencil inscription, "C761," which may refer to Bartlett's cabin number. A search for the ship's manifest turned up nothing, so "C761" will remain a mystery. Bartlett was undoubtedly aided in his attempt to make postal history by the newness of the duck stamp and the route the cover traveled. The 1934 duck stamp had been issued only twenty-eight days prior to its use on this cover when knowledge of the regulations pertaining to its use was still not widespread. Had the letter been posted say, six months hence, it is likely a postal worker would have caught the mistake and told Mr. Bartlett that this duck would not fly. If the regulations governing duck stamps were new and unfamiliar to U.S. postal workers, imagine what a mystery this strange stamp with flying ducks must have been to the foreign mail handlers who saw it as it flew to South America! The Graf Zeppelin cover now resides in the Smithsonian Institution's National Postal Museum, courtesy of Mrs. Jeanette Cantrell Rudy.

There are probably as many different types of duck stamp collectors as there are ducks. Some focus on amassing a complete set of mint stamps, ones that were never used and still retain their original gum on the back. Others seek used stamps, with hunters' signatures across the face. There are those who want

The famous Graf Zeppelin cover, front and back. Credit: Jeanette Cantrell Rudy and the National Postal Museum, Smithsonian Institution (photo by Larry Gates).

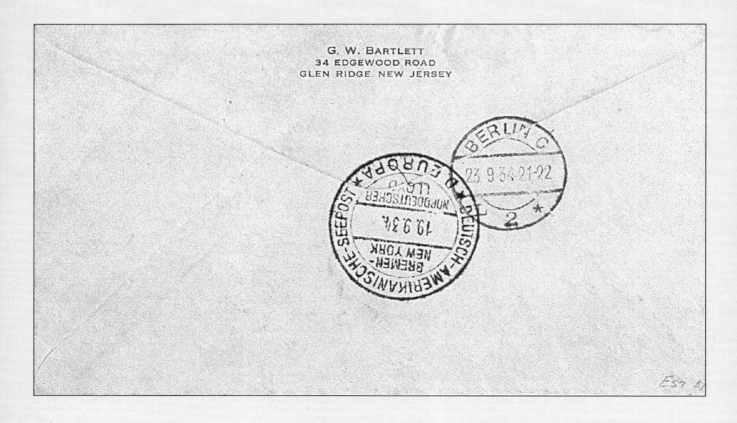

artist-signed stamps, stamps with printing errors, plate blocks, and full panes. Collectors of U.S. stamps or hunting licenses would certainly include ducks in their collection to round things out. Topical collectors specializing in stamps that depict birds or which relate to hunting might add duck stamps to their albums. First Day Cover collectors will also find plenty of ducks. There are numerous variations on these themes. A collection can be customized to fit the personality and creativity of the collector.

Whatever you choose to collect, someday you may be called a philatelist. Don't take offense, philatelist is simply another term for stamp collector, and philately is the activity of stamp collecting. These terms were coined in 1864, in an article by M. Georges Heprin in the French journal *Le Collectionneur de Timbres-Poste*. Twenty-five years earlier, in 1840, postal reformer Rowland Hill of Great Britain instituted the use of the "Penny Black", the world's first adhesive postage stamp,

and the hobby of stamp collecting was born. Mr. Heprin was casting about for a formal way to describe the new hobby and those that pursued it, when he hit upon philately and philatelist, which are derived from the Greek roots philos, meaning "love of", a, indicating a negative, and telos, "charge." The last part of the word can also be derived from the Greek, atelia, "exemption from payment" or "free from charge." Thus, philately means, "love of that which is without charge." It refers to the how the use of stamps replaced the earlier postal practice of having the sender and/or recipient of a piece of mail pay a direct fee for this service, as opposed to pre-paying the fee with a stamp.

No matter what you are called or what you collect, there is really only one main requirement in this hobby - enjoy it. Collecting duck stamps connects you to a broader community of interesting and interested people who share your passion.

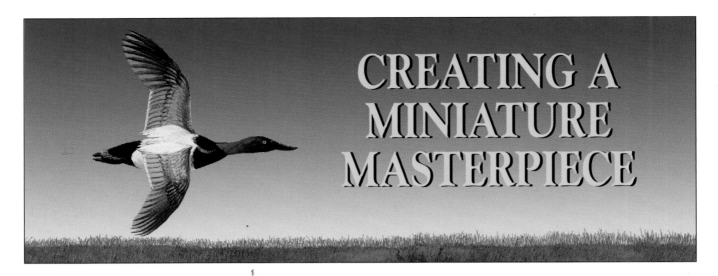

CREATING A MINIATURE MASTERPIECE

In order to collect a stamp someone has to print it. With duck stamps, the honor of creation goes the BEP. There are many steps in the transformation of a winning duck stamp design from artwork to stamp, all of which require the talents of a diverse cast of characters. Their combined efforts annually produce what are arguably among the most beautiful of all United State's stamps - true miniature works of art. The first step in this transformation is ensuring that the artwork selected at the annual art contest for federal duck stamp will translate well into a philatelic form. According to Leonard Buckley, former Assistant Foreman of Product Design and Engraving at the BEP, "if there is any detail you cannot easily recognize, it probably won't reproduce well in stamp size miniature." The BEP representative at the judging for the art contest helps to ensure that the judges are informed of the intricacies of producing a stamp and the need for a certain level of detail in the original artwork. Largely because of this preparation, the BEP has had few problems. As Buckley notes, "none of the images we have received has been particularly difficult to deal with." There was one instance, however, where both the BEP and the U.S. F&WS were concerned about the reproducing a winning design, not because of the level of detail in the artwork, but because of its color, or lack thereof.

Alderson Magee's winning design of Canada geese for the 1976 stamp was in black and white, even though color entries had been the norm since 1970. When Magee got word from Robert Hines of the U.S. F&WS that he had won, he also was told that the service and the BEP planned to produce the stamp in color. This got Magee very upset. He felt that "It was judged as a black and white piece and that is what it should have stayed." Magee wasn't the only one upset. Immediately after the judging was over, Hines and the representative from the BEP told the judges that they were going to add color to the design when it was turned into a stamp. This angered the judges who also felt strongly that the

stamp's design should be true to the original design. Two of those judges, George Reiger and Les Line knew that the art editor of *The Washington Post* was sitting in the audience. They called him up and asked Hines and the BEP representative to repeat what they had just said. When they did, the art editor exclaimed "boy, that's my story right there!" Two days later, the paper ran a story on Magee's win highlighting the controversy over color. By this time, however, the Department of the Interior began to waffle. In the article, an Interior official was quoted as saying, "[t]here's no controversy here. Black and white or color? A Committee will decide."

The "committee" ultimately decided to leave good enough alone and print the stamp in black and white. It is likely that the *Post* article, and the publicity it generated, tipped the balance in favor of that decision. But Magee points to one other factor that might have played a role. Soon after the contest, Magee was at the Easton Waterfowl Festival where he met Senator Barry Goldwater (R-AZ), a hunter and waterfowl enthusiast. During the conversation Magee confided his concern over colorizing the stamp. Shortly after Magee returned home, Hines called to say the stamp would be black and white. While Magee is not sure Goldwater intervened on his behalf, he thinks that is likely the case.

The BEP decides on the lettering, the border, how the colors will be separated, and what printing methods and equipment will be used to produce the stamp to its best advantage. While the BEP has some flexibility in deciding what portion of the original artwork will be on the stamp, it cannot make any final decisions on this issue without the approval of the U.S. F&WS. In the past, just after the contest the BEP received the original painting so that it could ensure the accuracy of the color and begin preparing the final model of the new stamp - a finished size, photographic reproduction of what the stamp actually will look like. Beginning with the 1999 stamp this process changed. Now, shortly after the contest

Alderson Magee's winning artwork for the 1976 federal duck stamp. Credit: Alderson Magee.

The 1976 federal duck stamp. Credit: U.S. Fish and Wildlife Service.

the BEP receives the artwork for a few days to make a digital scan of it. The BEP uses the scan to produce souvenir prints and for pre-press operations for the gummed and self-adhesive stamps. The original artwork then begins its "victory" tour of stamp shows and waterfowl festivals, returning to the BEP briefly at the end of December, when the engraving process truly begins.

The master steel die of the intaglio (pronounced in-tal'-yo) image is engraved by hand. Intaglio, which is Italian for "below the surface", refers to a method of printing in which the design is recessed into the face of the printing plate. During printing, the ink, which is held in the depressions on the plate, is transferred onto the paper. The depth and pattern of the engraving and the pressure applied during printing are the factors that determine the amount of ink that is pulled out of the depressions and transferred to the paper. The more ink that is transferred, the higher the relief on the paper.

Engraving is a skill that is not easily acquired. At the BEP, letter and script and sculptural engravers serve a seven-year apprenticeship and portrait (picture) engravers serve a ten-year apprenticeship with an instructor, after which they ascend to journeyman status. During Gary Chaconas' 30-year career with the BEP, he has engraved six federal duck stamps, the 1989, 1990, 1991, 1993, 1994, and

BEP engraver, Gary Chaconas, working on the 1994 federal duck stamp. The photo shows the model, an engraving proof, and the die for the stamp. The engraver's many tools can be seen to the right of the model. Credit: U.S. Bureau of Engraving and Printing.

1996 issues. Gary characterizes his job as "interpreting the painting into lines, dots, and dashes that will convey the value [light to dark] and texture of the design, and then engraving that interpretation into steel." The size of the steel dies can vary, with most of the ones for the duck stamp being 3.5 inches x 4 inches and one-quarter inch deep. The dies start out in rough shape and the plate finishers and engravers burnish the surface to a mirror-like finish, which allows for more consistent cutting and etching of the steel. The engraver then transfers the image of the design to the face of the die through an elaborate process. The first step is making an acetate tracing of the design using a sharpened steel point. This is actually an intaglio process, only that the cuts are made into acetate not metal. The steel point leaves finely recessed lines that are so small that the engraver rubs a red powder over the surface in order to see them. Next the engraver rolls a thin layer of wax onto the acetate which adheres to the surface but does not go into the design. Placing the acetate on the steel die, wax side down, the engraver rubs the back of the acetate, transferring the wax to the die. Now the only part of the die that is exposed is the design. A diluted solution of nitric acid is poured over the surface of the die. Where there is wax, nothing happens, but where the acid touches the exposed design it discolors the surface of the steel like a stain. Thus, once the wax is removed with a solvent, an outline of the design remains that is used as a guide for the actual engraving. Because of the way in which both letters and the design itself are transferred to the die, the image that the engravers work on is reversed. Preparing a tracing for the design can take a week or more. It is particularly important to get it right during this stage, because the outline of the image that is left on the surface of the die determines where the engraving will appear. If the tracing is poor, so too will be the engraving and ultimate image that appears on the stamp.

With the die stained, the next decision is whether to use hand tools or to etch away the design with acid. Usually it is a combination of both methods and it is up to the engraver to make the call. For example, if a deep recessed line is needed, that will probably be done by hand, using a graver or burin to cut the steel. If finer lines were required, say for feathers, a solution of acid would likely be used. As with the original tracing, here too it is critical that the engraver be careful. Going too deep with the graver or leaving the acid on the surface a bit too long can ruin long hours of work. While it is sometimes possible to repair mistakes during the engraving process, it is not easy.

The process of engraving the letters and the design can take upwards of two months. And on rare occasions engravers will have to scrap a die they have worked on for days, weeks, or months because it just wasn't coming together. Chaconas had this experience with Miller's 1993 stamp. "We just weren't getting the results we needed," Chaconas recalls, "and we decided to start it again." At various stages of the engraving process, the master die is taken to a plate printer ("prover") who pulls a hand-proof of the image on a small press. These proofs enable the printer and engraver to marry the intaglio die image with the background color images of the stamp, the latter of which is usually produced by offset lithography. This enables BEP personnel to see how the overall stamp is coming together in terms of balance, color, fidelity and detail. The engraver can draw on the proof and decide where more color needs to go and then return to the die to do the additional work. For particularly intricate parts of the design, the engraver will make trips to the prover once a week or even more frequently. Another way of checking on the progress of the engraving is to compare the die with the original painting. Because of the demand for the painting on the "victory tour" and for other events, the BEP engravers only see the painting fleetingly at various times during the production process. When the actual painting is not available the engraver has plenty of high-quality photos, scans and working models to use as references.

There was a time when virtually all U.S. stamps were engraved. But with advances in other forms of printing, including offset lithography, which is less time-intensive and less expensive, the amount of engraving has dramatically dwindled. This trend has been evidenced to some degree in the duck stamp series. With the earlier issues, virtually the entire stamp was engraved. Today, the balance of engraving versus offset-lithography in a duck stamp varies depending on the availability of press time, the budget, and the nature of the design itself. Some stamps, like Wilhelm Goebels surf scoters in 1996 and Neal Anderson's red-breasted mergansers in 1994, have heavily-engraved designs. Others such as Howe's King Eiders in 1991 have very little engraving, largely because of limitations on press time. Each year, duck stamp collectors eagerly wait to see how much of the new stamp is hand-engraved because engraving is special, even if only because it is so rarely used in our increasingly mechanized world.

The engraver's role has not only varied based on the amount of engraving on the stamp, but also because of the nature of the original art. In the early years of the program the engravers often had to add considerable detail in translating the art onto the stamp. Perhaps the best example of this is Benson's artwork for the 1935 stamp. The relatively sparse and almost abbreviated artwork was given more detail during the engraving process, while still retaining the strong design. The early engravers, such as Carl T. Alt, Alvin R. Meissner, and James R. Lowe and their successors are the unsung artists who helped to give the stamps their incredible beauty. When comparing today's artwork with the finished stamp, you'll note very little alteration from the original. This is not a slight on the engravers. The ones working today are every bit as skilled as their predecessors. It is just that today's winning artists are well aware of the need to create detailed and well-balanced images that will reproduce well at stamp-size. Modern duck stamps invariably require less creativity of design on the part of BEP personnel, although the actual engraving process is much the same as it was in years past.

Plate printer, Mike Bean, making a die proof for the 1996 federal duck stamp on the Spider Press. Credit. U.S. Bureau of Engraving and Printing.

When the BEP is satisfied with the quality shown by the proof, preparation begins for printing production in early May. The first step is the creation of the printing plates. In the past, the master die was used to create a steel transfer roll to produce an intaglio printing sleeve. In 1999, however, a new process was put into place. The master die is now used to produce a negative from which the printing sleeve is photo-engraved in preparation for printing. This change has resulted in substantially lower costs during pre-press production. Once the copper sleeve is etched, it is chrome plated to protect it during the printing process where it is exposed to the abrasive wear and high pressures. In order to have the intaglio fall exactly in place over the offset print, the sleeve has to be exactly the right diameter. The tolerances are extremely tight. If the sleeve is even a little bit off, the printing process and subsequent perforating will not work properly and the quality of the stamp will suffer.

From 1934 through the 1958-59 issue, intaglio printing was done on a single-color flatbed press. Hence, all stamps produced during this period were printed in a single color; however, the varied depths of the engraving result in heavy and light ink areas that provide a wide tonal range from shadow to highlights. Between 1960 and the 1986 issue, intaglio printing was done on a rotary, sheet-fed press that could print up to three colors from a single plate. The

Artist Frank W. Benson's original black and white design. This comparison indicates the importance of the engraver's role for the early issues in particular. Credit: Jeanette Cantrell Rudy and the National Postal Museum, Smithsonian Institution (photo by Larry Gates).

The 1935 federal duck stamp. Credit: U.S. Fish and Wildlife Service.

offset colors were first printed on a sheet-fed offset press. This multi-press printing process was supplanted, in 1988, by the nine-color capability "D" press, which did everything on one pass through the system. The D press was the workhorse of the duck stamp printing program through 1995, when it was replaced by the "F" press. Giori, located in Lausanne, Switzerland supplied the F press for $12,000,000, but it was actually manufactured by Koenig and Bauer, located in Wurzburg-1, Germany. The F and D presses are quite similar, one difference being that the F press has the capacity to print four offset colors from a single tower unit, while the D press could print six. Even though the F press only has seven-color capability (both offset and intaglio), it runs better than D and offers a tighter image register and higher print quality. The first duck stamp printed with the F press was the 1996 issue.

Beginning in 1998, duck stamps were produced in two formats, traditional gummed and the new pres-sure-sensitive, self-adhesive (peel and stick) stamp (the self-adhesive is being issued on a three-year trial basis, beginning July 1, 1998). The gummed version uses LP-736 paper and a standard polyvinyl acetate gum applied by the paper manufacturer. Self-adhesives are printed on LP-800 paper, using a permanent acrylic adhesive also applied by the manufacturer. The printing process used for both versions of the stamp is identical. On the F press, the intaglio and offset steps are melded over the course of 200 feet and the printing speed is 300 feet per minute. First, all the offset colors are printed. Then the paper goes to the offset drier oven and chill roller, followed by an intaglio print station where the paper can be printed in one, two, or three colors. Next, the paper flies to the intaglio drier and chill roller. The printing of the new self-adhesives created some challenges for the BEP team. One of the first things to be considered was the thicker paper with a layer of adhesive in the center. Setting the drier ovens and chill rollers to achieve proper drying of the inks proved difficult, because at the normal settings the adhesive was becoming fluid, causing the paper and the liner to shift position. All of these problems were overcome during the testing phase and at present cause very few problems.

Another potential printing problem that affects both formats, to varying degrees, is snowflaking, or voids in the ink coverage because of valleys in the paper. Since the paper must have a coating that will accept both intaglio and offset printing, the paper manufacturer is sometimes forced to use a less than ideal coating for the offset part of the process, which can lead to snowflaking. This is less of a problem with the self-adhesive format because the paper used for it is much more forgiving in all phases of the printing process.

Once the stamp is printed, the process for the gummed and self-adhesive stamps diverges. After exiting the intaglio drier and chill rollers the gummed stamps move to the flexo unit, which flips them over and prints the prescribed words on the pregummed back of the paper. Next, the rolls of stamps are sent to roll examination, where errors and mistakes are removed, and then on to the off-line perforating section, where the rolls are perforated and cut into 120-sheet subjects. The off-line perforator creates a perfect "bull's-eye" hole where the corners of the stamps meet. The sheets are then sent to the bindery divided into panes of thirty subjects each and hand-inspected. Self-adhesive stamps also move to the flexo unit after exiting the intaglio drier and chill rollers, but instead of printing a back

The "F" press at the Bureau of Engraving and Printing, which prints today's federal duck stamps. Credit: U.S. Bureau of Engraving and Printing.

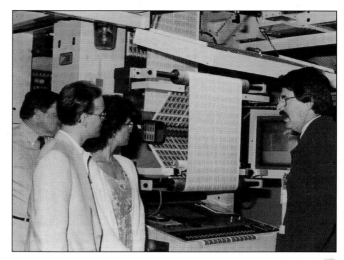

Artist for the 1996 stamp, Wilhelm Goebel, and his wife, Christine, watch as his stamp design is printed at the BEP. Credit: U.S. Bureau of Engraving and Printing.

inscription on the stamp, this is where all the text and images that appear on the back of the sheetlets is applied. Self-adhesives duck stamps are printed in sheets of twenty-four. Next, the sheets are sent to the Book Section where they are die-cut, separated into individual sheetlets and wrapped in one operation.

Perhaps the most impressive attribute of the F press is its speed. Early printing methods could require up to two weeks to produce the year's supply of duck stamps, whereas the F press can do the same run in a day. For example, the order for the 1999 federal duck stamp called for 9,950 sheets of the gummed variety and 116,650 self-adhesive sheets. Each format took half a day to print. Once BEP finishes the run, it packages the stamps and ships them to post offices nationwide, usually a month in advance of the issuance date.

For the BEP staff, producing the federal duck stamp is pure pleasure. According the Jerry L. Hudson Sr., Chief, Postage Stamp Printing and Processing, "We do it because we really want to. There is a lot of pride that everyone takes working on this particular job. Usually it is a lot prettier than other stamps, and it only happens once a year." Part of the joy of working on the federal duck stamp has to do with routine and rhythm. Each year the process unfolds in a familiar manner. The judging in the early fall, modeling over the holidays, proving through winter and early spring, printing in early May, and shipping by June. If a problem arises, the BEP has plenty of time built into the schedule to work it out.

COLLECTING DUCK STAMPS

There is no right or wrong way to collect duck stamps, but there are many tools that can make collecting more enjoyable. The first thing to learn are the terms for describing stamps, the language of the hobby. The most basic term is the name of the stamp. When discussing a particular stamp with someone how would you know you are talking about the same item if it didn't have a name? The most recognized naming system for all stamps, not just duck stamps, is the one employed by Scott Catalogue Company. Under this system, duck stamps are identified by the letters "RW," followed by a number which identifies where the stamp is in the series from the first stamp up through the most recent. "RW" stands for Revenue Waterfowl, denoting the fact that duck stamps fall into the category of revenue stamps and have as their subject waterfowl. Thus, RW1 refers to the very first duck stamp, and RW2, the second, RW3, the third, and so on. Another popular cataloguing system is found in the Krause-Minkus Standard Catalogue of U.S. Stamps. Like the Scott system, this one is simple, using letters and the number of the stamp in the series. Instead of "RW" each duck stamp is identified by "RH" which stands for Revenue Hunting. Finally, the stamps might be referred to by year alone. Thus, the first duck stamp, which was issued in August of 1934 and was valid until June 30, 1935, could be referred to either as the "1934" or the "1934-35" stamp. In this book we refer to all federal duck stamps by their year of issuance. Thus, Darling's stamp is the 1934 issue, and the next stamp is the 1935 issue, etc. To determine the number of the stamp in the series, subtract 1934 from the date printed on the stamp. For example, if a stamp is void after June 30, 1954, subtract 1934 to discover that the stamp is the 20th issued.

A name alone, however, conveys little information. Before a collector purchases a duck stamp, he/she needs to know the shape it is in, for that determines its value aesthetically and monetarily. In order to ensure ease of communication and under-standing among collectors, the hobby has developed a set of generic terms used to describe the quality of a stamp. Key ones relating to the face of the stamp include the following:

Condition - The condition of a stamp encompasses a variety of factors, including the brightness of color, clarity of design, the sharpness of perforations, integrity of the paper and gum, and the attractiveness of the signature. Stamps that are creased, stained, torn, have thin spots, or are missing perforations are considered to be in poor condition and are priced appropriately. There is no formal way of defining a stamp's condition, but once you have seen a number of examples of the same issue, the variability and importance of condition become apparent. With experience, you'll know a quality stamp when you see it.

Grading System - The grading system focuses on the centering of the design on the stamp. There are many grades of stamps, but the most widely used are extremely fine (XF), very fine (VF), and fine (F):

Extremely Fine (XF) - A stamp with a virtually perfectly centered design, with even edges, out to the perforations, on all sides. Duck stamps are difficult to find perfectly centered. Hence the collector will pay a premium for one that is XF.

Very Fine (VF) - The same as XF except that the design is slightly off-center on one side, but this does little to detract from the beauty of the stamp.

Fine (F) - The same as VF, except the design will be more off center, often on more than one side. This is the lowest grade of stamp that most collectors will accept.

Mint (M) - A stamp that is in the same condition as the day it was printed. In other words, as one would purchase it at the post office.

FINE
(F)

VERY FINE
(VF)

EXTREMELY
FINE
(XF)

The 1934 federal duck stamp showing the differences between the three primary grades of stamp. Credit: Sam Houston Duck Company.

Used - A stamp that has been signed by the hunter, or anyone else for that matter, or is somehow postally canceled. With regular postage stamps, this term refers to those that have been sent through the mail and canceled, either by hand or machine. Of course the famous Graf Zeppelin duck would classify as "used" under this definition, as would other postally-used duck stamps. The latter ducks, however, are quite different from the Graf Zeppelin stamp. While the Graf Zeppelin flew on its own power, other postally-used ducks are invariably ones that were "tied to" or set alongside regular postage stamps which covered the cost of mailing the envelope (see discussion under first day covers, below).

There are other early duck stamps that did not go through the U.S. mail but are nevertheless hand-canceled. This fact has led to some confusion among collectors who happen upon these stamps and think they have found an extremely rare duck like the one on the Graf Zeppelin cover. Visions of great wealth are dashed when such collectors learn the reason for their find. The original postal regulations governing duck stamps required that they "not be defaced in any way." This stipulation was requested by Darling in order to preserve the artwork on the stamp's face. Postal officials, however, soon realized that unsigned/canceled stamps could be transferred from one hunter to another, with everyone but the first in this chain gaining the privilege of hunting without paying the price for the stamp. To keep this from

happening, the postal regulations were changed with the issuance of the second duck stamp. From that point forward, hunters were to sign the stamps on their face. In neither case were postal workers supposed to cancel duck stamps. However, all postal workers did not carefully read or apply the regulations. Some did cancel duck stamps. While canceled, and therefore "used" specimens of the 1934 stamp and some other early issues are not common, they are not rare. Since many of the hand-canceled stamps have a circular cancellation with the name of the town or city, state and date, they are sometimes referred to as "socked on the nose."

If you think the gradings of XF, VF, and F and the condition of the stamp are subjective you're right. Stamp dealers with years of experience can disagree on the grading, especially of those specimens that fall on the cusp of two grades. Assessing condition is not an exact science either. Nevertheless, these terms form a workable identification system and no one has developed a better alternative. As a collector, the most important question is does the stamp look good to you? If the answer is yes and you are happy with the purchase, then the formal grading and condition is of secondary importance. However, if you're buying federal duck stamps for investment purposes, the quality of the stamp is critical. If you have any doubts, get an expert opinion, especially on the more expensive items.

The back of a stamp is as important as its face. Here, too, generic terms have been created to ensure that collectors are speaking the same language.

Gum - On the back of every mint federal duck stamp there is a gum layer which, when wetted, enables the stamp to be affixed to another object, usually a hunting license. Presence of the gum is one way to determine if the stamp is unused. But this can be tricky. As noted earlier, the 1934 through the 1945 stamps had no inscription on the reverse. For the 1946 through the 1953 issue, the inscription was printed directly on the stamp, with gum applied over it. Thus, for all of these issues it is possible to take an unsigned used stamp and re-gum it to sell as mint. Unfortunately, there are unscrupulous collectors and dealers who will perform this type of fakery, but they are the exception, not the rule. It takes an experienced eye to spot the fakes. One way to tell is to look at the perforation hairs. It is extremely difficult to apply gum to a stamp and avoid getting it on those hairs. If the hairs are gummed, the odds are that the stamp has been doctored. Re-gumming virtually disappears with later issues, 1954 up through the present. For these stamps, the inscription is printed on top of the gum. Therefore, if the gum is gone, so too is the inscription. However, there have been instances where fakers go to great length to recreate not only the gum but also the inscription on top.

Collectors of unused duck stamps not only look to see if the original gum is intact, they also consider its condition. The 1934 through the 1953 stamps were wet-printed and therefore it is not uncommon to find them with gum bends or skips. These imperfections are not considered a fault and do not detract from the stamp's value. Indeed, if you find such stamps with an exceptionally smooth gum, there is a good chance it has been re-gummed. If it's too good to be true, it probably is. Since the issuance of the 1954 stamp, however, a dry printing process has been used and stamps with gum bends and/or skips are considered abnormal and should be priced accordingly.

Hinged (H) - One of the ways in which duck stamps can be displayed in albums is by using little pieces of gummed paper, generally resembling wax paper, which are bent over in the middle. Once moistened, the hinge sticks to the back of the stamp and the album page, keeping the stamp from falling off. Hinges were invented as long ago as the 1860s. Careful use of high-quality hinges, which peel off easily, leave little trace on the stamp. Poor quality hinges, on the other hand, can wreak havoc on the stamp's back. If you see a stamp with a square or rectangular discoloration on the back or a similarly shaped patch of rough paper, chances are you're seeing the remnants of an overly zealous hinge that didn't want to come off. Or maybe you're looking at a piece of the hinge that simply stayed behind when the flap attaching the stamp to the album was ripped or cut off. Hinges went out of fashion with the invention of stamp mounts, enclosed, see-through pieces of plastic that shield the stamps without disturbing them. For the collector who is primarily interested in the design on the front of the stamp, purchasing hinged duck stamps is a great way to save money while obtaining a great-looking stamp, since dealers usually heavily discount hinged specimens. Stamps that have never been hinged are referred to, sensibly enough, as never hinged or NH.

Federal duck stamps come in many different formats. The most widely collected of these is the individual specimen, and one goal shared by many collectors is to have a complete set of duck stamps. While this is an expensive goal, it is one that the determined collector can clearly achieve. There are many other directions in which collectors can head, should they so choose, and for each one of the duck stamp formats listed below, there are many devotees.

Artist-signed - Ducks stamps are the only type of stamp which stamp artists routinely sign for collectors. The value of autographed duck stamps depends in part on whether the artist is dead or alive, with the former usually being the most expensive. The artists for the first fourteen stamps are all deceased, as are ten artists for later issues. Since some artists

have more than one win, the actual number of living artists is now twenty-seven. These artists represent about forty stamps, so a collector can obtain nearly two-thirds of the sixty-six artist-signed stamps with little difficulty and expense. Most of them will cost little more than the stamp's face value.

The 1934 stamp signed by Darling is one of the most desirable of all artist-signed duck stamps. Since he was one of the main reasons why the post office regulations for duck stamps originally forbade defacing them in any way, Darling originally was opposed to signatures and cancellations. Even after the law changed, Darling resisted requests for his signature, and he signed very few stamps in those early years. Nevertheless, later on Darling turned out to be a prolific signer, attending numerous public events around the country with pen in hand. There is great demand for Darling-signed stamps, but, unfortunately, many of them exist without gum or are faded from exposure to light. This has caused the value of quality singles to skyrocket to $3,000, depending on condition. Darling-signed stamps are even more interesting to collect because of their variety. He used at least four different signatures - J.N. Darling, Ding, 'Ding,' and J.N. Darling, alias Ding. Sometimes he added a "yours truly" or "your friend." As one would expect, the signature affects the price of the stamp, since some are more common than others. A more modern rarity is the artist-signed 1968 stamp. The artist, C. G. Pritchard died after signing about 100 stamps. He was on his way to a signing event when he suffered a medical emergency and died in a related car crash. While these stamps are not as valuable as Darling's, they come close.

Some artists used more than one signature due to health problems. Both J.D. Knap (1937) and Jack Murray (1947) suffered strokes. Their pre-stroke and post-stroke signatures are quite different. The former are smoother and in script. After the stroke, both men printed their signatures with apparent unsteadiness. The most difficult signatures to obtain are those of Roland Clark (1938) and Francis Jaques (1940), both deceased. Clark disliked signing and usually made the person requesting the signature agree not to sell it. Any dealers who asked him to sign would have their stamps returned, often with a caustic note. Jaques had a similar attitude. The few stamps he did sign are usually in bad shape since he used a brown ink pen that not only matched the sepia color of the stamp, but also tended to be unstable and susceptible to fading.

Whenever valuable autographs are involved there is always the threat or forgery. Fortunately, fake artist-signed duck stamps are rare. Only scarce stamps are eligible for forging, and the provenance of these can serve as a check against fakery. The majority of early signed stamps come from contemporary

Two 1934 federal duck stamps, each signed with a different Darling signature. Credit: Jeanette Cantrell Rudy and the National Postal Museum, Smithsonian Institution (photo by Larry Gates).

The 1938 federal duck stamp singed by the artist, Roland Clark. Credit: Jeanette Cantrell Rudy and the National Postal Museum, Smithsonian Institution (photo by Larry Gates).

autograph or print collectors who received the stamp as a gift from the seller, most often with a print. Such collections give credibility to the signature when all factors are present. If in doubt, ask an expert.

Certificates of Appreciation/Souvenir Cards - In the late 1950s, severe droughts threatened duck populations, necessitating stricter hunting regulations and shorter hunting seasons. Sales of federal duck stamps plummeted. This created a Catch-22. Fewer duck stamp sales meant less money to purchase lands to help the ducks make it through this bad time. In an effort to boost sales among hunters and non-hunters, the U.S. F&WS distributed the first certificate of appreciation for purchasers of a duck stamp, which were sent to post-season purchasers of the 1959 stamp. These 5-inch x 7-inch cards

are quite scarce because they were poorly publicized and have lack-luster appeal, printed in black and white on imitation parchment. The second and third certificates, with the 1960 stamp affixed, were issued the following year, 1961, and were as unpopular as their predecessors, making them very scarce and therefore valuable. Perhaps singed by this experience, the U.S. F&WS stopped issuing certificates until they resurrected the process in 1971, for a single year, and then again in 1984. In 1986, the U.S. F&WS issued an appreciation card for AMERIPEX, an international stamp exhibition and show held in Rosemont, Illinois. This kicked of a series of appreciation cards that were handed out at a wide variety of stamp shows, at national wildlife refuges, and directly from the Duck Stamp Office. Up through 1996, with a couple of exceptions, certificates of

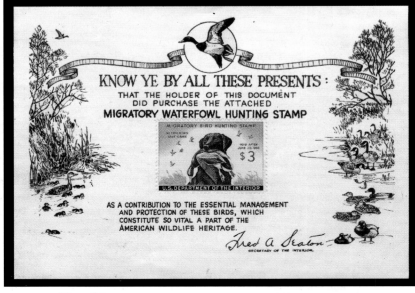

The 1960 certificate of appreciation presented to purchasers of the federal duck stamp, with stamp affixed. The certificate was part of an effort to get more people to buy duck stamps. Credit: Sam Houston Duck Company.

Two photo essays for the 1934 federal duck stamp. Neither was final, but the right one is very close to the design actually used. Credit: Sam Houston Duck Company.

appreciation accompanied all federal issues free of charge. Beginning with the 1987 issue and continuing up through the present, an upgraded card has been created in full color, and printed for the U.S. F&WS by the BEP. These cards are termed "souvenir cards," through their official status of being prepared by the BEP. Souvenir cards are sold in various formats — numbered, unnumbered, mint, first day cancels, artist-signed, and combinations thereof. According to the Duck Stamp Office, the souvenir card program will be continued. However, the gratis appreciation cards were discontinued in 1996 because of increases in printing costs and declines in customer participation. The quality of most souvenir cards is excellent, and they are highly collectible.

Essays - These are stamp designs not accepted for the issued stamp. The "dry-runs" on the way to a finished product. The sequence of essays traces the evolution of a stamp. The differences between early essays and final designs can range from relatively minor to fundamental. Another term you might hear is "photo essay." As expected, this is simply a photo of an essay stamp. In the early 1980s, Scott Auctions, of New York offered a group of photo essays. The holdings belonged to the widow of Alvin R. Meissner, the designer of the essays for the first six federal duck stamps, the 1934 through the 1939, as well as numerous other postage stamps. At the auction, four sets of photo essays for the 1934 issue were offered, two stamps per set. One essay had a divided border with the "$1" in a circle at the bottom. The second essay is essentially how the stamp was issued, except for the size of the "$1", which is larger than on the eventual stamp. The release of these photo essays was not authorized by the BEP and caused quite a stir when the auction was announced. Rather than confiscate the material, BEP decided to allow the sale for the widow, since her husband did design the essays and they were not legitimate stamps anyway (they sold for roughly $200 a set). While the

photo essays sold at this auction have been observed, the other duck essays, for the 1935 through 1939 issues, have remained hidden in a collection somewhere.

One of the most interesting set of essays are those created for self-adhesive federal duck stamp, which debuted July 1, 1998. While the first self-adhesive depicted Robert Steiner's design of a barrow's goldeneye, the essay proofs exhibit Wilhelm Goebels' 1996 stamp of surf scooters. The BEP used the engraving plates for Goebels' stamp to test the integrity of the self-adhesive paper under the extreme pressures of the intaglio printing process. Two sets of three different essays were created. Each essay was hand-cut to simulate the die-cut process and demonstrate the quality of the peel-and-stick feature of the new stamp.

At the end of 1998, the Federal Duck Stamp Office auctioned one set of the self-adhesive stamp essays, with proceeds going to the Migratory Bird Conservation Fund for the purchase of waterfowl habitat. The other set resides at the National Postal Museum. Bids were accepted by mail or fax and the opening bid was set at $25,000. Surprisingly, only one person bid — a "collector in the northeast" — and got the proofs for the minimum amount (a bargain since the bidder's submitted bid was more than double that amount). Presented in a blue portfolio adorned with the gold embossed emblem of the U.S. F&WS, the three proofs are accompanied by a special dossier tracing the changing design and evolution of the stamp.

First Day Covers (FDC) - When a postage stamp is issued there is often a special event where the new stamp is introduced and put on sale. These events are commemorated with FDCs, consisting of an envelope that has the new stamp affixed which is canceled on the first day of issue. First day events are usually held at a specially designated post office or location associated with the stamp. The cancel often indicates

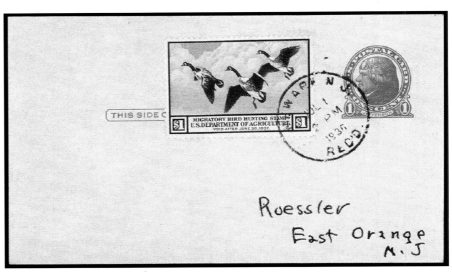

Third time is a charm for A.C. Roessler. After two failed attempts to create a FDC with a duck stamp, he succeeded on July 1, 1936, making this the very first federal duck stamp FDC. Credit: Jeanette Cantrell Rudy and the National Postal Museum, Smithsonian Institution (photo by Larry Gates).

the special nature of this philatelic item by stating that it is a "First Day of Issue." Since duck stamps are not legal for mailing, creating a FDC for them is done a little differently. On the first day of issue, both the duck stamp and a first class postage stamp are affixed to an envelope. Once the cancel is applied (tying the two stamps together), the duck cover can either begin its journey through the mail to the addressee or go directly into a person's collection. Since addressed FDCs are usually not wanted by second generation collectors, most collectors will send a second envelope to the Postal Service with the proper postage so that the FDC can be returned in the unaddressed condition. Naturally, the Postal Service loves this idea since they collect postage twice.

Early duck FDCs were created with little fanfare, invariably by a collector or dealer in search of a special philatelic item. One such dealer was A.C. Roessler, of East Orange, New Jersey. He was one of the first to make FDCs for postage stamps. In 1934, Roessler decided to make a FDC using the first duck stamp. The cover indicates that it is a first day issue, but the postmark is August 27, five days after the official first day of sale, August 22. The date is probably the first day of sale at his New Jersey Post Office, but not the national first day of sale. Roessler tried again with the 1935 stamp, but also missed the mark, in this case by a day. Finally, with the 1936 stamp, Roessler succeeded with a FDC canceled and dated July 1, 1936, making it the earliest known duck FDC with a nationally recognized first day of sale. If he performed this feat again with later issues they haven't surfaced. Despite Roessler's proclivity to publicize his philatelic activities there was little publicity surrounding these duck covers. The reason for this might be gleaned from a *Linn's Stamp News* article dated July 15, 1933, and titled "Roessler Pleads Guilty." The story recounts how Roessler admitted to using the mails in a scheme to defraud, "and the other [count] that he caused to be printed and did use

prints in similitude of obligations of the United States." His year and a day sentence was suspended by the judge and Roessler was placed on probation for three years. The judge was Guy L. Fake, a particularly appropriate name given the nature of the judgment.

Duck stamp FDCs began in earnest with the issuance of the 1980 federal duck stamp. The 1980 covers, however, remain very elusive, selling in the range of $150-$300. Soon, the popularity of FDCs soared, and more dealers began preparing and selling them. The number of dealers peaked at between 75 and 100 by the late 1980s, and has since began to decline. Many FDCs bear a design, called a cachet (ka-shay), usually near the left edge of the envelope. Cachets are purely aesthetic and present an image that has some relationship to the stamp being honored by the FDC. According to Mellone's Specialized Cachet Catalog of Ducks and Express Mail First Day Covers, the 1976 duck stamp is the earliest duck FDC with cachet, so Mallone was unaware of the Roessler cover of 1936. It must be assumed that other early, privately prepared FDC's, both with and without cachets, exist but have yet to surface.

A beautiful, hand-painted First Day Cover designed by Nina Enroth, a wildlife artist who lives in Mexico. Only 50 covers were issued. Credit: Sam Houston Duck Company.

While first day cancels have always been an annual event, it wasn't until 1987 that duck stamp first day ceremonies became an annual event. They are usually held in Washington, D.C., and have become mini-celebrations, replete with special cancellations, the winning artist, government dignitaries, and collectors in search of another FDC for their collection. The first day of sale for duck stamps is usually on July 1, although there have been a few exceptions. One was for the first stamp, which was issued on August 22, 1934. Given all the turmoil and last-minute negotiations surrounding the creation of the duck stamp program, it is no surprise that the stamp was issued a little late, just in time for hunting season. Another notable exception came on September 1, 1949, the latest date of a duck stamp issue. The cause was Congress debating the merits of increasing the duck stamp rate from $1 to $2, which met with study, objections, and inevitable bureaucratic delays. June 21, 1997, the earliest first day ceremony to date, was the opening day of the NAPEX stamp show in McClean, Virginia. The first day event was held there on the assumption that more stamp collectors would be likely to attend than was normally the case with the Washington event usually held on July 1. Despite the success of NAPEX, the first day ceremony has since reverted back to Washington and is currently held at the Smithsonian Institution's National Postal Museum, on July 1. If you happen to be in or near the nation's capitol on that day, take time to attend the ceremony. It's a great way to experience the duck stamp program.

Another tradition that has developed is the artist's first day of sale, accompanied by a special commemorative. The first such event was in 1987, when Arthur Anderson had one in his hometown, Onalaska, Wisconsin. Dual ceremonies continue to this day, and in some cases the artist's hometown ceremony is earlier than the first day ceremony in Washington, D.C.. In such cases, the first date of sale is considered the "first day" of issue, although not the first day of national sale.

First Day Of Sale and First Day Ceremony Programs - In recent years, on the first day of issue, either an independent publisher or the U.S. F&WS produces a limited quantity of special programs to celebrate the event. With the 1998 federal duck stamp, for example, the U.S. F&WS printed 1,500, 10-inch x 6-inch First Day Ceremony Programs on heavy-stock paper which folds open and has four pages of printed material, including a beautiful picture of the stamp, the schedule of events, and a bio and photo of the artist. Although the programs do not come with a stamp affixed, many collectors will purchase a stamp at the ceremony, apply it to the program, have it postmarked, and get the signatures of attending dignitaries and the artist.

Front cover of the First Day Ceremony Program for the 1996 federal duck stamp, which also celebrates the opening of the National Postal Museum's new exhibit "Artistic License: The Duck Stamp Story." Credit: U.S. Fish and Wildlife Service.

Forms 3332, 3333 and 3334 - If you were a hunter in 1934 in an area that did not issue hunting licenses, where were you supposed to affix your federal duck stamp? According to the law in 1934, "each stamp shall, at the time of issuance, be affixed adhesively to the game license issued to the applicant under state law . . . or if the applicant is not required to have a State License, to a certificate furnished for that purpose by the Post Office Department at the time of issuance of such stamp." This meant that only one stamp per hunter was legally permissible. The certificate referred to is Form 3333, a light blue card, 2.5 inches x 4.5 inches, with a space for the stamp, postmaster's signature, and a separate cancellation. On the back of the form was a line for the hunter's signature and some text that essentially absolves the owner from needing a state game license to legally hunt. As mentioned earlier, the initial regulations governing the duck stamp forbade defacing the stamp in any way, including cancellation. That fact accounts for the unusually high number of both unsigned, no gum and unsigned, re-gummed examples of the 1934 stamp. Two weeks prior to June 30, 1935, when the first duck stamps were to be withdrawn from sale and destroyed, the law was amended, discontinuing the need to use Form

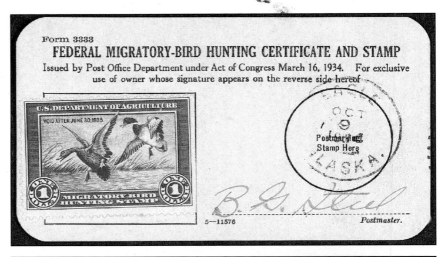

Top: Form 3333 from Eagle, Alaska (October 9, 1934). Credit: Jeanette Cantrell Rudy and the National Postal Museum, Smithsonian Institution (photo by Larry Gates). Bottom: Reverse of Form 3333. Credit: Sam Houston Duck Company.

3333. This created a two-week window during which hunters could purchase a 1934 stamp that was neither affixed to a state license or a Form 3333. This change also allowed the purchase of multiple stamps, thereby making plate blocks and full panes available to the general public.

Form 3333 was distributed upon request, mostly to third- and fourth-class post offices because landowners were not required to have licenses for hunting on their own land but still needed a duck stamp to hunt. Also, in Washington D.C., where hunting was illegal, collectors would have to purchase their stamp on Form 3333. And there were times when smaller post offices did sell the stamps on Form 3333 if a hunter, who had a license, requested this format. Finally, hunting licenses might not have been available in very rural areas, creating a need for Form 3333.

The policy of distributing copies of Form 3333, upon request, leads to an intriguing question. How did the Post Office Department know how many copies of Form 3333 to send to far-flung post offices

in order to ensure no shortages cropped up? Up until the early 1990s there was no evidence that any such shortages occurred. Then, two "temporary" Form 3333s were discovered, both hailing from Texas. One, issued in Houston and bearing a cancellation date of October 30, 1934, states at the bottom, "[t]his form to be used temporarily in lieu of blue card form which has become exhausted." Other examples are probably out there, but have yet to be found.

Robert Schoen's 1954 study of duck stamps estimated that 3,175 Form 3333s were issued. That number alone makes them scarce, but adding to their rarity is the probability that only 10 percent to 15 percent of them have survived. The rarest are the Hawaiian Form 3333s. A scant 137 copies of the 1934 stamp were issued in Hawaii (at the time a territory) and only two Form 3333s with that stamp have surfaced. One has a June 25, 1935 cancellation. Since this is only five days before the second duck stamp was issued, hardly a propitious time to begin hunting, a collector likely created it. Another Hawaiian Form 3333 was discovered in 1998 with a

The latest known use of Form 3333, with a 1955 federal duck stamp affixed. It was issued in Hyder, Alaska. Credit: Jeanette Cantrell Rudy and the National Postal Museum, Smithsonian Institution (photo by Larry Gates).

September 12, 1934 cancellation from Honolulu. The condition of the forms is critical to determining their value. They were normally folded, cut or creased to fit into a hunter's wallet, with corresponding soiling a virtual certainty. Form 3333s in pristine condition are usually collector-generated and command a premium. A typical price for a Form 3333 with the 1934 stamp affixed and properly canceled is about $500 in perfect condition. Ones that have more damage range between $100 and $200. Form 3333's with especially unusual cancellations or having multiple stamps can command a huge premium.

Postal clerks were required to place a cancel on the Form 3333 after a customer purchased a duck stamp. Some even canceled the stamp itself, which was improper for that issue, of course. The most frequently used cancellations on Form 3333 are Registered, M.O.B. (Money Order Broker), Parcel Post, and Duplex, a two-part postal killer cancel. The first three were usually double circle, purple or magenta ink, and the duplex always black. Some of the scarcest cancels are Stamp Window, Assistant Postmaster, Central Accounting, Cashier, and General Delivery. These cancellations are very hard to acquire and often command a premium. Colors other than black or purple/magenta with any cancel are considered very scarce and command a premium. A Trolley Car cancel was found on a single stamp. This rare cancel was in use in a small Michigan town which used a trolley for cross-town transportation. The vehicle was also used to transport mail, and the operator could sell stamps to patrons. Someone obviously purchased a duck stamp, and the conscientious postal employee affixed the cancel. The only known example of this stamp is in the collection of Jeanette Cantrell Rudy.

Because Form 3333 was specifically intended for use with only the first duck stamp, it is rare to find it with later issues attached. The latest known exam-

ple is one with a 1955 stamp, issued in Hyder, Alaska. Prior to this discovery in 1992, the latest known usage of Form 3333 was with a 1943 stamp, issued in Lake City, Colorado. There are also examples of Form 3333 with the 1935 through the 1940 stamps. The most unusual of these is one bearing a block of four 1934 stamps, issued in St. Paul, Minnesota and postmarked October 3, 1934 (it is not a plate block, which, for this stamp would have six stamps with the plate number opposite the middle). It might have been placed on there as a postal "favor" for a collector who wanted a most unusual item. Since neither the form nor the block is bent or creased, it is quite likely that this was created by a stamp collector and not used by a hunter, or a group of four hunters for that matter.

One of the most interesting and unusual Form 3333's is without a stamp. On November 26, 1936, a McLean, Virginia postmaster issued a Form 3333 to J. Sinclair Rector. The form has a machine cancel that runs across the space where the stamp was to be affixed and a second hand cancel at the top, barely visible. The presence of the machine cancel makes it a virtual impossibility that the form ever had a stamp on its face. Another puzzle on this form is the double signature on the postmaster line. The top name is Henry Storm, the postmaster. The identity of Myrtle Redwell, who is indicated beneath the line, is unknown, but it is likely that she was a clerk at the post office. What is particularly interesting about the signatures is that they are almost assuredly by the same hand - probably Storms. As to how this unusual Form 3333 came into being one cannot be certain since the participants are no longer around to ask, but the odds are it was the result of an emergency of sorts. Mr. Rector, a respected banker, avid hunter and ornithologist, lived near the post office where he had purchased his duck stamps in 1934 and 1935. On November 26, 1936, he ventures forth

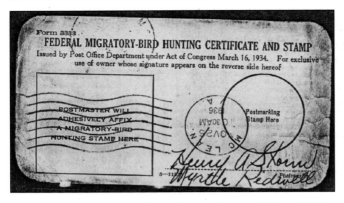

The intriguing J. Sinclair Rector Form 3333. Credit: Sam Houston Duck Company.

to purchase the 1936 duck stamp so that he can legally hunt. That day happens to be Thanksgiving. It wasn't until 1941 that this became a national holiday, but still many people informally took it off and perhaps one of those who did is the post office clerk with responsibilities for maintaining the duck stamp stock, a one Ms. Myrtle Redwell. In walks Mr. Rector. He requests a duck stamp but is told that the clerk who can sell it to him is off or, more likely, that the post office has simply run out of the stamps. Either way he appears to be out of luck. But, the postmaster wants to accommodate Mr. Rector's request if at all possible since he is an important and busy man in the community who wants to hunt on the up-and-up and would prefer not to miss another weekend of sport for lack of a stamp. So postmaster Storm devises a solution. Why not take the defunct Form 3333, many unused copies of which are laying about, cancel it and sign it, verifying that the $1 fee was paid, thereby confirming Mr. Rector's rectitude despite the stamp's absence. Myrtle Redwell's name could have been added so that Rector could return after the weekend and retrieve his stamp from her. Seeing her boss's signature and the cancellation would have given Ms. Redwell all the information she needed to hand over a duck stamp without any money changing hands. The hand cancel at the upper left of the form was Ms. Redwell's way of indicating that the stamp had been received by Rector.

(The authors would like to thank Mr. Mark Meany, a Form 3333 specialist, for his help in reconstructing this story.)

Before receiving Form 3333, the hunter had to fill out another form, 3332, an "application for migratory-bird hunting stamp" which enabled the postmaster to issue the Form 3333. These are very rare since few people bother to save paperwork. Up until the 1990s, only six copies were known to exist. Then a dealer found an unused pad of 20, but unfortunately it was stolen at a New York stamp show in the fall of 1998. Therefore, should any Form 3332s

Blank Form 3332. Credit: Jeanette Cantrell Rudy and the National Postal Museum, Smithsonian Institution (photo by Larry Gates).

become suddenly available be very suspicious and ask probing questions about its provenance.

As if two forms were not enough, there was also a Form 3334. Don't expect to see one, however. Form 3334 served as a summary-of-transactions register, basically a record tracking the sale of Form 3333s. All copies of Form 3334 were retained by the Post Office, and no known examples have been seen in philatelic circles.

Panes - The part of the original sheet usually offered for sale to the public. The number of duck stamps on a pane has varied over the years. Prior to the 1959 issue, there were 112 stamps per sheet, meaning four panes of 28 stamps each. After that, the printing method changed, and the number per pane bumped up to 30. Early panes, in particular, are quite rare and expensive. The late 1930s and on into the early 1940s was not an era of prosperity, being impacted by both the Great Depression and World War II. For someone, even a serious collector, to purchase an entire pane of duck stamps for $28 would be a major investment, especially when entire panes of regular

postage stamps could be had for much less. For example, it is believed that only five or six full panes of the 1934 stamp exist, with the last one selling for $60,000. With recent catalog values for mint 1934 stamps running around $675, it is clear that the price of a pane is much greater than the price of the twenty-eight individual stamps that make up the pane. Even for those early issues, between 1935 and 1941, where more panes are available, the price of a full pane significantly outstrips the cumulative price of twenty-eight individual stamps. If, however, suddenly and unexpectedly hundreds of additional panes of these issues surfaced, prices would drop considerably. Beginning with the 1942 duck stamp issue, the actual value of panes comes closer to the catalog value of the individual stamps.

Plate Blocks - A group of connected stamps, four or six, which has a plate block number on the attached selvage. The latter term refers to the paper margin that it attached to the edges of some stamps, but which is not a part of

Full pane of the 1958 federal duck stamp (above), the last of the 28-stamp format, and a Full pane of the 1959 federal duck stamp, the first of the 30-stamp format. Credit: Sam Houston Duck Company.

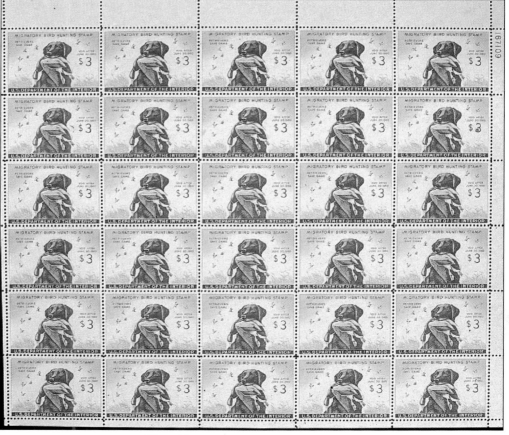

95

the stamps. From the 1934 through 1958, a plate block consists of six stamps in two horizontal rows of three. Plate blocks since then consist of four stamps, with two rows of two. To be considered a true plate block, the selvage on two sides of the block should be intact. For the flat press years, 1934 through 1958, each full sheet of 112 stamps contained four panes of 28 stamps, with there being upper left (UL), upper right (UR), lower left (LL) and lower right (LR) panes. Each of these panes contains a plate block number in the bottom or top selvage, so two plate-block positions for each pane is possible. The position is determined by the location of the side selvage and the top or bottom selvage. Where the two meet will determine that position. If the selvage meets in the LL corner, it is a LL plate block, etc. Particular positions generally do not command a premium, unless a specialist collector needs a certain position and is bidding in open competition against another collector needed the same position. The most popular position among collectors seems to be the upper right, possibly because early plate blocks have large top selvage and smaller bottom selvage. From 1959 to the present, sheets have been printed on a rotary press, with plate numbers on the side selvage rather than the top or bottom. The singular exception is the 1964 stamp, on which the plate number was incorrectly placed in the same position as the former flat press. Accordingly, it is collected in a plate block of six. The 1964 stamp plate block catalog value of $2,000, versus $500 for plate blocks issued in the same time frame, is because of the initial cataloging which indicated that 1964 plate blocks need consist of only four stamps. It wasn't until a few years later that the Scott Catalog modified the requirement that 1964 plate blocks have six stamps, catching many collectors two stamps short, and causing the price to skyrocket.

The rarity of early plate blocks was in evidence at the Shreves Philatelic Galleries auction on May 8, 1998. On the "block," so to speak, were single plate blocks of the 1934 and 1935 stamps. Both had problems. The 1934 block, while well centered and beautiful in color, had trimmed side selvage and the 1935 was hinged and a bit off center. Nevertheless, the realizations were astounding. The 1934 block sold for $12,100; 1935 for $11,000. Both prices were thousands of dollars more than the value listed in contemporary catalogues. The iron law of supply and demand made it a particularly good day for Shreves. In the early 1990s, Bob Dumaine was commissioned by collector Jeanette Cantrell Rudy (see profile on page 116) to obtain a complete matched set of all the U.S. federal duck stamp plate blocks. The plates were to have full selvage and be well centered and, if possible, never hinged. Since complying with this request required Dumaine to acquire sixteen plate blocks each for both 1934 and 1935, the balance of plate blocks available to other collectors was greatly diminished. Dumaine's extensive research on this topic has uncovered only about thirty plate blocks from 1934 and a few more than forty from 1935. There are certainly more than this number in existence, but unless someone is hoarding a great stash, the number is not large. Any time one of these early plate blocks comes up for sale, collector interest is likely to be high.

Proof/Die Proof - A proof or die proof is a trial printing of the stamp using the final design. They can be run in black and white, color, or both. If the proofs are run in different colors than that used for the final stamp, they are termed trial color proofs. While proofs are created for every federal duck stamp, they rarely become available to collectors. In most cases the proofs are retained by the BEP. When proofs do make it into general circulation it is an exciting event. In May 1995, at Compex 95, Jacques C. Schiff offered for sale large die proofs of the 1941 and 1943 stamps. Bidding was vigorous and they each sold for $4,620, much more than expected. At the Robert A. Siegel 1997 Rarities of the World auction, large die proofs of the 1936, 1937, and 1938 stamps were offered. The first two realized for $5,500, but the third did not sell. The 1937 proof was particularly interesting, being printed in a striking

1938 federal duck stamp plate block of six. Credit: Sam Houston Duck Company.

DEPARTMENT OF THE TREASURY
BUREAU OF ENGRAVING AND PRINTING

Engraving Approval and Provisional Color Approval:

Director, U. S. Fish and Wildlife Service
U. S. Department of the Interior

Large die proof for the 1987 federal duck stamp. Credit: National Postal Museum, Smithsonian Institution (photo by Larry Gates).

light red violet. Green was the ultimate color chosen for the 1937 stamp. Apparently the BEP liked the light red violet, just not for the 1937 stamp. The next year's stamp, Clark's pintails, used that color to good effect.

Sheets - A duck stamp sheet contains four panes. Collectors cannot buy full sheets and none are known to be in private collections. The 50th anniversary special printing of federal duck stamps is the only exception to this rule, and it is discussed further on this chapter, in the section on rarities.

An excellent way to learn about the great variety of duck stamps and their value is to browse through stamp catalogs. The information below lists the major catalogs along with information on their content and contacts.

There are many ways one can acquire a collection of duck stamps. Hunters get a new stamp each year. In the early years, most hunters undoubtedly either forgot about where they had placed their old stamps or just threw them out. With the increase in stamp value, many hunters, even if not stamp collectors,

are now saving their old stamps, and those who misplaced or threw away their licenses are kicking themselves for not buying more when they had the chance. It's never too late to start collecting, whether your goal is investment, enjoyment or both. The best time to get a new duck stamp is within three years after it is printed, when copies can be purchased directly from the postal service, for face value. If your local post office doesn't stock duck stamps, you can order directly from the service through there "USA Philatelic" catalogue (call 1-800-STAMP 24, or visit their web site: www.stampsonline.com). For other places to order newly released federal duck stamps, check out the Duck Stamp Office's home page http://duckstamps.fws.gov/

Attending stamp shows can be a very exciting and informative way to build your collection. At small shows, there are often dealers who have a nice selection of ducks to thumb through. At the bigger shows, dealers who specialize in ducks are likely to be on hand. Inspecting the stamps in person is the best way to assess condition, and if you have questions there is somebody to ask, oftentimes a person who is quite knowledgeable. You can also reach duck

MAJOR DUCK STAMP CATALOGS

Some of these catalogs include price lists, and if the issuing company sells stamps, that is noted.

BROOKMAN STAMP CO.

10 Chestnut Drive
Bedford, NH 03110
603-472-5575

Federal, state, and Indian reservation on nine pages which are part of a larger catalog. Grades for federal are F-VF, VF NH, plate blocks, as well as used. Some photos. Sells stamps.

WEB: www.brookmanstamps.com

DAVID R. TORRE NON-PICTORIAL WATERFOWL STAMPS

P. O. Box 4298
Santa Rosa, CA 95402
707-546-4859

A 78-page specialized catalog of non-pictorial U.S. waterfowl stamps. Includes unused, used and signed categories for many local, state, and Indian Reservation stamps. Informative explanations of the stamps' history and background. Many photos. Sells stamps.

DUCKS 97
HOWARD RICHOUX

6721 Shamrock Road
Lincoln, NE 68506
402-488-8345

CD ROM, disc of duck hunting, as well as fishing and conservation stamps, and general game through 1997 issues. Grading is for fine to very fine stamps. Requires Windows 3.x/95/98. Sells stamps.

KRAUSE-MINKUS, STANDARD CATALOG OF U.S. STAMPS

700 E. State St.
Iola, WI 54990
715-445-2214

Federal duck hunting stamps only listed; part of a larger catalog, ducks on 9 pages, prices for very fine grade only, includes mint, used, and plate blocks. Federal photos.

WEB: www.krause.com

MICHAEL JAFFE STAMPS

P. O. Box 61484
Vancouver, WA 98666
1-800-782-6770

A 48 page catalog/price list of federal, state, foreign, duck stamps, Indian Reservation stamps, and duck stamp prints. Grades from average to XF, faulty to mint, includes mint, used, no gum, and plate blocks. Many photos. Sells stamps.

WEB: www.brookmanstamps.com

SAM HOUSTON DUCK CO.

c/o Bob Dumaine
P. O. Box 820087
Houston, TX 77282
1-800-231-5926

A 68-page catalog of federal, state, foreign, Indian Reservation, fishing and conservation stamps graded fine to XF, mint, used, no gum, plate blocks, prints, First Day Covers, albums and supplies. Includes artists species, errors, and frames. Partial color, many photos. Auctions available. Sells stamps.

WEB: www.shduck.com

SCOTT SPECIALIZED CATALOGUE

P. O. Box 828
Sidney, OH 45365
937-498-0802

Duck Hunting Stamps Only - Part of larger catalogue; 33 pages of federal and state stamps, prices for very fine grade only, mint, used, and no gum singles, mint plate blocks, and errors. Includes prices for early text stamps and Indian Reservations. Some photos.

WEB: www.scottonline.com

THE DUCK STAMP IMAGE COLLECTION - U.S. FISH AND WILDLIFE SERVICE

1849 C Street NW
Room 2058
Washington, DC 20240
202-208-5508

Information pages, federal only, one stamp per page. Contains data on stamp, artist, designer, quantity sold. Space for mounting stamps on each page. Must be downloaded from web site and printed. Photos of federal duck stamps included.

WEB Only: www.fws.gov/r9dso/dkhome.html

stamp dealers through the mail. Many general stamp dealers have price lists which include ducks, and dealers that specialize in ducks, of course, have extensive offerings that appeal to the beginning, intermediate, or advanced duck stamp collector. As the sidebar on page 98 indicates, some duck stamp catalogs are supported by dealers who also sell stamps. For an extensive list of dealers, go to the National Duck Stamp Collectors Society listing on the web at www.hwcn.org/link/ndscs, or e-mail ndscs@hwcn.org

More adventurous collectors can acquire stamps through auctions. Sam Houston Duck Company, out of Houston, Texas, is the only auction house in the United States that specializes in duck stamps. Other stamp auction houses offer duck stamps on a regular basis, including Robert A. Siegel, New York; Ivy and Mader, West Caldwell, New Jersey; Charles Shreve, Dallas, Texas; Superior Auctions, Beverly Hills, California; H.R. Harmer, New York; and Jacques C. Schiff, Jr. Ridgefield Park, New Jersey. Major auction houses, such as Sotheby's and Spinks will occasionally offer rare duck stamps for sale. In these venues, the bidding can become fast and furious, quickly moving prices towards the rarefied air that only truly wealthy collectors can breathe. For example, on October 25, 1990, Christie's (now owned by Spinks) auctioned off panes of the 1936, 1937, 1938, and 1939 stamps, and some later issues. The price realizations were off the charts, all of which were records for these panes. The 1936 pane, for example, which had numerous gum problems, went for $18,150. That's roughly $648 per stamp, including ten straight-edged examples, quite high as compared to the $325 that the Scott Catalog listed for a very fine, never hinged single. Christie's had expected the pane to go for $4,000. It was the particulars of the competition that drove up the price. Five of the major duck stamp collectors needed the pane to round out their collections and none of them wanted to give up without a fight.

With the phenomenal growth of the Internet, it is not surprising that there are plenty of places to buy duck stamps on the web. Many dealers have home pages with images and prices of stamps. There are also many on-line auctions which can keep you up in

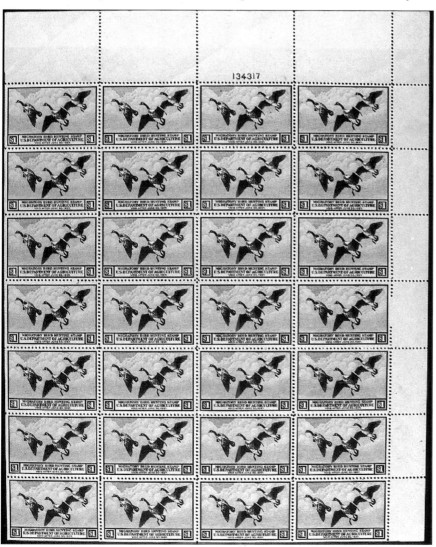

Mint pane of the 1936 federal duck stamp. Credit: Jeanette Cantrell Rudy and the National Postal Museum, Smithsonian Institution (photo by Larry Gates).

front of your monitor until the wee hours of the morning, battling it out with other collectors. Some of the major ones where you're likely to find a good selection of ducks are www.collectit.net; www.stampauctions.com, and on eBay, the world's largest on-line auction house for collectibles — www.ebay.com.

Purchasing stamps is only the first step in collecting. Knowing how to handle and house the stamps is equally important. The first rule is to avoid touching the stamps with your fingers, unless your hands are very clean and dry. Oil, dirt or other substances on your skin can damage stamps over time. It is better to use a specially designed stamp tong to inspect and move your stamps. Tongs, unlike most tweezers, have flat ends with no ridges so as to avoid leaving marks on the stamps. Another useful tool is a magnifying glass. A lens with five- or ten-power magnification will reveal the true craftsmanship of the engraver as reflected in the stamp's intricate design. Magnification will also enable you to better judge the condition of the stamp.

There is quite a range of options for housing duck stamps. The lowest-tech and worst way is to shove them into a drawer where the odds of damage are greatest. A significant step up from this method is to use stock books, which contain cardboard or paper sheets with plastic strips into which the stamps slide. For the more systematic collector, there are a variety of albums to choose from. General stamp albums, such as the Scott Minuteman, cover virtually all U.S. stamp issues, and have a number of pages devoted to federal duck stamps, each of which contains black and white images of the stamps. There are also a few specialized albums, devoted specifically to federal duck stamps, which are listed below.

There are many ways to place stamps into albums. Hinges are still available and used by some collectors, but as noted earlier, are not a preferred choice since they invariably detract from the stamp's condition and reduce its value. If you really want to use hinges, save them for stamps without gum or poorer quality stamps. There are a variety of companies that produce high-quality mounts that allow stamps to be placed in albums without any damage. Mounts are usually made of some sort of plastic, with the front of the mount being clear to facilitate viewing of the stamp, and the back of mount having a wettable (gummed) adhesive layer that affixes the mount to the page. The stamp is slid into the space between the front and back of the mount. You can purchase mounts which are pre-cut to fit duck stamps or you can buy mount-strips and cut them up yourself. The most ambitious of collectors can create their own album pages, giving them the option of displaying their treasures in whatever form they fancy.

One of the most satisfying aspects of being a collector is learning about your collection and sharing that knowledge with others. Conversing with stamp deal-

ers and fellow collectors, as well as reading the information provided in stamp albums are excellent ways of satisfying these goals. If you want to delve deeper you can. There are a number of duck stamp books that do an excellent job of presenting various aspects of the duck stamp story. These include David McBrides, *The Federal Duck Stamps* (Winchester Press, 1984); Laurence F. Johnson's *The Federal Duck Stamp Story* (Alexander & Company, 1984); Joe McCaddin's *Duck*

(Note to reader: If you are interested in purchasing one of these albums, please contact one of the dealers listed under the section on Major Duck Stamp Catalogs)

Coastal Bend Federal Duck Album
One volume that holds single stamps. Lighthouse binder, in brown, black, red, green or blue, with matching slipcase. Pages are three-hole punched, printed on heavy ivory stock. One or two stamps per page with accompanying information on the stamp and artists. It can be purchased with or without pre-cut mounts in place.

Scott Combination Federal and State Duck Album
Holds single issues. Green binder imprinted in gold, Federal and State Duck Stamps, with matching slipcase. Over 150 pages on ivory stock, with photos/spaces for federal and state stamps. Blank pages are included and yearly supplements are available. You have the option of paying a premium for album pages with pre-cut Showguard mounts already in place, or you can purchase pre-cut mounts separately. This is the most popular duck stamp album.

SHDC Federal Singles
Prepared by the Sam Houston Duck Company, the ivory pages fit Scott binders and they contain spaces for the major errors, plate number single (PNS), and special issues.

Stearns & Fink Federal Album
A two-volume set which has space for single stamps and contains extensive information on the stamps and the artists. Burgundy and gold binders with matching slipcases. Pages are three-hole punched and printed on heavy stock. Art images are in color from the 1970 issue on (except 1976). Supplements are available.

White Ace Federal Duck Pages
Holds single stamps. Pages are three-hole punched with colored and decorated borders. The three-ring binders are black with a white ace on the cover. Slipcase can be purchased as well as supplements which come out every four years.

Linn's Stamp News
Weekly. For more than 12 years, this newspaper has run a monthly duck stamp column by Bob Dumaine.
P.O. Box 29
Sidney, OH 45365

WEB: www.linns.com

Scott Stamp Monthly
Scott Publishing Co.
P.O. Box 828
Sidney, OH 45365-0828

WEB: www.scottonline.com

Stamp Collector
Bi-weekly.
Krause Publications.
700 E. State St.
Iola, WI 54990-0001

WEB: www.krause.com/stamps/

State Revenue News
The Journal of State Revenue Stamps, including state ducks.
P.O. Box 629
Chappaqua, NY 10514

The American Philatelist
Monthly journal of the American Philatelic Society, published since 1887. With than 50,000 members in more than 110 countries, APS is the largest, nonprofit membership society in the world for stamp collectors.
P.O. Box 8000
State College PA 16803 USA

WEB: www.stamps.org/aps/services/ap/theap.htm

The American Revenuer
The Journal of the American Revenue Association, published ten times per year.
President
P.O.Box 1663
Easton, MD 21601

WEB: www.ericjackson.com/ara.htm

Topical Time

The Journal of Thematic Philately, published bi-monthly by the American Topical Association.

P.O. Box 50820
Albuquerque, NM 87181

Stamps & Prints, the Complete Federal and State Editions (Park Lane, 1988, 1991); Scott Weidensaul's *Duck Stamps* (Gallery Books, 1989); and Michael Ruscoe's *American Waterfowl, The Federal and First-Of-State Duck Stamps and Prints* (Hugh Lauter Levin Associates, 1989); All of these are out-of-print, but you can find them at libraries, used book stores, or through stamp dealers.

Another place to find up-to-date information on duck stamps is through the philatelic press. The major publications are listed below. While only one of them, *Linn's Stamp News*, currently has a regular column devoted to duck stamps, all of them occasionally cover this area. These publications are important for the general background they provide. Articles on all aspects of stamp collecting, news about stamp shows and events, and other exciting information these publications contain will enrich your understanding and enjoyment of duck stamp collecting.

For those who seek further specialized knowledge, there are two other options. The National Duck Stamp Collectors Society (NDSCS) is the only stamp collecting society devoted exclusively to ducks. *Duck Tracks*, the official journal of the NDSCS, is a quarterly publication that is full of interesting articles and news about duck stamps and duck stamp collecting. The society's home page also contains information collecting duck stamps and links to other web pages of interest to collectors (www.hwcn.org/link/ndscs or e-mail, NDSCS@hwen.org). To contact the society write to NDSCS Secretary, P.O. Box 43, Harleysville PA 19438-0043.

Another great source of information is the monthly *Duck Report, A Journal for Duck Stamp Collectors*, published by The Sam Houston Duck Company. It can be accessed through the web for free (http://www.shduck.com) or through the company (13310 Westheimer, #150, Houston, TX 77077).

DESIGN MISTAKES, VARIETIES, ERRORS AND RARITIES

Despite the best of intentions, things can go wrong. Everyone associated with the creation of the duck stamp tries to get it right each year by producing a stamp that is biologically and technically perfect. Sometimes, however, there are problems. One class of these is design mistakes. The most common of which is when an artist depicts an impossible situation. For example, both the 1937 and 1938 stamps have concept problems with wind currents. White caps in the designs or blowing marsh grass indicate wind direction, and an approximate 15-20 knot wind speed. In both cases, the ducks are shown taking off or alighting with the wind. That's a bit odd given the aerodynamics of the situation. Ducks, like airplanes find it difficult, if not impossible to take off or land with the wind since resistance is minimal or non-existent in strong wind. The result of most flying attempts will be helter-skelter takeoffs and landings, and very embarrassed ducks.

The 1960 stamp shows a pair of redheads with four ducklings in tow. It's a beautiful family portrait. However, after redheads mate the male heads for the hills and is not seen again, so this hen should consider herself lucky indeed. The 1962 stamp depicts two pintails coming in for a landing. It is a pretty picture, except that the tail feathers are reversed. The flight result here would be that the air would pass through the feathers, causing a loss of control during landings, and the ducks probably would cartwheel as they hit the water.

Sometimes a mistake in the design is caught before the stamp is printed. Such is the case with the 1961 stamp, which pictured mallard ducklings without clear definition of wing markings, which were added later. The 1984 stamp, apparently based on photographs of captive ducks, showed birds with clipped wings. In the final design the ducks were shown in their natural state. Even the granddaddy of them all, Ding Darling, made a mistake that the BEP caught in time. In his sketch for the 1934 stamp, the hen was shown with nearly 30 primary and secondary wing feathers, when there should be only 10 of each. There is no doubt that Ding knew the correct number. Given the haste with which he had to sketch that first design, perhaps he used a little bit of artistic license or just got a bit too excited.

The 1937 and 1938 federal duck stamps both have wind direction problems. Credit: U.S. Fish and Wildlife Service.

A redhead male who is a little too doting, on the 1960 federal duck stamp. Credit: U.S. Fish and Wildlife Service.

There are also design mistakes that involve the wording of the stamp. For example, the 1967 stamp has wording indicating that the pictured birds are "Old Squaws," when the correct spelling is "Oldsquaws."

Design mistakes are inherent in the stamp. Every high-quality example of the 1960 stamp, for example, will depict a pastoral scene of family tranquillity that is just plain wrong, just as every mint condition 1937 stamp will show aerodynamically challenged greater scaups. Duck stamp varieties and errors, on the other hand, are altogether different breeds of philatelic material. In these cases, the problems arose during the printing process. Something goes wrong and the stamps that come out of the printing press are not quite right. Errors are distinguished from varieties by the severity. Stamps that are unintentionally not perforated, have the wrong colors, or are missing a major design element qualify as errors. Varieties, by contrast, are printing flaws of a less serious nature, such as color shifts, partial perforations, partial serial number, color shades, crazy perforations and the like. In both cases, to be considered true errors and varieties, the stamps must be unintentionally issued, and sold over the counter by federal agents, e.g., the USPS or other officially sanctioned vendors.

With most products, the closer it is to perfection the more desirable it is, and the higher the premium that is paid to possess it. This logic is turned on its head with stamp collecting. The most valuable and sought-after stamps are often the ones that have problems - the more serious the problem the better. Witness the storied history of the "inverted Jenny," the famous 1918, 24-cent airmail stamp error with the upside down image of a Curtiss Jenny biplane, which today is one of the most expensive of all U.S. stamps. Thus, varieties and errors are among the most highly prized of all duck stamps. While only

eleven major errors are known, there are more than fifty different varieties. As one would expect, there are many more specimens of varieties than errors. (See the Appendix titled Duck Stamp Errors and Varieties on page 196, for a listing of the major errors and varieties). Many varieties are within the financial reach of the average duck stamp collector, however most errors are very rare, and therefore expensive. Set your sights accordingly.

Varieties are the result of printing problems. Gradations in color and shadings might be due to over- or under-inking, improper color mix, or uneven ink distribution. Dirty printing plates or ink transfer rollers can wreak havoc on stamp quality. A small blob of dirt can mask a color from being printed, causing a light spot or a miscoloration on the stamp. For example, if red is being overlaid on blue to make purple, and the red screen is blocked, a blue spot will appear in the purple field. The result of such miscues depends on the colors that are being combined. Printers refer to these spots as "hickeys," but stamp dealers often opt for the prosaic designations like "firefly," "shot duck," "light on the tail," "moon over the mountain," and the like.

One interesting duck stamp variety was discovered just minutes after the stamp's issuance. On June 27, 1996, the first day of sale for the 1996 stamp, a collector and a dealer perusing a pane of stamps noticed something odd - broken inner frame lines around the design. Further investigation showed that the broken frame lines were not constant, showing up in various locations on all four panes of the stamp. When asked about this problem, Leonard Buckley, foreman of engraving at the BEP, stated that "a review . . . shows that we lost the fine line on the inside border of the printing sleeve because of excess wiping pressure on a portion of the run. Unfortunately, this was missed by [the] examining [department]. The entire run, however, was not

A pintail with reversed tail feathers on the 1962 federal duck stamp. Credit: U.S. Fish and Wildlife Service.

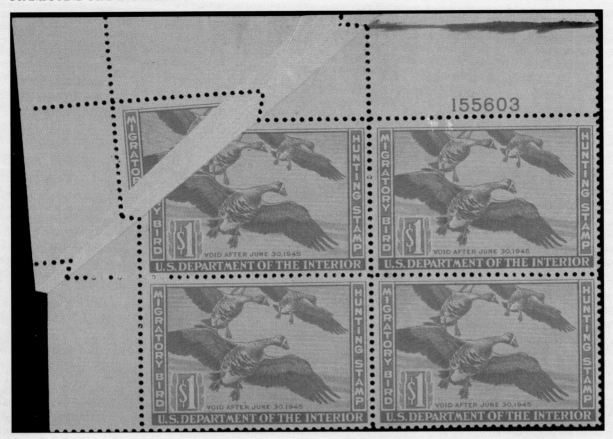

Above: Block of four 1944 stamps, foldover variety. Credit: Jeanette Cantrell Rudy and the National Postal Museum, Smithsonian Institution (photo by Larry Gates).

Right: The 1967 federal duck stamp with foldover variety. Credit: Jeanette Cantrell Rudy and the National Postal Museum, Smithsonian Institution (photo by Larry Gates).

Right: 1987 federal duck stamp with color shift. Credit: Jeanette Cantrell Rudy and the National Postal Museum, Smithsonian Institution (photo by Larry Gates).

Below: 1935 federal duck stamp, block of twelve with vertical misperforations. Credit: Jeanette Cantrell Rudy and the National Postal Museum, Smithsonian Institution (photo by Larry Gates).

1997 federal duck stamp, normal and with breast-feather break variation (right). Credit: Jeanette Cantrell Rudy and the National Postal Museum, Smithsonian Institution (photo by Larry Gates).

affected." This is not a rare variety and obtaining a single specimen costs less than $40. Another unusual variety shows up on certain specimens of the 1997 stamp of a Canada goose standing on the edge of the lake. On the vast majority of the issued stamps, the goose's breast is finely shaped, but on some there is a break in breast feathers, subtle but definitely noticeable. There is even a variety within this variety. Sometimes the printing flaw extends downward to the lake. Upon inquiry, the BEP's Larry R. Felix, Director of External Relations, offered the following technical explanation of the printing problem that created these two varieties. "The migratory bird stamp in question is the result of a miscut during the pantograph operation when preparing the inking-in-rollers for the multicolor setup required for the design on the 1997-98 issue. The pantograph operation occurs when the intaglio design is printed on either two or three inking rollers, depending on the total number of colors desired. Each roller is then cut with a high-speed drill removing all the rubber surface except for the area of the design that is to be printed in a specific color. Each roller will have [a] different cut and [a] different piece of the design left on it. Each individual roller is placed in a different fountain with its own ink train allowing for selective inking. Selective inking is up to three color printings with one plate sleeve with only one pass. Only the area not cut will transfer ink to the plate or sleeve so any miscut that was supposed to print will not receive ink so it will not print."

For the collector interested in color variations, there is a bevy to choose from. You can get the 1952 stamp in a deep ultramarine shade, 1973 with an image shift that causes a white halo to appear over the drake's head, 1985 with a red color shift, 1988 in yellow/tan or deep rose, 1990 in either dull bluish-

gray or deep lavender, and 1995 in green, deep purple or with an orange split in the sky.

The eleven major federal errors are the royalty of the duck stamp collecting world. They are extra-special because of the great care that the BEP takes in printing each year's allotment of duck stamps. One can imagine how varieties occasionally slip through the bureau's intricate quality control system. They are only minor variations of the desired product. It is more difficult to understand how the much more grave printing flaws represented by errors ever see the light of day, especially when one considers the jumbo size of the stamps. The fact that there are so few errors and that they are printed in such limited numbers is a testament to the skill and care that the BEP employs in printing stamps. The errors are flukes in an otherwise exceptionally well-run operation and that is why they are so fascinating

1934 Stamp Imperforates, vertical and horizontal

Stamps without perforations around the edges are labeled imperforate. Those with perforations on two opposing sides are referred to as partially imperforate. Only vertical imperforate pairs of the 1934 issue are known to exist, including a few strips of three, all without gum and ostensibly from one pane of 28. Some examples of the partially imperforate 1934 issues may have been trimmed to create the completely imperforate stamps. By so doing, it is likely an off-center imperforate multiple would be created. All examples of vertically imperforate pairs are extremely rare and desirable, although they may have been printer's waste. Most have small faults and have an estimated value of $35,000 per strip.

1934 federal duck stamp, group of eight horizontally imperforate. Credit: Sam Houston Duck Company.

As for imperforate pairs, lacking only horizontal perforations, the largest multiple known is a block of eight, 2 x 4 with gum on the face and internal creasing. This example, complete with a Philatelic Foundation Certificate of authenticity, also has gum on its face and none on its back (in fact none of the imperforate 1934s have gum on the reverse). This block of eight is believed to be the only surviving stamps that are not totally imperforate. Pairs and strips of three are possible, but not known. Totally imperforate horizontal pairs are unknown, and if a full pane of such existed, it would have certainly shown up by now. The value of this error is the same as the totally imperforate examples, an estimated $35,000 per pair. The largest known multiple would be valued much higher than the four pair singularly.

1934 federal duck stamp, imperforate strip of three. Credit: Jeanette Cantrell Rudy and the National Postal Museum, Smithsonian Institution (photo by Larry Gates).

The 1946 federal duck stamp with the normal red-brown color (above), and the rose-red color error. Credit: Jeanette Cantrell Rudy and the National Postal Museum, Smithsonian Institution (photo by Larry Gates).

1946 Stamp Color Error

Normally, the 1946 stamp is reddish brown. The color error of this stamp, first discovered in the late 1980s, is rose red. Over the years, many color variations of the 1946 stamp have been found, but all were concluded to be variations of reddish brown. Assessing color variations in stamps is a tricky business. Many dealers and collectors have, with other stamp issues, seen blue stamps that should be green, pink stamps that should be red, or brown stamps that should be orange. Such variations are better termed "changelings," and are not true errors. Changelings result when stamps are exposed to chemicals or intense light which can fade or alter colors. There is no doubt, however, that the rose red version of the 1946 stamp is a major error. Color

experts agree that change from reddish brown to rose red is not possible. How this error arose is a mystery, but the color is very similar to the 2-cent Presidential stamp (John Adams) issued in 1938 and used up through the early 1950s. Less than ten examples of the rose red 1946 duck stamp error are thought to exist. The estimated value for a single specimen is $20,000.

1957 and 1959 Stamps
With Inverted Back Inscription

The most recent error discovery took place in 1998, when a single example of the 1959 stamp was found with an inverted back inscription. This is a particularly difficult error to detect for two reasons. First, many people don't take the time to examine

The only recorded example of a 1959 stamp with an inverted back inscription. The reverse image is the error stamp. The stamp on the left is a regular 1959 stamp shown for image only. Credit: Jeanette Cantrell Rudy and the National Postal Museum, Smithsonian Institution (photo by Larry Gates).

the back of the stamp, focusing most of their energy on the image on the front. Second, unlike a missing back inscription, one can flip a stamp with an inverted inscription and still be fooled because the writing is present as it should be. It depends on how you flip the stamp. If the writing it placed correctly, one should be able to turn the stamp over from side to side, like reading a book, and have the inscription appear upright. If you flip an inverted inscription stamp top over bottom it will appear as if nothing is amiss. The only other issue with an inverted inscription is the 1957 stamp of which there are six known examples. The estimated value of the 1957 error is $5,000; 1959 is $25,000.

1982 Stamp Missing Orange and Violet Colors

Very few examples of this error are known. The orange and violet colors are unstable, and many stamps have been observed coming from prints exposed to ultra-violet light with fading. It is necessary to obtain a certificate of authenticity for this issue since light-bleached copies are on the market. All known examples have full, undisturbed original gum, without any trace of the orange or violet color. Examples have surfaced from various parts of the country and no multiples are known. The estimated value of an authentic example is $7,500.

1982 federal duck stamp missing orange and violet (Top), and normal stamp. Credit: Jeanette Cantrell Rudy and the National Postal Museum, Smithsonian Institution (photo by Larry Gates).

1985 federal duck stamp missing blue color. Bottom four rows of stamps with normal color. The fifth row up has lost partial blue. The top row is completely missing blue. Credit: Sam Houston Duck Company.

1985 stamp missing blue color

Created as a result of sheet splice, which prompted a color shutoff. Only one pane exists, top row of five without blue. The error pane is valued at $65,000.

1986 Stamp Missing Black Engraving

Normal examples of the 1986 stamp show a fulvous whistling duck sitting peacefully atop the water. A significant amount of the stamp design is engraved with black ink. With the black engraving missing, the stamp becomes strange looking indeed, making for an impressive error. The duck no longer has eyes or feather tips and there is no text or denomination on the stamp's face. A collector found a sheet of these errors in Alaska. Later a second sheet

turned up in Michigan. Two other panes, on partial, were also discovered in Michigan, and it was rumored that they were turned in to the BEP and destroyed. If that is the case, between only sixty and seventy examples of this error exist. The estimated value of this stamp is $3,500.

1990 Stamp Missing Back Inscription

On a visit to a local post office, a duck stamp collector from Richmond, Virginia saw something odd. While looking through the stock for a high-quality specimen of the 1990 stamp, he noticed one that was missing the gray inscription on the back. Realizing he had stumbled upon something quite unusual, the collector purchased approximately 170 error stamps. It is the first missing back inscription on a federal duck stamp. An unusual characteristic of this major

1986 federal duck stamp missing black color (left), and normal stamp. Credit: Jeanette Cantrell Rudy and the National Postal Museum, Smithsonian Institution (photo by Larry Gates).

error is that since the inscription for this issue is placed over the gum, once the gum is removed the error disappears. Therefore it is vital to ensure the existence of original gum for this to be a true error. The estimated value for this stamp is $400.

1991 Stamp Missing Black Engraving

The 1991 stamp shows a pair of king eiders at water's edge. Only the lower chest of the drake and the front and top of the hen were engraved, much to the consternation of collectors who relish the engraved look and feel of the federal duck stamp. In the normal stamp the engraved portion of the two birds' chests is black, and the engraving is rather heavy and can easily be felt. On the error, of which only six specimens have been identified thus far, the black engraving is missing. Its absence creates a grayish-mauve shade on the drake's chest and a much lighter brown for the hen. The first example of this error was discovered in 1992 by Dan Harshman, of Sport'en Art in Sullivan, Illinois, who questioned the stamps odd appearance when he purchased it

from collector who had coupled it with a print of the stamp art. All known examples of this error originated in the San Francisco, California area. The estimated value for this error is $12,500.

1993 Stamp Missing Black Engraving

Shortly after the 1993 stamp was issued, a collector entered the Hastings, Nebraska Post Office to purchase a stamp. He was attempting to add a plate number single to his collection, but neither he nor the clerk could locate the plate numbers on the panes that the postal clerk had in stock. The collector left with a single stamp, and soon realized something was amiss since the ducks were nearly without feathers. The black engraved portion of the stamp was missing entirely, which explains why there was no plate number to be found, since the engraved plate number is printed on the pane. Another collector and his son stumbled on the error and purchased five panes. Once the word of this discovery hit the philatelic press, people started searching for this error. Thus far, five full panes, plus several singles have

1991 federal duck stamp missing black engraving (left), and normal specimen. Credit: Jeanette Cantrell Rudy and the National Postal Museum, Smithsonian Institution (photo by Larry Gates).

been found. Four panes have all the stamps missing the black; the other is a transition pane, which has partial black on the left two vertical rows and is void of the black engraving on the third through fifth rows. According to the Hastings postmaster, only a few other panes were sold before the error was noticed, most of which were placed in the lobby automatic vending machines. He removed the remaining panes from sale and sent them to Washington for destruction. All known panes are from the upper-right plate position. However, the postmaster indicated the possible existence of an upper-left position among those sent to be destroyed. The estimated value for a single of this error is $4,000.

Finding a duck stamp error is like winning the lottery since many of them sell for many thousands of dollars. Whether more errors will surface is anyone's guess. That new errors were found in the early 1990s, many decades after the original stamps were issued, points strongly to the possibility that more surprises await the keen-eyed collector. If you think you might

have a major duck stamp error, one of the best things you can do is send the stamp in for verification to one or both of the following organizations.

American Philatelic Society
P.O. Box 8000
State College, PA 16801
Phone: 814-237-3803

The Philatelic Foundation
501 Fifth Ave. Room 1901
New York, NY 10017
Phone: 212-867-3699

These organizations examine and render opinions on whether stamps and postal documents are genuine. They are non-profit and offer only opinions, which may not be accurate all the time.

If varieties, instead of errors, are what you're after, then the chances of success are even greater. As for the future, few things in life are perfect, and try as they might the BEP is bound to experience

Sheet of six 1993 federal duck stamps showing a transitional loss of black color from upper left to lower right corner.
Credit: Jeanette Cantrell Rudy and the National Postal Museum, Smithsonian Institution (photo by Larry Gates).

Plate block of the 50th anniversary duck stamp. Credit: Sam Houston Duck Company.

other printing mistakes, and some of those mistakes are going to make it to the general public. So next time you visit the post office or your local stamp dealer and see someone examining every little detail of the duck stamps on hand with the intensity of a prospector, don't laugh, they might just find a new variety or error.

Many of the duck stamp rarities are the errors and some of the more unusual varieties that were covered above. There are, however, a few others that must not be overlooked. One is the special issue of uncut sheets produced for the 50th anniversary of the duck stamp program. Creating these was not as straightforward a task as one might imagine. The major hurdle was deciding which stamp should receive the honor of being the official anniversary stamp, 1983 or 1984. The confusion was caused by the dates that appear on the stamps. The first duck stamp was issued on August 22, 1934 and was void after June 30, 1935, the date printed on its face. Counting fifty years from the August 22 date of issue, which has evolved to a July 1 issue date, you end up at August 22 or July 1, 1984. Thus, the 1983 stamp, which is physically the 50th stamp in the series, and expired on June 30, 1984, misses the issuance-date 50th anniversary by either a day or 53 days. The 1984 stamp, W.C. Morris's wigeons, however, was issued on July 1, 1984, and that is the one the Department of the Interior chose as the 50th anniversary stamp, even though it is not actually the 50th stamp.

The Department of the Interior's math caused some uncomfortable moments for Phil Scholer. After winning the contest in 1983, he began production of the first poster to be released along with the limited edition prints. He assumed his was the "golden anniversary" stamp and was planning to use that hook to his advantage in marketing. Soon after, however, he was contacted by government lawyers who presented him with a cease and desist order. Since they had anointed the 51st stamp as the one to be honored as the anniversary stamp, they didn't want Scholer claiming otherwise. According to Scholer, "following months of stress, we were allowed to do our thing and

needless to say, the 'controversy' was the kind of promotion money can't buy."

Congress approved the printing of fifteen uncut, fully perforated sheets of 120 stamps each of the 1984 stamp. Each sheet has overprinting on the selvage indicating that it is a commemorative printing and identifying which number it is among the fifteen. The sheets were to be sold via sealed bid, at a $2,000 per sheet minimum, cashier's checks up front and the limit of one to a customer. Only four sheets sold at prices ranging from $2,000 to $4,151. Part of the reason for the poor showing is that the sale was advertised mainly to art dealers rather than stamp collectors. A year later, the remaining sheets were put up for sale again. This time bidders could buy multiple sheets and advance funds were not required. While eleven sheets remained, one of those, number 15 was donated to the Smithsonian, leaving ten for sale. With better advertising and relaxed terms, the auction was successful. There were ninety bids from forty-nine bidders and all ten sold. Commemorative sheets are both rare and expensive. In the late 1980s, a full sheet sold at auction for $36,850. The estimated value of a full sheet today is $45,000, and only three such full sheets are believed to have survived, one of which resides in the National Postal Museum.

There is always something special about the first anything. Your first date, your first car, your first paycheck — you name it, if it's your first time you'll remember, for good or bad. The same holds for the first duck stamp. There is something extra special about it. It launched the program, set the standard, and captured the imagination of the people who first laid eyes on it and all of those who have followed. If the first duck stamp is special, what about the actual "first" copy of the first stamp ever sold? Wouldn't that be an amazing find? Bob Dumaine, co-author of this book, had the pleasure of discovering just how thrilling this once-in-a-lifetime event could be, and rather than paraphrase the story, here is his first person account of the rarest of the rare — the first duck stamp.

Form 3333

FEDERAL MIGRATORY-BIRD HUNTING CERTIFICATE AND STAMP

Issued by Post Office Department under Act of Congress March 16, 1934.   For exclusive use of owner whose signature appears on the reverse side hereof

U.S. DEPARTMENT OF AGRICULTURE
VOID AFTER JUNE 30, 1935
ONE DOLLAR 1   ONE DOLLAR 1
MIGRATORY BIRD HUNTING STAMP

WASHINGTON, D.C.
AUG
1934
Postmarking Stamp Here

5—11576

Postmaster.

The very first Form 3333 issued, with Darling's signature across the face of the 1934 stamp.   William M. Mooney, Postmaster of Washington, D.C., to whom Darling gave the very first duck stamp ever purchased, also signed it. Credit: Jeanette Cantrell Rudy and the National Postal Museum, Smithsonian Institution (photo by Larry Gates).

The Very First

For nearly 55 years, August 14, 1934, was listed by the Department of the Interior as the date of sale of the first duck stamp. In 1989, a most unusual event occurred.

I received a phone call from a stamp collector who told me that a friend of his had the "very first" duck stamp ever sold, affixed to a Form 3333. I mentioned that many people "thought" they had the first duck stamp sold, but many such stamps were sold in 1934. He stressed it was the very first duck stamp sold, and his friend had an affidavit to prove it. He was correct. The date on the form was August 22, 1934, and it was accompanied by an affidavit of authenticity signed by Clinton B. Eilenberger, Third Assistant Postmaster General and Ding Darling. Eilenberger sold the stamp to Darling, Chief of the Biological Survey, and artist of the stamp, who in turn presented the item to

William M. Mooney, Postmaster of Washington D.C., and a stamp collector.

Mooney owned the stamp until 1939, when Mrs. Weir, a Treasury Department employee and friend, suggested that he meet one of her employees, a messenger boy with an interest in stamps named George Elam. At the brief meeting, Mooney sold his collection comprised mostly of first day covers, and the first duck stamp to Elam for $50.

In 1943, for $100 Elam, sold his entire stamp collection, except for the first duck stamp, to help finance his family's move to California. George served in the Armed Forces during World War II, and after the war relocated to Indiana, his birthplace, always carrying the stamp in the family's box of valuables. The stamp and the accompanying affidavit moved with him to Wisconsin, Texas, Louisiana, then finally back to Texas. During that time, Elam would tell people about his prized possession, and many of them no doubt took his story with a grain of salt. George and Wyllia, his wife of fifty years, considered the stamp a part of the family.

It was a touch of great providence that Elam and the first duck stamp settled a few miles away from me in Texas, and that a friend of Elam's contacted me about the stamp. After discussing the stamp with Elam, he decided to hold it for awhile. At his request, I followed-up in about six months, offering $10,000, the most ever paid for a single duck stamp at that time. He considered it, and consented to sell with the provision it be displayed by a future buyer or myself.

Over the years, Elam had kept the stamp exactly as he bought it, in a browned glassine with a paper clip holding it in place. Fifty years of residence in a steel box with family papers had taken a toll on the condition. The stamp was in perfect condition, but there was light flap toning and a rust spot from the paper clip on the Form 3333.

I made two attempts to sell the stamp to dealers for about $12,000, but they both declined. Since I was a dealer in duck stamps, I decided to keep the stamp and display it at shows. Approximately two weeks later, I was speaking to Gene German, a serious collector in New Jersey (see profile on page 120). My enthusiasm spilled over to him, but I told him I was going to keep the stamp. Gene then shocked me with his unsolicited offer of $150,000. Since I had just told him I was going to keep it, I was in a dilemma, as that amount exceeded my wildest expectations, especially since two dealers had denied me for $12,000. I sort of gasped and told Gene I would think it over.

The next amazing event occurred 20 minutes later. Another advanced collector, John Gieser of South Carolina, called me and we were chatting. Gene's offer was still throbbing in my head, and I told John what transpired. Gieser has a dynamic personality, and immediately decided he wanted the stamp, and offered $200,000. I was in a state of "lotto" shock.

Now this was looking like a once in a lifetime stroke of good luck. To be fair to the seven major duck stamp collectors at that time, I decided to offer the stamp to all. I readied a proposal, sent it via Express Mail, and the first to pay $275,000 would own the item. Almost immediately Jeanette Rudy of Nashville, Tennessee, called and told me it was "sold." I was sitting on top of the world from my unexpected good fortune.

Naturally, I wanted to tell the duck stamp collecting world about the discovery, so, once the sale to Mrs. Rudy went through, I gave the story to Mike Read, stamp writer for the *Houston Post*. The same day the story was published, Elam called me and told me I would be hearing from his attorneys. Now that was a very cold feeling for the luckiest day in my life.

Framed reproductions of the stamp and affidavit were presented to President George Bush; Secretary of the Interior, Manual Lujan; Director of the U.S. F&WS, John Turner; Chief of the Duck Stamp Office, Norma Opgrand; Elam, and many others, so there was no intent to keep it a secret.

Although all the paperwork receipts, funds transfer, and the like had been in order, and the extraordinary offer from Jeanette Rudy was a true accidental escalation of value, I now had a problem. I was positive I had done nothing wrong, but somehow Elam did not know that. Since it was now a legal issue, I could not explain it to him either, due to the code of silence requested by the attorneys. So the lawyer war was on, and I was the target. About two years passed and legal papers showered everybody, depositions, and all the other fun things of a lawsuit. The dealers I had offered the stamp to for $12,000 confirmed my offer and their refusal. Professionals had declined to pay $12,000, so it obviously had no predetermined value. I soon found out that the paperwork and unending meetings were taking a tremendous toll on me personally, and my duck stamp business. I truly understood why Elam was upset since the stamp brought so much, but then I figured certainly he could understand the freakish nature of the sale. Maybe he did; the lawyers apparently did not. After much agonizing, I decided to settle out of court, and get along with my stamp business. There was no admission of wrongdoing, but the aggravation and suspicion associated with the whole event tarnished my feeling for the stamp, but just for a short time.

When Jeanette Cantrell Rudy displayed the stamp and then bequeathed it to the Smithsonian's National Postal Museum, all the sour feelings turned to lemonade. The precious stamp had been resurrected from its steel lock box coffin and could now be enjoyed by people forever, thanks to J.N. Darling, William B. Mooney, George Elam, Jeanette Rudy, and humbly, myself.

— Bob Dumaine

GREAT COLLECTORS

It is not so much the desire to the best or the biggest, but the love of the hobby and the thrill of the chase that leads so many duck stamp collectors to add to their holdings and build a collection of which they are proud. For a few individuals, this pursuit has resulted in a collection that is among the greatest in the world. Three of the great collectors are profiled below. Through a combination of drive, determination, knowledge, resources, and a little luck, each of them has assembled an array of duck stamps and related items that are so unique and impressive that they are worthy of being exhibited in a museum. One collection already is!

Jeanette Cantrell Rudy

Growing up in Sheffield, Alabama, Jeanette Cantrell Rudy knew nothing about duck hunting or duck stamps. That changed in the fall of 1949, when her new husband, Daniel Clees Rudy asked her to go the post office to get a duck stamp. She looked at him quizzically and said "what the Sam Hill is a duck stamp?" He explained the purpose of the stamp and then she announced, "if you go hunting, I go too." "All right, then," he said, "get two stamps." She purchased two of the green 1949 stamps depicting goldeneyes. "I had a license," Rudy recalls, "but the stamp was so beautiful that I didn't want to lick it and put it on or sign it, so I didn't." Every year thereafter, on hunting trips with her husband, she would take her license and mint stamp along, always ready with a pen in case a game warden came by to check on things. It wasn't until the 1960s that Jeanette started "officially" collecting duck stamps. Since that time she has put together what is arguably the most impressive federal duck stamp collection ever created, a portion of which is now on permanent exhibit at the Smithsonian Institution's National Postal Museum, in Washington, D.C.

Sometime around 1965, Rudy saw an advertisement for a nearby stamp show in Nashville, Tennessee, and off she went. "People were running back and forth like maggots. It was very exciting." There she learned about the Nashville Philatelic Society and decided to join. At her first meeting of the society she brought along her mint ducks and showed them to a few people who said it was a nice collection. One person asked if she was specializing in ducks and Rudy thought for a moment and said "yes." She started studying up on duck stamps and buying more here and there. It was through her exposure to duck stamps that Rudy first learned the true meaning of conservation.

Jeanette Cantrell Rudy. Credit: Jeanette Cantrell Rudy.

Mr. Rudy's sausage business, which he ran with his brother, was beginning to take off at this time, but it was nothing compared to the major business it is today. The family budget was tight and her husband didn't exactly see purchasing duck stamps as a high priority, so Rudy was forced to become creative. "Sometimes I took the grocery money and bought some stamps. We wise wives don't tell our husbands everything. If he got chicken instead of steak then I bought a stamp. So he ate a lot of chicken!" When, some years later, Rudy was finally able to pull together nearly $300 to purchase her first mint copy of the 1934 stamp, she thought she had "really arrived" and that she was "the only one in the world who owned one." No sooner had she bought the 1934 stamp, then she started saving up for the 1935.

Rudy didn't want to keep her collection hidden from view so she began showing her stamps at stamp shows around the country. In the process, she won a number of awards and displayed her collection at the Federal Duck Stamp Contest and Congressional Reception in Washington, D.C., as well as numerous other events. This recognition not surprising since it reflects the time and effort Rudy puts into preparing her exhibits and the amazing depth of her collection. Rudy's prized possession is the very first duck stamp issued to Ding Darling on a Form 3333, which Bob Dumaine sold to her. After she had submitted her winning bid of $275,000, Bob visited Rudy in

Nashville to show her the Form 3333. She had spoken to Bob over the phone, but never met him. Just to be safe, Rudy had a policemen friend come to the house in plainclothes, to keep an eye on Bob in the event that anything should happen. Bob placed the Form 3333 in front of Rudy and she picked it up with tongs to inspect the front and back. "He was sitting on the edge of his chair," Rudy recalls. "He just about had a fit because he was concerned I might damage it. But if I was going to buy it I had to look at it." Bob and the Form 3333 passed the test and Bob left with the check. As Bob was walking out the door, Rudy told him "if the check bounces you can take it out in sausage." According to Rudy, "he just looked at me. It would take him a long time to eat up that much sausage."

Rudy especially likes the hard-to-acquire duck stamps, the errors, unusual varieties, and special formats. One of the most difficult parts of her collection to piece together was a complete set of plate blocks for every number plate that has ever been printed. She has almost done it and is on the lookout for the last few holdouts - some plate blocks from the earliest issues. Other prizes in her collection include an error pane of the 1993 stamp, missing the black engraving, the 1946 plate single of the rose red error, and the unique 1959 stamp with inverted back inscription. Rudy also had an extensive collection of artist-signed federals, and of state, local, and Indian duck and waterfowl stamps. Most

Two pages from the exquisite album owned by Mrs. Rudy, which has hand-drawn images by Joe Hautman accompanying every stamp. The album is opened to a drawing of mallards and multiples of the 1934 stamp. Credit: Jeanette Cantrell Rudy and the National Postal Museum, Smithsonian Institution (photo by Larry Gates).

of Rudy's stamps are housed in albums of her own design and the more valuable stamps are kept in lockboxes at the bank. Some of her most beautiful albums are handmade in England and are illustrated by federal winner Joe Hautman. Choice specimens of each stamp issue are combined with beautiful artwork of the same species in the stamp, making the album a very special expression of her individuality.

Rudy's entire life is suffused with a strong sense of giving back to the community. She is involved in numerous charitable and philanthropic endeavors, and sits on a variety of boards of directors for non-profit organizations. The most spectacular outgrowth of her desire to give back, at least with respect to duck stamps, is on display in Washington,

D.C. On June 27, 1996, the National Postal Museum opened the Jeanette Cantrell Rudy Gallery, which houses a permanent exhibit titled "Artistic License: The Duck Stamp Story." Rudy donated $500,000, the largest amount received by the museum from a single donor, in addition to loaning portions of her collection for the exhibit. Rudy plans to maintain her collection until she dies, at which point it will go to the museum. In the meantime, the museum will be able to choose items from her collection for display. Additional support for the gallery came from the J.N. "Ding" Darling Foundation, DU, Inc., the BEP, and the U.S. F&WS.

Rudy didn't want to be the only person to see and be inspired by her collection. "It was really selfish on my part to want to collect and keep the stamps,"

Artistic License: The Duck Stamp Story

At the entrance to the National Postal Museum's gallery, Artistic License: The Duck Stamp Story, pairs of Canada geese and mallards hanging on invisible wires appear to be swooping down to take a gander at what's inside. A beautiful mural depicting a typical American wetland, replete with reeds, water, and trees covers the walls of the gallery, from floor to ceiling. The wetland, however, is not merely two-dimensional. The epoxy floor appears to be mud or sand with impressions of leaves all around, as if scattered by the wind. Beyond the railings and display cases that curve around the inside perimeter of the gallery, are stands of authentic dried marsh grass, various waterfowl (including a Great Blue Heron), smaller birds, squirrels, a realistic-looking body of water, and even artificial trees, including oak saplings and a couple of large trunks that rise into the ceiling. Among the flora and fauna are three very life-like mannequins. One is of Rudy, standing ready for the hunt, in her camouflage clothing with shotgun in hand. Further along sits Jim Hautman sketching a scene. Nearby is Jack Gregory, a

long-time associate of Rudy's, birdwatching. The faces of the mannequins were made from plaster casts of Rudy, Hautman, and Gregory.

Visitors are guided through a series of state-of-the-art exhibits. The gallery's advanced fiber-optic lighting system uses varying light levels to protect the stamps. Higher light intensities are used for stamps containing blacks and browns and lower intensities for those with reds and oranges. Directional sound systems confine sounds to limited areas, making it easier for viewers to focus on the video materials before them. The technical aspects of the exhibit, however, are secondary to the stamps. The gallery's holding have already been changed once since its inception in 1996. Rarities that have been on view in

The entrance to the National Postal Museum's gallery, "Artistic License: The Duck Stamp Story." Credit: Jim O'Donnell, National Postal Museum, Smithsonian Institution.

Rudy notes. "Having them at home hidden away doesn't do any good, but sharing them through the museum relieved me of my selfishness - that way I would not be a selfish old biddy." Speaking during the dedication ceremony, Rudy stated, "I am thrilled about the opportunity to leave my collection to the National Postal Museum, where it will be cared for and seen by many people for years to come. . . . I consider this a part of my personal legacy as well as an effort to preserve the history of our great country." Rudy also sees this exhibit as a way to spread awareness of the need for conservation and to let people see how important the duck stamp program is in the fight for conservation.

Rudy was one of the judges for the 1992 duck stamp competition. "I thought I'd died and gone to heaven. I wanted to do right. Be sure I was taking everything into consideration. I went into with all my heart. I was in a nervous tizzy the whole time. Voted for the winner [Joe Hautman] - gave him five, five times." Rudy is not the only person in her family to be a judge. In 1994, her sister, Geneva C. Barry, of Lacombe, Louisiana, was a judge in the contest that selected Jim Hautman's mallards the winner. Rudy is still actively collecting, always searching for something new and exciting. "It's still a thrill, collecting and seeing ducks. Every time I see a flight of geese or ducks go over head I feel like it is the very first time." She advises collectors to "just enjoy what they are doing. Take one stamp at a time and one day at a time and show pride in what you have."

the past include the Graf Zeppelin cover and a series of six of the 1993 canvasback error stamps showing a gradual loss of the black engraving. Today, the gallery includes a whole series of mint panes, including some of the earliest years, A.C. Roessler's 1936 First Day Cover, and the 1959 stamp error with the inverted back inscription.

Other display cases contain historical pictures of the types of market-hunting which led to declines in waterfowl populations, state and local duck stamps, and beautiful original artwork for recent federal and junior duck stamp winners. There also are three videos for museum visitors to view. "The Duck Stamp Story" describes the history of the duck stamp program and the events and individuals who helped to create and sustain it. "A Stamp for the Future," emphasizes the importance of the duck stamp to hunters, conservationists, artists, and stamp collectors. Finally, an untitled video shows waterfowl, quacks and all, landing, taking off from, and flying over wetlands.

The National Postal Museum is located just blocks away from the Capitol Building in Washington, D.C., right next to Union Station. Its hours are 10 a.m. to 5:30 p.m., every day except December 25. Guided tours are offered Monday through Friday at 11 a.m., 1 p.m. and 2 p.m.; Saturday and Sunday at 11 a.m. and 1 p.m. For more information about museum activities and to arrange group tours, call 202-357-2991.

Above: *A life-size mannequin of Mrs. Rudy, shotgun in hand, ready for the hunt. Credit: Jim O'Donnell, National Postal Museum, Smithsonian Institution.*
Left: *An interior view of "Artistic License: The Duck Stamp Story," showing two of the illuminated cases and some of the background diorama. Credit: Jim O'Donnell, National Postal Museum, Smithsonian Institution.*

Bob Lesino (right), Program Manager, The Federal Duck Stamp Program, handing Gene German an Artist Commemorative Issue certificate at the first day ceremony for the 1995 stamp. German was one of the judges for that contest. Credit: Dave Gallagher.

Gene German

In the late 1980s the Wall Street chapter of DU held a charitable auction. Gene German, one of the founders of this group and a member of the New York Stock Exchange, was sitting in the audience. When a New Jersey Duck Stamp print, framed with two duck stamps, went on the block, German bought it. As a resident of New Jersey, part of his interest in this item was geographic. But German also was impressed with the beauty and order of the presentation, the numbered print and the matching stamps, one signed by the artist. Although he didn't realize it then, he was hooked. What began as a charitable impulse became a passionate pursuit. In a relatively short period of time, German has amassed one of the premier duck stamp collections and he has the distinction of owning the largest number of original federal duck stamp paintings - seventeen.

Shortly after the auction, German read an article on duck stamps in the DU magazine and decided he wanted to learn more. In the advertising section of the magazine, he spied an advertisement for Sam Houston Duck Company, gave them a call and was directed to the President, Bob Dumaine. At the end of a long conversation, German commented that he had taken up a lot of time and to make it worthwhile

he asked Bob to set him up with an album and stamps, adding up to a total of $10,000.

When the Scott album arrived, some stamps were already on the pages in pre-inserted mounts, but many were loose, allowing German the chance to physically go through the motion of placing them on the pages. The beauty of the stamps and their vibrant colors piqued his interest. With Bob's assistance, German set his sights on collecting complete sets of both federal and state duck stamps, all in extra-fine condition. Today, he has three complete sets of the federal and state issues, housed in various Scott albums. Each year, the albums are updated.

German also has two books of federal errors and varieties and an almost complete set of plate blocks. Of all his stamps, his favorite is a transition pane of the 1993 stamp, on which some of the stamps are missing the black engraving. There are only two panes of the 1993 error. On one, all the stamps are missing the black engraving. On the one German owns, the stamps have partial black on the left two vertical rows and is mostly void of the black engraving on the third through fifth rows. When these two panes were first discovered, German was offered the option of selecting either one. He chose the transition pane because felt it was so unique, showing the evolution of an error as the entire sheet of stamps passed through the printing press.

Other prized possessions include the number two of the special printing of uncut sheets of the 50th Anniversary issue and a special duck stamp album which runs up through the early 1950s, that was custom-made for an now-deceased collector and contains pages to match each stamp, along with special cutouts for the stamp and the artist's autograph. German is in the process of updating the album, carrying the initial design throughout.

As often happens with duck stamp collectors, their interests move them into related areas of collecting. For German, one direction led to artwork. Slowly and quietly he began acquiring original duck stamp paintings. At first, these could be had for between $5,000 to $7,000, but then word got out that a major buyer was on the lookout for new acquisitions and the price shot up to the point where some of German's later purchases were in the neighborhood of $25,000. The sharply climbing prices combined with German's shifting interests led him to move away from duck stamp art collecting.

Sixteen of his seventeen original paintings are propped up against the wall in one of the rooms in his house. Asked about this unusual style of display, German responded, "I've literally run out of wall space." The seventeenth painting, Richard Plasschaert's mallards, hangs in his office. It was the first winning painting he purchased, but more importantly, it is also the art on German's favorite stamp, the 1980 issue, chosen as his favorite because his kids like it best. One year they even bought him a woodcut of the stamp as a present, which also hangs in his office. Perhaps the most unusual duck stamp-related items in German's office are the three original paintings by Bob Hines. While Hines' artwork graces the 1946 stamp, the three paintings German owns are ones that Hines submitted in other years that did not win the competition. Everyone focuses so much attention on the winning artwork that they often forget the other beautiful paintings and drawings that were not chosen.

In 1994, German had the honor of being a judge in the federal contest, the one where Jim Hautman's painting of two mallard scored a perfect 25 for the win. While German was somewhat "overwhelmed by the whole thing," he found that experience "very enlightening" and a "great pleasure." German was so impressed by the winning art that he asked a scrimshaw artist to make a duplicate of Jim's two mallards on a piece of fossilized walrus tusk. At a dinner in Washington, German showed the carving to Jim who was amazed.

German's family thinks he's a bit "crazy" for collecting duck stamps and related items. They are not alone. German often wonders, "am I crazy for spending all of this money?" Nevertheless, he still has a fire for collecting. "I'm doing it for me. . . I'm a little boy in a toy store, it's very exciting." His advice to other collectors is simple. "Start slow. Not everybody can do what I do. One of the great things about ducks stamps is that a determined collector can create a complete collection for a reasonable cost. At whatever level you collect, there is a sense of achievement, accomplishment and beauty . . . All of the duck stamps are connected and when you have them all you have something really unique. Just do it at your own pace and enjoy."

Richard W. Plasschaert's winning design for the 1980 stamp. He chose this design because he "wanted something simple, thinking that it would have the best chance to win. I chose mallards because they are very common." Credit: Richard. W. Plasschaert.

William B. Webster

William B. Webster, of Minnesota, is a great believer in things happening because they are supposed to. He also believes that good timing, hard work, and good judgment can help position people in the right place at the right time, in effect creating good luck. All of these factors have helped Webster amass one of the great duck stamp collections in the world. If you had to pick one event that best proves this point it would be his visit to a doctor in Red Wing, Minnesota, who lived just twelve miles from his home.

The year was 1962 when a Minneapolis stamp dealer told Webster about the doctor's duck stamp collection and recommended that he see if the doctor had any duplicates he might wish to sell. One day Webster happened to be driving through Red Wing and decided to stop by. The doctor's wife answered the door and told Webster that her husband had died the week before. Having no idea what do with his large stamp collection, she asked Webster to leave his phone number and said she would talk to her attorney and see what he suggested.

Webster continued on his journey home, doubtful that he would hear anything more about the doctor's "ducks." But two months later he did get a call from a banker in Red Wing who invited him to see the collection, on the wife's recommendation. She very much wanted Webster to purchase the stamps rather than send them to an auction house. He had no idea what to expect. As the banker began pulling out mint sheets, plate blocks of four and six, plate number singles and singles, Webster was awestruck. The extent and quality of the collection was astounding. "Once I saw them all," Webster remembers, "I now had the concern of how would I ever be able to buy some 4,500 mint 'ducks.' Clearly the largest and finest collection of federal duck stamps ever assembled."

Asking for a few days to think it over, Webster went back to the stamp dealer for advice on what to offer. They arrived at a number and, upon the dealer's recommendation, Webster went to a bank in search of a loan. "With a growing family, our first five by this time, and a house mortgage, I obviously needed outside financing to purchase the stamps." He visited a boyhood friend who was a Vice President of the First National Bank in St. Paul, and asked for $6,000. Did Webster have any collateral, the VP wanted to know. Not really came the reply, how about the stamps? "Well," said the VP, "we don't take duck stamps as collateral." The VP suggested that Webster ask his life insurance company for a loan. He did and it worked.

With money in hand, Webster visited the wife and her banker, offering face value for the stamps. They accepted. According to Webster, that "turned out to be one of the best buys of my life." By today's standards purchasing such stamps for face value might seem like a steal, but at the time it was a fair price. Duck

William B. Webster and one of his beloved dogs. Credit: William B. Webster.

stamp collectors were few and far between and, consequently, stamp dealers had little interest in stocking duck stamps, especially since they had no face value. If the stamps had gone to auction, they likely would have sold for less than what Webster offered.

At the time of this purchase, Webster was already an avid duck stamp collector, but his first connection to duck stamps came much earlier. The first stamp he purchased for hunting was the 1940 issue, Francis Lee Jaques' black ducks. During his three years in the Air Corps during World War II, as an aerial and ground photographer, Webster's father continued to purchase duck stamps on his behalf. When Webster returned from the war he continued the practice, placing the stamps in the hunting log his father had begun in the 1920s. "Figuring they were not only attractive but designed by the very best of the wildlife artists of the time," Webster felt that "collecting the stamps would be a noteworthy and interesting venture." His first step was to go back and fill in the years he had missed, 1934-1939, with mint copies. Webster also became friendly with a knowledgeable philatelist who gave him sound advice on putting together a significant collection of ducks.

Webster's purchase of the "doctor's ducks" in the early 1960s brought his collection to a new level, and since that time he has continued adding to it each year, with both regular issues and unique items. As a result, he has a very complete set of mint singles, artist-signed stamps, plate number singles, and all but four years of full sheets (1936, 1937, 1938, and

1939). His prized possessions include: a vertical strip of three of the 1934 stamp, horizontally imperforate; Form 3333 with 1934 stamp signed by Darling; a 1935 plate block of four signed in the margin by Darling; and a die proof for the 1945 stamp singed by the artist, Owen J. Gromme. He keeps his collection in a bank vault which he periodically visits.

Webster also has one of very two unique collections of duck stamp prints known to exist. Not only one print of each year but one print of each edition offered to collectors for that particular year. He also owns two of the original duck paintings. His interest in wildlife art came early and as a youth he thought he might be an artist. While Webster did a number of drawings, his focus soon shifted from wanting to be an artist to collecting art. His interest in duck stamp prints was sparked in the early 1950s when a friend showed him a Crossroads of Sport catalog, which listed all of the duck stamp prints from 1934 through 1951. As was the case with the early stamps, the prints were not the collecting sensation they would later become. Each could be purchased for a relatively reasonable $10 to $15, and Webster updated the entire set, to which he has added in subsequent years.

By the mid-1960s, Webster was a noted authority on duck stamps and wildlife art, but it was still only a hobby. By day, Webster was a manufacturer's representative with Master Lock Company for eight Midwestern states. In 1967, while on a hunting trip with noted wildlife artists David Maass and David Hagerbaumer, Webster's career began heading in a new direction. Both artists complained about the lack of wildlife art publishers who had the requisite skills to produce high-quality prints. Webster saw an opportunity and decided to become the type of publisher his friends couldn't find. Upon his return

from the trip, he and his father devised a name for the new venture. They each wrote down five candidates on separate sheets of paper and the only duplicate on their lists was Wild Wings. In 1968, Webster incorporated the company. Two years later Wild Wings published its first print, Owen Gromme's Wintering Quail, and sent out the offering to 6,000 people. The phenomenal response told Webster he was on to something. From that small beginning, Wild Wings has grown into one of the nation's leading publishers and distributors of wildlife art, with nearly 150 employees, annual catalog mailing list of upwards of 6.5 million, and numerous retail stores.

Webster is very involved in efforts to preserve waterfowl, serving since the early 1980s as a trustee of the Delta Waterfowl Foundation and since 1973 as an Honorary Trustee of DU. He is the founder of the American Museum of Wildlife Art located in the University of Minnesota's Bell Museum of Natural History, of which he is also a founding board member. The nucleus of the American Museum of Wildlife Art's collection is comprised of items donated by Webster himself.

Every time Webster talks to someone about stamps, whether family, friend, or casual acquaintance, he urges them to buy a mint pane of duck stamps as an investment. Few have taken this advice, much to his surprise. Then again, they haven't seen what he has. Webster has witnessed the evolution of duck stamp collecting, from a hobby shared by few to a passion pursued by many, and he has watched prices rise consistently over the years. He knows there is value in "ducks" and his enjoyment of this hobby has not lessened in the six decades since he purchased his first duck stamp.

Die proof for the 1945 stamp depicting the artwork of Owen J. Gromme. Credit: William B. Webster.

Artistry & Marketing

Daniel Smith's majestic snow goose that appeared on the 1988 federal duck stamp. Credit: Daniel Smith.

THE CONTEST

A pair of mallards landing in a marsh, black ducks soaring in tandem over reeds bowed by the wind, Canada geese guarding their brood, a majestic snow goose rising off a wetland on a golden morning, and a spectacled eider angling over white-capped waves and an amber Alaskan sky. Each duck stamp design offers the artist an opportunity to capture the beauty and grace of one of our North American migratory waterfowl. The best of these designs invokes a strong emotional response, pulling the observer into the scene to share the artist's vision. Look at them closely and feel the wind rushing by, smell the fresh scent of water, and relax with the serenity of the scene. Since 1934, art has been the foundation upon which the Federal Duck Stamp Program has been built. The selection of the artwork is the first step in the annual cycle leading up to the printing of a new duck stamp. Over the years, the selection process has gone through many twists and turns. Today, the duck stamp art competition is an elaborate affair, replete with rules and regulations that serve to orchestrate what is the only federal art contest in existence. In the beginning it was quite different.

Necessity, it is said, is the mother of invention, so perhaps the father is the great skill necessary to

Francis Lee Jaques wash painting of black ducks soaring over swaying reeds is often cited by his fellow artists and other observers as being the most beautiful of all federal designs. Credit: U.S. Fish and Wildlife Service.

Maynard Reece's wash and gouache buffleheads which were chosen to be on the face of the 1948 federal duck stamp. Credit: U.S. Fish and Wildlife Service.

bring that invention to a reality. In mid-1934 what was desperately needed was a design for the first duck stamp. The law creating the duck stamp program was passed in March of that year, and Darling, as the new head of the Bureau of Biological Survey, was handed the task of launching the duck stamp program. Part of that task was creating a design to go on the new stamp. Darling, much to his surprise, became the first "duck stamp artist" when his hastily sketched ideas were adopted by the BEP as the foundation for the 1934 stamp. Perhaps chastened by this experience, Darling instituted a more formal procedure in 1935. That year the Survey began the practice of inviting one artist to submit a design. This invitational process, subsequently administered by the U.S. F&WS, continued up through the late 1940s. While some have referred to these early artists as being "commissioned" to submit their work, that is not the best term since the process was not that formal and the artists were paid nothing for their work, although they retained the rights to the art and were free to sell prints of it, as many did. Some of the most talented artists of the day submitted their work during these early years, including Benson (1935), Francis Lee Jaques (1940), and A. Lassell Ripley (1942), all of whom had established reputations that went well beyond wildlife art.

Toward the late 1940s, as recognition of the duck stamp program grew, the U.S. F&WS began receiving unsolicited submissions. Maynard Reece, who would go on to win the duck stamp art competition an unequaled five times, first became involved in the duck stamp program in 1947, when Darling invited him, as well as at least one other artist, to submit

drawings for consideration. Reece submitted two designs and was awarded third place. In 1948, however, Reece submitted two more designs "without any request from anyone," as he recalls, and it was his design of three buffleheads that was selected to be on that year's stamp. His other submission came in third. The next year there were eight unsolicited submissions.

Hines, an artist-illustrator for the U.S. F&WS and designer of the 1946 stamp, saw a trend developing and suggested to his colleagues that the U.S. F&WS officially open up the duck stamp competition to anyone who wanted to enter. The idea took hold and the era of "open competition" began. For the 1950 stamp, sixty-five artists submitted eighty-eight entries. The competition has been fierce ever since, reaching an all-time high for the 1982 stamp, with 2,099 entries.

For the first two contests there were no formal rules of submission for the artists to follow, but this changed with the third competition for the 1952 stamp. The designs were to be five by seven inches, in black and white, with the name of the species and the artist clearly indicated at the bottom of the design so that the judges could see them. The choice of medium, scene, and species was left to the artist, with the only limitation being that the design had to depict "wild American waterfowl."

One exception during these early years to the laissez-faire attitude towards the design was the 1959 stamp. In its press release about the competition that year, the U.S. F&WS requested that artists submit designs showing a retriever in action. The idea was suggested by a number of conservation

King Buck, Reece's most famous duck stamp design. If you compare this painting with the stamp on the front page of the Stamps and Stamp Collecting section you will notice that the artwork has eleven flying ducks, while the stamp has only seven. Credit: Maynard Reece.

organizations that wanted to bring attention to the problem of crippling losses of waterfowl, which were estimated at the time to constitute twenty-five percent of the annual death toll of migratory waterfowl. It was hoped that by highlighting the important role of retrievers, such losses could be reduced. Artists were free to incorporate any species of waterfowl in the design.

Reece, who had already won in 1948 and 1951, hadn't planned to enter that contest when he got a call from John Olin, owner of Nilo Kennels. Would Reece be interested, he inquired, in painting one of his dogs, King Buck, and submitting it to the contest? King Buck wasn't just any dog. Although he had started off life as an ailing puppy, he went on to win two National Championship Stakes in 1952 and 1953. According to Reece, the call came because they "thought I might have a better chance of winning, given my track record." Reece consented, and visited King Buck, worked with him in the field, and made a number of sketches. The black and white tempera drawing that Reece entered in the contest won top honors.

The King Buck stamp, as it has come to be known, was immediately ensnared in controversy. A number of contestants declared, with disgust, that "a dog, not a duck, won the contest." Many non-hunters were upset by the image of a dead mallard on the stamp. On the flip side, many retriever lovers raved about the stamp. To Reece, the opposition to his design "was absolutely wrong because the purpose of King Buck was to show how important retrievers are in the cause of conservation." The tempest quickly died down, and King Buck has gone on to become one of the most popular of all duck stamp designs. Still,

the controversy might have had a chilling effect on subsequent entries and judging. It wasn't until 1999 that another winning design, Jim Hautman's greater scaup, showed a dog in the design (albeit as a minor element). However, many state stamps have capitalized on the popular theme by featuring retrievers on their stamps, and the federal contest rules have now been modified to allow for other than a waterfowl species as a theme.

The requirements for art-submissions changed over the years. Up until the competition for the 1970 stamp, artists were at liberty to submit as many designs as they could muster. That year artists were limited to three; in 1976 it was lowered to one. 1970 also was the first year that allowed color entries, and Edward J. Bierly won with a watercolor painting of two Ross' geese standing in shallow water, with the goose in the foreground preening. From that point forward, all winning designs, with the exception of Magee's in 1976, have been in color. During the 1950s and 1960s there was nothing to stop a winning artist from submitting entries year after year. Although many winners voluntarily dropped out of the competition for a while after their win, there were some who didn't. Edward A. Morris even won the contest twice in a row, in 1961 and 1962. In 1971, to keep the same artist from winning too often, entry was limited to those who had not won in the preceding five years; the next year the rules were changed again and winners were not allowed to compete for the three years following their win.

In 1975, James P. Fisher's design of a canvasback decoy with three canvasback flying overhead in an inset set off a controversy reminiscent of the one swirling around King Buck. Many people protested that a decoy should not be on a duck stamp, despite the fact that decoys play an important role in the history of waterfowl hunting. To avoid a repeat, the U.S. F&WS began requiring that the dominant image in the design be a live bird. Twenty-one years later, in 1996, the artwork of second-place finisher in the contest precipitated another change in the rules. That year, Hank Buffington submitted a beautiful rendition of a pintail leaning over for a sip of water. It just missed beating out all 474 entries for the coveted title of winning design. It was only after the contest was completed, however, that it became known that Buffington's entry had been created on a computer and put on paper with a high-quality, Iris printer. Buffington had done nothing wrong. The contest rules did not exclude computer-generated images and he stated clearly on his entry form that his submission was created on a Macintosh, listing the computer as the "medium" for the piece. Neither the U.S. F&WS staff nor the judges noticed this until after the competition was over, and it is not clear what they would have done had they noticed, since Buffington's was a valid entry. But when people crowded around the winning designs, someone noticed the dot pattern on the Buffington's pintail

and wondered whether the image had been computer generated. A check of the entry form confirmed this suspicion. According to Buckley, BEP's technical advisor during that competition, "none of us could identify it as a computer image during the competition, . . . but everyone looked at the competition as original hand-rendered artwork with no mechanical assist." To square perception with reality, the contest rules were changed. From that point forward, designs could only be "hand drawn," original creations. There can be no original for a computer-generated work, since the computer is capable of recreating the exact image indefinitely.

The U.S. F&WS's practice of allowing artists to pick their species was perceived as a problem by the late 1980s. While there are only forty-two species of North American waterfowl that could be shown on a duck stamp, even with more than fifty years worth of stamps there were still nine species that had yet to be depicted - lesser scaup, king eider, spectacled eider, surf scoter, black scoter, Barrow's goldeneye, black-bellied whistling duck, mottled duck and the red-breasted merganser. To ensure complete coverage, the U.S. F&WS changed the contest rules. Beginning with the 1988 stamp only certain species,

Edward J. Bierly's winning design of Ross' geese for the 1970 issue won on the first year that allowed colored entries. Credit: Edward J. Bierly.

James P. Fisher's design chosen for the 1975 federal duck stamp, with its prominent use of a decoy, stirred up controversy. Credit: U.S. Fish and Wildlife Service.

Hank Buffington's pintail captured second place in the 1996 art contest. It was only after the competition that the judges discovered Buffington's image was generated on a computer. Credit: U.S. Fish and Wildlife Service.

Neal Anderson's winning artwork of lesser scaup for the 1989 federal duck stamp. Credit: Neal Anderson and Wild Wings.

usually a choice of five or fewer, were eligible each year. As of the year 2000, only the black scoter had failed to be immortalized on a stamp. Its time has come. In the competition for the 2001 stamp, artists will be able to choose from five species, all of which have previously been depicted on a stamp, but then for the 2002 stamp only the black scoter will be eligible. After that, the yearly lists of eligible species will begin cycling through again.

Today, aspiring duck stamp artists are supplied with a detailed set of contest rules and regulations to help them prepare their submission. In addition to the requirements already covered above, artists are told that a fee of $100, in the form of a certified check, cashiers check or money order must accompany the entry. To enter, one must be a U.S. citizen, national, or resident alien, and 18 years or older. Each entry must be matted only in white, and the mat's outside dimensions should be nine by twelve inches. The image size seen within the cutout portion of the mat must be seven by ten inches, horizontally positioned, not the five by seven inches with which earlier submissions had to comply (the size change began with the 1987 stamp). Not only is computer-generated art forbidden, so too is any

design duplicated from previously published art, including photographs. While the design must have one of the eligible species as its dominant feature, it may also include, but is not limited to, hunting dogs, hunting scenes, use of waterfowl decoys, NWRs as the background of habitat scenes, and other designs that depict the sporting, conservation, stamp collecting and other uses of the stamp. All entries should be drawn with fullest attention to clarity of detail and the relationship of tonal values. These are the characteristics that the engraver and other BEP staff will rely on to interpret the design as it makes the transition from a piece of art to an image on a stamp. Thus, if an image is beautiful, but is very difficult to translate into stamp form, it will probably not be chosen. Finally, the front of the artwork is no longer signed by the artist to help ensure that the judging is not biased.

To help artists prepare for the competition, the Duck Stamp Office offers art workshops during the spring and summer, at various professional art centers/schools around the country. Aspiring artists hear from U.S. F&WS staff about the history of the contest and the rules and regulations that govern entries and judging, giving them a better understanding of what the judges are looking for. Winning artists often attend the workshops to offer a firsthand account of the process. Strategies for improvement are offered along with professional critiques of participants' work.

The rules governing the judging have also significantly changed over time. During the early years of open competition judging was relatively informal. Panels comprised of U.S. F&WS personnel, dignitaries, artists, waterfowl experts, BEP staff, and journalists, sometimes with as many as twenty-two members, would review and vote on the entries, talking amongst themselves, comparing notes. According to one participant who judged one of the contests in the mid-1950s, the process was less than "scientific." "Viewing the paintings, we were all wandering around looking a bit confused. Then, Ira Gabrielson [former Director of the U.S. F&WS] goes over and says I like this one, and everybody else gravitates over and, what do you know, they all like that one too!"

Over time the judging process grew more involved. George Reiger, currently Conservation Editor for *Field & Stream*, and judge for the contests that chose the 1976 and 1977 stamps, recalls beginning the judging at mid-morning. The first step was a short presentation by a staffer from the BEP who told the judges about the importance of picking a design that had clarity and was not too busy, so as to ensure reproducibility of the image at stamp size. Next came the preliminary screening, during which time the judges winnowed the group of artwork, eliminating those that either didn't impress or were otherwise inappropriate. For the 1976 contest, in particular, Reiger saw some memorable designs that failed to survive the first screening. One was a scene of Revolutionary War drummer boys looking skyward towards the flying ducks overhead. Apparently the artist had gotten a bit too caught up in the excitement surrounding the bicentennial celebrations. Another showed a duck coming in for a landing on the end of a hunter's layout boat. The perspective was way off, making the duck appear huge, upwards of 200 pounds. Reiger doubted if the hunter's gun was large enough to shoot such a monster out of the air, and he wondered whether such a shot would be more in self-defense than for the purpose of hunting. Reiger remembers another painting of wood ducks flying through a swamp that "was quite aesthetically pleasing, but it didn't make the grade because it was too busy, too many branches to translate well into stamp size." With these and their peers out of the running, the judges next chose eight to ten finalists, and then in the final round they chose the top three, with the one receiving the highest cumulative ranking being crowned winner. The judging was completed by early afternoon. Throughout the process, the judges were free to discuss their likes and dislikes with one another. Reiger found the exchange of ideas very useful. "Part of the pleasure of judging is talking and learning from others," he said. If a question arose, the judges addressed it together. In one instance during the judging for the 1977 stamp, there was dispute over the wing feathers in a painting of Ross' geese. Some wondered if it had the right number of primaries. The judging was held up for twenty minutes while one of the staffers ran up to the office of the director of the U.S. F&WS to get a reference book on waterfowl. The painting, by Martin Murk was determined to be correct and it went on to win the contest.

Today, judging is more formalized, with detailed regulations spelling out the requirements. Five judges, and one alternate, are selected annually by the Secretary of the Interior. All of the judges must have one or more of the following characteristics: recognized art credentials; knowledge of the anatomical makeup and the natural habitat of the eligible waterfowl species; an understanding of the wildlife sporting world in which the duck stamp is used; an awareness of philately and the role the duck stamp plays in stamp collecting; and demonstrated support for the conservation of waterfowl and wetlands through active involvement in the conservation community. According to the contest regulations, the judges are supposed to judge the art submissions on the basis of anatomical accuracy, artistic composition and suitability for engraving in the production of a stamp.

The judging process usually spans two days (although it can be bumped up to three if the number of entries gets quite large). At the start of the first day, U.S. F&WS and BEP staff brief the judges on all the judging procedures and other details of the competition. This is when the judges first get to preview the eligible artwork. The Duck Stamp Office has already weeded out any ineligible pieces. The entries are displayed in the cavernous Department of the Interior main auditorium in numerical order, with the number signifying only when the art was received and processed by the U.S. F&WS. The artist's name is not included on the front of the design and, therefore the judging is blind. Prior to the first round of judging and before the opening of the contest to the public, the judges are given two hours to review all the entries. If they have any questions, they are free to ask U.S. F&WS or BEP staff for clarification, but they are not to talk amongst themselves or compare notes. Throughout the entire contest, when it comes to the artwork, there exists a wall of silence between judges. This helps to ensure fairness and avoid collusion. During the first round, all qualified entries are shown one at a time to each of the judges, who are sitting on stage, whereupon they vote "in" or "out." Those entries receiving a majority

Alderson Magee's winning artwork for the 1976 stamp being shown to the judges prior to their final selection.
Credit: Alderson Magee.

of "in" votes become eligible for the second round. The remaining entries are placed in a group for public viewing. During the voting in this and subsequent rounds, the judges are seated at a table and separated from one another with opaque dividers, further ensuring the integrity of the vote.

Prior to the second round, each judge is afforded the opportunity to select up to five entries of those that were eliminated during the first round and pull them back into the competition. All of the still-eligible entries are now hung at the front of the auditorium, in numerical order. As the judges view the entries, the technical advisors from the Department of the Interior and the BEP provide a critical analysis for each design, pointing out any serious anatomical problems and/or serious design problems for the engravers. With the judges seated back on stage, each entry is passed before the panel for another vote. In the second round, the scores can range from one to five, which is indicated by numbered card that the judge holds aloft. The total

across all five judges is the score for that entry. The entries receiving the five highest scores advance to the third round of judging, which takes place the next day. Usually more than five entries make it to the final round, since tie scores are all eligible.

In the third round of judging, the judges vote on the remaining entries using the same method as in round two, except they indicate a numerical score from three to five for each entry. The Contest Coordinator tabulates the final votes and presents them to the Director, U.S. F&WS, who announces the winning entry as well as the entries that placed second and third. In case of a tie vote for first, second, or third place in the third round, the judges will vote again on the tied entries, using the same method as in round three. When the winner is in the audience, he or she is called forward for congratulations. When the winner is not present, which is usually the case, congratulations are offered via telephone. The odds are good that the winner will be there to answer the call since the artists who have

The cavernous auditorium at the U.S. Department of Interior, set up for the judging with all the artwork hung and waiting for inspection. Credit: Dave Gallagher.

Judges for the 1997 Federal Duck Stamp Contest listening to contest officials outline the judging process From left to right, they are Emily Pels, Doug Grann, Karen Hollingsworth, and Lillian and Donald Stokes. Credit: Dave Gallagher.

Tom Fegley, judge for the 1998 contest, taking notes on some of the entries. Credit: Dave Gallagher.

advanced to round three are called before the final judging and asked to stay within reach.

Every year the federal duck stamp contest follows a familiar pattern. In the spring and summer, contest guidelines are mailed to prospective artists, and are also made available on the Duck Stamp Office home page. Any time after issuance of the new stamp, usually on July 1, artists can submit their designs for consideration during the next competition. Entries must be postmarked by the middle of September, and the contest is held at the end of October or the beginning of November. Judging is a time of intense excitement. To be selected as a judge is a true honor, and many past judges cite the experience as one of the greatest of their lives. Karen Hollingsworth, nature photographer and conservationist, even gave up a chance to visit Pantanal, Brazil, a place she had wanted to photograph for years, to participate in judging the 1997 contest. For Jameson Parker, a writer, actor and host of the outdoor television program, The World of Ducks Unlimited, being asked to judge the contest for the 1999 stamp was not only an honor, but also a means of reconnecting with his past. As Parker relates it,

[m]y grandfather, historian and writer Mark Sullivan, was a friend of Ding Darling's and maintained a correspondence with him for many years. I attended the same college as . . . Darling (Beloit College in Beloit, Wisconsin) and that connection actually helped me graduate from there. I got caught with a bottle of booze in the girl's dormitory and the college was considering expelling me. At some point in the ensuing furor, my mother, who had clearly learned a thing or two about political negotiation from her father, mentioned that she still had piles of Ding Darling's letters for my grandfather and that she had been thinking about donating them to the college. I ended up with a one year's suspension and, finally, a degree; the college ended up with the letters."

A couple of months prior to the annual contest, the Duck Stamp Office contacts prospective judges and invites them to be part of the upcoming panel. Rather than run out and tell everyone about their appointment, judges are instructed to remain silent. This is for their benefit and further ensures the integrity of the contest. The Federal Duck Stamp Program seeks to eliminate outside influences on judges such as that of artists, publishers, or any one else with a personal motive for selecting the winner. Prior to arriving in Washington, many judges have already begun "boning-up." Mary Ann Owens, an active stamp collector and exhibitor and judge for the 1995 contest, took the list of eligible species to the library and read as much as she could about each of them. Others have studied past winners to learn what types of designs have been successful. Hollingsworth took a slightly more unusual step in her preparations for the contest. "I got a stronger prescription for my reading glasses . . . I thought it would be a good idea to actually be able to see the artwork!"

When judges first view all of the entries lined up along the sides of the Department of the Interior auditorium, the response is usually equal parts amazement and moderate panic. Jim Jude, Executive Director of the Australian Wildlife Fund and judge for the 1991 stamp contest, looked over the 626 entries, thinking "it hardly seemed possible" that a single winner could be selected from such a large group. Surprisingly, even with so much high quality artwork in the competition, the field narrows rather quickly. For example, after the first round, Jude and his fellow judges had brought forward just 38 designs. Similarly, during the 1993 contest, 629 entries were whittled to 29 before the second round began.

USFWS Director, Jamie Clark and Jameson Parker at the judging for the 1999 federal duck stamp. Parker was one of the judges. Credit: Dave Gallagher.

One of the most interesting features of the judging is its openness. According to Gary "Radar" Burghoff, Emmy Award winning actor, director, wildlife artist, and judge in 1993, "the contest is a national art gallery once a year and it's open to the public. It's a wonderful thing to bring the family to." While the auditorium is seldom filled, many people do filter in and out during the judging. The audience is like a sixth judge. Visitors will wander the same aisles as the judges and come to their own conclusions as to which design should be crowned winner. While audience members do not get an official vote, nor are they allowed to express their opinions to any of the judges, they can keep track of the competition to see if the judges' selection squares with theirs. For Hollingsworth, having the judging take place "independently, out in the open for all to see [was] the most difficult part" of the experience. "Knowing that I was going to be facing the folks in the auditorium holding up my vote, was a bit unnerving at first." As is usually the case, the judges get used to the company. Hollingsworth became much more "relaxed" after the first few entries.

To assist the judges in their difficult task, the Duck Stamp Office provides each with a special hand-held lens that reduces the visual size of the image and gives them a better idea of how the art would appear if reproduced at stamp size. Other assistance comes from two technical advisors, as well as the Duck Stamp Office staff, who are available

throughout the contest to answer questions. If a judge would like to know whether an anatomical feature is correct, the U.S. F&WS wildlife biologist is there to help. Similarly, the BEP technical advisor answers questions about the engraving and stamp production process. If a judge asks a question that might interest the entire panel, the question is stated and answered aloud for all to hear. Sometimes when a particularly detailed or sensitive question arises, the audience is asked to leave the auditorium for a brief period while the judges confer with the technical advisors.

A camaraderie develops among the judges, encouraged in part by the social functions that take place outside of the auditorium, such as dinners sponsored by groups related to the duck stamp program. But however friendly the judges become, they are forbidden from discussing the artwork or their selections with each other. This silence combined with the lack of artist identification on the artwork helps to ensure fairness in judging and has worked quite well. Some judges find the process a bit unsettling. To Owens, "the silence during the . . .contest was very spooky at times." In her many years of experience as a philatelic judge she was encouraged to work and talk with other judges. And when she was a member of the Citizen's Stamp Advisory Committee, it was expected that the group would actively discuss the designs considered for each postage stamp. During the duck stamp contest Owen recalls, "It was difficult at first to have to think and just talk with myself and to have no interaction with the other judges." Another feature of the contest designed to ensure fairness is the "pull-back" opportunity just prior to the beginning of round two of the judging. By allowing each judge to bring forward up to five entries that didn't survive the "in-out" voting, quality work is given a second chance and the likelihood of making a "mistake" is reduced.

With the field greatly narrowed, the second round of judging commences. Prior to opening the auditorium to the public, the judges have some time to critically compare and contrast the remaining entries. The judging becomes a bit more difficult and the field is narrowed once again. The artwork that makes it to third and final round is truly remarkable. The tension mounts as each judge critically reviews and votes on the art that passes before them. Often "oohs" and "aahs" come from the audience after the votes are cast. Despite the stiff competition, usually one painting stands out and rarely is there a need for a tiebreak to determine the winner. In the 1998 contest, for example, after the first round, 337 entries were whittled down to twenty-four. Then the judges pulled back seventeen of the paintings that had been graded "out," leaving forty-one pieces of art for the second round. There was a

Neal Anderson winning artwork of red-breasted mergansers for the 1994 federal duck stamp. Anderson's children referred to the species as "punk ducks." Credit: Neal Anderson and Wild Wings.

wide variation in scores during the second round, with the lowest ranked artwork receiving a total of nine, and the highest, twenty-four out of a possible twenty-five. Only ten competitors made it to the third round. One round of voting determined the winner. Jim Hautman's greater scaup, which had received a score of twenty-four in round two, moved up a notch to twenty-five, only the second perfect score in the history of the competition. The first perfect score also went to Jim for his 1995 stamp design of two mallards. Two paintings tied for second, each garnering a score of twenty, while the lowest two finishers during this round received scores of sixteen. After two tiebreaks, the second and third place finishers were determined. Interestingly enough, when Jim Hautman first scored a perfect twenty-five, there was a dramatic tiebreak to determine the winner.

Waiting for the judging to finish is not easy on the artists, especially those who progress to the later rounds. Scholer, whose pintails appear on the 1983 stamp, was the first artist to attend the judging. He and his wife sat in the audience, getting more excited and agitated with each round. "Watching my entry progress through the judging process was really nerve-wracking." The night before the final voting for the 1998 contest, Jim Hautman, at dinner with friends, expressed deep reservations of his painting's chances. As one of his dinner companions noted, "he was concerned it was too dark, in the wrong place on the display board or not properly lighted. He wondered if he should have left the boat out of the scene or selected a different species."

For Joe Hautman, who won in 1991, the judging went smoothly until the last round. After his spectacled eiders received the highest score in the second round, Joe felt he was in a strong position for the final judging. But before the third round could begin, Joe and everyone else had to wait for the arrival of the Secretary of the Interior who was supposed to be present for the final votes and then announce the winner. Other commitments detained the Secretary for a long time, and in the meantime the judges were asked to look over the finalists once again. Hearing this and fearing that the judges might change their minds, Joe thought to himself, "no, no, don't look again, just vote!" The wait for the final vote "seemed like ages." Robert Steiner, winner of the 1997 contest, received word at 8:30 in the morning (West Coast time) that his painting of a Barrow's goldeneye had made it to the finals. The caller recommended that he not only stay near the phone, but also think of what type of speech he might give if chosen. Steiner was told that if he won he would be contacted within the hour. He tried painting to pass the time, but accomplished nothing.

When the winning artist is in the audience, the shock and joy of winning can be seen on their faces. If the winner is called via telephone, learning the outcome can be just as surprising and sweet. When Daniel Smith, winner for the 1988 stamp received the call, he remembers his "...heart was racing for an hour. My blood pressure was probably off the chart." For Steiner, "...when they called to say I won, it was a total miracle." Morris, winner for the 1961 and 1962 stamps, was more low-key. "My reaction to hearing was, 'How about that!'" Some artists who get the call can't believe it's real. When Bob Hines called Murk to tell him he his Ross' Geese had been chosen for the 1977 stamp, Murk said, "Sure I did." A couple of his buddies had already called, telling him he had won, and Murk thought this was more the same. When Hines convinced Murk it was real

Judges for the 1994 contest give Jim Hautman's mallards a perfect score of 25. Credit: Dave Gallagher.

he was "flabbergasted." Similarly, when Arthur G. Anderson first got the call that his redheads would be on the 1987 stamp, he said he "thought it was one of . . . my friends playing a joke." When contacted at his home about his first win, Jim Hautman said, "I can't believe it. How do I know you're not kidding? Wow!" When the Secretary of the Interior invited Jim to meet President George Bush the following afternoon, he said, "I guess this isn't a joke." Then there are those artists who get the call and don't know how to react because they haven't a clue as to what winning entails. Magee, whose Canada geese grace the 1976 stamp, had totally forgotten about the contest when he picked up the phone in his kitchen. Hines said, "are you sitting down?" Magee recalls that "I still had no idea why I should be sitting down or what was about to happen to me." Upon learning that he won, Magee thought, "that was nice to hear, a real honor, but I was completely unaware of the financial and other consequences of winning." With all the publicity surrounding the contest in recent years, it is safe to say that no future winners will be as "unaware" as Magee when they get the call.

In at least one case, the process of informing the winning artist went awry. In 1992, Bruce Miller's canvasbacks walked away with top honors. Manual

Lujan, then Secretary of Interior, called Miller to tell him the good news. The call was played over the public address system in the Interior auditorium for all to hear. "Hello, Bruce Miller, this is Manual Lujan and I have a surprise for you." The surprise was on Lujan, however, when the voice on the phone said, "this is Daniel Smith's office, not Bruce Miller." Smith's painting of canvasbacks was the fourth place finisher. After a moment of stunned silence, the Secretary apologized and hung up. The correct phone number was quickly found. When Miller actually answered the second call, he yelped "hot damn!"

The judges' selection is not always greeted with universal acclamation. No matter how structured and fair the judging process, it is still the cumulative result of five people's subjective choices covering a whole range of attributes. Different panels of judges might very well select different winners from the same pool of applicants. As Maass notes, "you have to have the right design for the right judges. For example, a lot of times you will get judges who are hunters and will pick a design that might look like a hunter would see it. Other times you will get judges with an ornithological bent who might pick a pretty design that shows the bird in a pretty setting. This variability is a natural outcome. I see no criticism in the way the judging is done. It is probably

Bruce Miller's winning artwork for the 1993 federal duck stamp. Credit: Bruce Miller.

good because there is no way you second-guess the judges." A review of all past winning designs does reveal a wide range of quality in terms of design, rendering, and general interest. Over the years there have been complaints that the "best" painting was not selected, and indeed, some observers have claimed that certain winning art is terrible. Some have placed blame on the judge selection process, which has been argued to be too political rather than based on the judge's abilities to actually choose quality art. In at least one case, the contest that chose Fisher's painting of a canvasback decoy as winner, there were claims made that the judging was rigged, although the charges were never formally proven. It is important to note, however, that, for every person who find faults with judging, many more believe that the judging is excellent and has generally led to selection of true winners. It is a testament to the high quality of the judging, though, that the number of instances in which observers have felt that the "wrong" design won are few and far between. Changes in the judging process have served to improve it, further reducing the chances of poor or suspicious selections.

Judges are often greatly affected by the experience. "For several days," Burghoff recalls, "I was in a state of euphoria and total delight, surrounded by hundreds of entries of people who were extremely involved in their art and had a love for nature. There was such an expression of beauty. The contest literally changed my life. It made me more aware that there are many people out there who care passionately about the environment. It also made me realize how much I loved painting." Using this experience as a launching pad, Burghoff began painting seriously. Coincidentally, during the duck stamp contest Burghoff found an art teacher, David Tomori, to help him pursue this path. Tomori was in town with one of his students who had an entry in the Federal Junior Duck Stamp contest, which took place the same time as the "senior" contest. They were introduced and discovered that they lived just fifteen miles apart in California. With Tomori's early assistance, Burghoff has gone on to create seventeen wildlife paintings, limited edition prints of which are on sale at galleries from coast to coast. What was once his avocation has turned into more of a vocation. As for his fellow judges, Burghoff found them "a total joy, a group of wonderful people. We had a lot of laughs."

For Parker, the most exciting part of the judging was hearing that his friend, Jim Hautman, had won. The moments that led up this announcement also shine a favorable light on the quality of the judging. During the last round, Parker thought he recognized a stylistic technique of Jim's in one of the remaining ten paintings. "It was an excellent painting," Parker recalls, "but there was one even better that my

A cacheted First Day Cover hand painted by Gary "Radar" Burghoff, for the 1990 federal duck stamp. Credit: Sam Houston Duck Company.

conscience made me vote for. I was convinced I was voting against Jim and knowing he was present made that an extremely painful decision. However, I followed my conscience and voted for the best piece. Picture my delight when I realized that I wasn't as good a judge of stylistic technique as I had thought."

However important an event judging is to judges, it is much more important to winning artists. Having one's design chosen for a federal duck stamp is often the single most significant event in an artist's life. The winner instantly becomes well-known in wildlife art circles, if they weren't already. Demand for their artwork invariably rises. As Smith notes, "winning the federal contest was an incredible thrill and boost to my career." But with the fame comes added pressures. The artist is required to go on a "victory tour," participating in events designed to promote the Federal Duck Stamp Program. Among these are the Waterfowl Festival (Easton, Maryland), The Wildlife West Festival (Redland, California), J.N. "Ding" Darling Birthday Event at the refuge that bears his name (Sanibel, Florida), the First Day Ceremony (Washington, D.C.), and the Wings and Water Festival (Stone Harbor, New Jersey). Artists are also expected to attend at least three major stamp shows. At each of these stops along the tour, the artist must sign autographs and generally be a spokesman for the duck stamp program, sometimes offering brief remarks to the assembled crowds, a task which can be more than a little stressful to some artists who are more comfortable performing on a canvas than before a crowd. Accompanying the artist is the winning artwork, which is put on display. The winner is also required to provide the Duck Stamp Office with separate line drawings to be used for postal cancellations at the stamp's first two days of sale.

In between all this traveling and promotion, the artist must attend to the business side of winning. While the official prizes for winning - publicity, a pane of duck stamps signed by the Secretary of the Interior, a limited edition artist's souvenir card, travel to certain events, and speaking engagements - are quite nice, it is the artist's right to market their design which is the most coveted prize of all. The artist is free to contract with a publisher or to self-publish prints of their design for sale to the public, with all proceeds to be split between the publisher and artist. This can generate serious money for the artist, with a number of them earning over a million dollars from these ventures.

Some artists have been overwhelmed by the attention winning brings. When Hines called Murk to tell him he had won, his advice was borne of experience. "Pour a glass of whiskey," Murk recalls Hines saying, "drink the damn thing and get out of town because everyone is going to be calling you." Murk had no idea what was to come, but reported that soon the phone was ringing off the hook with "well-wishers and dealers wondering what I was going to do about publishing prints. Since I had no clue at the time, that's when I took off with my son and went duck hunting in Canada. When I'd call home to see how my wife was doing, she kept saying I had to come home to the never-ending phone calls and I kept saying 'I can't, we're duck hunting.' We were home two weeks later - my son and I full of good memories of a great hunt together and my wife never happier to see us and turn the phone over to me."

Stanley Stearns' blue geese (left) which appeared on the 1955 federal duck stamp. Credit for the art: Stanley Stearns; Credit for the stamp: U.S. Fish and Wildlife Service.

Winning "changed" Scholer's life. He reported, "it brought financial freedom, enabling me to become a full-time wildlife artist. It also changed the way people related to me and vice-versa. And it forced me to become a businessman in a hurry. It was a hectic year and very stressful but absolutely the best thing I had happen to my career." When Richard Plasschaert got the call that his mallards would be on the 1980 stamp, he was sitting at a light table at the printing company where he worked. Four years earlier he had quit that job to, as he remembers, "become a world famous artist but I went broke in a year. Then I went back. Right at the time of the duck stamp contest I was on the verge of quitting again." After Hines told him he had won, Plasschaert said, "you've got to be kidding." He stayed at his table for a half-hour, but he couldn't concentrate on work, in large part because of the well-wishers who were already calling. "I knew what I'd won and the impact of winning on my career," Plasschaert recalls. "I walked up to my boss and said this ain't going to work, I can't keep my mind on anything. My boss said 'I don't' imagine I'll see you for while,' and he was right. I punched out for the last time." One of the funniest aspects of Plasschaert's learning he had won happened before he found out. Hines had first called Plasschaert's home and gotten his wife on the line. Hines asked where Plasschaert was, but his wife wanted to know what the call was about. When Hines balked, Mrs. Plasschaert said, "If you don't tell me what it is, I won't tell you where he is." Hines let her know and, according to her husband, "she just about died and gave him my phone number."

Ironically, the pressures and commitments of winning often take a toll on the artist's first love - their art. "The downside of being a stamp artist," according to Smith, "is the shortage of painting time. You spend most of your time doing business, signing prints and stamps, traveling for promotional purposes, painting remarques, etc., . . . You can't improve and progress as an artist if you're not painting." After each of his three wins, Stanley Stearns recalls, "we had a constant stream of visitors from all over the country. Sometimes people would come in the morning, stay all day and take us out to dinner. I had a heck of a time trying to get work done." These visits were doubly hard for Stearns because they were often unannounced. He didn't have a phone at the time, so instead of calling first, people would sometimes just arrive.

While the lack of time for painting in the year following the win is a common refrain, winning artists can take some measure of hope from Jim Hautman's experience. In the year after his first win in 1989, he, like most other artists, became extremely busy and painted very little. "Not being prepared for winning, I started saying yes to all sorts of opportunities and quickly became way overcommitted." This experience prepped him for the next time, and in the year after his second win, in 1994, Jim's improved time-management skills and willingness to say "no" allowed him to complete an impressive fourteen paintings. Of course, few artists get the opportunity to ascend this learning curve.

The possibility of achieving financial freedom is one of the factors that has had the greatest impact on

The 1963 federal duck stamp featured Edward J. Bierly's design of pacific brant. Credit: Edward J. Bierly.

the popularity of the duck stamp art contest. During the first few decades of the contest, the main reason for entering the contest was not financial gain, but the honor of having one's work grace the face of a stamp and to be part of an important conservation program. It is not that the early artists were uninterested in money, but the opportunity to make large amounts of money from marketing the design simply did not exist. Print runs were generally small and prices fairly low. While some of the early artists earned respectable profits, they were just that, "respectable." Starting in the early 1970s, profits from prints began their slow ascent towards the stratosphere and artists began taking notice. Print runs became larger and the number of buyers grew. The addition of color to the designs certainly helped, as did the evolution of printing techniques and more aggressive marketing of artists and publishing houses.

Bierly, winning artist for the 1956, 1963, and 1970 stamp, saw how the evolving popularity of prints could translate into monetary rewards and increased freedom. "Profits from selling prints for the first stamp were moderate [$2,000]. The second better [$6,000]. The third was a Godsend. Just after winning the third time, I found out that my office at the National Park Service was moving to Harper's Ferry, West Virginia. To follow work would have meant selling our home in Virginia, which we loved. Sales from the prints for the third design allowed me to take early retirement and keep our home. I earned the equivalent of more than two years worth of my salary [$50,000]." When he thinks about the huge amounts of money later artists have gotten, Bierly laughs and adds, "I wouldn't resent it at all if I could win again."

By the late 1970s, winning artists were earning significant amounts; nevertheless, the number of artists vying for the win hovered consistently around 300. One article changed all that. In the December-January 1979 issue of *National Wildlife* magazine, Sam Iker wrote a piece titled "The World's Richest Art Competition?" In it, he recounted how recent winners had become rich men almost overnight. Murk's winnings were placed at an impressive $450,000, a sum which was noted as being four times larger than the Nobel Prize. The most recent winner at the time of publication was Albert Gilbert. Iker speculated that Gilbert was likely to earn more than $1 million from the sale of a record-sized edition of 7,150 prints. As for the future of print sales, the article predicted soaring profits driven by an expanding market.

The magazine's large circulation guaranteed that many people, including aspiring artists, would now know how lucrative duck stamp art could be. With visions of wealth spurring them on, thousands of people took up their pens and brushes and other assorted implements, and entered the contest. There were 1,362 entrants for the 1980 stamp, 1,507 in 1981, and an all-time high of 2,099 in 1982, when Maass won with his canvasbacks. Up through the mid-1980s, interest remained high and the number of entrants held at around 1,500. Many who entered were serious artists in search of both the honor and wealth that came to the winner. Some had different motivations and skills. More than a few Donald and Daffy Ducks were sent to Washington. Other curious entries included a duck dressed in hunting clothes, a duck punching a hole through an American flag, and ducks jumping out of birthday cakes. There was a "trumpeter swan," showing the bird with a trumpet behind it, a sleeping hunter in a blind with a duck atop his head, and a duck flapping its wings while standing on the shore, the only problem was that while one wing was fully-feathered, the other was in

The year that David Maass' canvasbacks took home the top prize in 1981 was the high point for entries to the federal duck stamp contest - 2099. Credit: David Maass and Wild Wings.

Nancy Howe's winning artwork for the 1991 duck stamp — a pair of king eiders exploring the subarctic tundra. Howe is the only women ever to win the federal contest. Credit: Nancy Howe and Lowell Thompson.

skeleton form with a single feather coming off the end.

The number of entries began to drop precipitously in the late 1980s; 884 for the 1989 stamp, 585 for the 1995 stamp, and more recently, 337 for the 1999 stamp. Part of this decline is a result of increasing the entry fee, in stages, from nothing for the 1982 stamp contest to $20, $35, $50 and finally $100. The expense greatly reduced the number of frivolous entries. Another factor, though certainly of relatively minor impact, was the decreasing financial rewards of winning. For some time after the initial boom in print sales, the winning design was truly a "million-dollar duck." Print runs skyrocketed and demand kept pace. But, eventually, frenzied buying subsided and the print market settled down to more sustainable levels. Winning artists still make a lot of money, however it is usually on the order of hundreds of thousands of dollars, not millions.

To better understand the fall off in entries the Federal Duck Stamp Office recently surveyed artists on the subject. Among the most common answers given for not entering were that the fee was too high, the same artist always wins, and there is not enough encouragement for artists to pursue different styles. One respondent wrote in "only a masochist would continue to pay $100 to be steamrolled by the Hautman boys [Jim, Joe, and Bob Hautman have won five contests between them]." Another commented that "if you are not going to allow freedom of expressions - styles - you might just as well hand out this as a commission since you dictate how it is to be painted, right down to having classes for it." Howe, winning artist for the 1991 stamp, echoes this last concern. "The contest has become too cookie-cutter like. Instead of rewarding creativity, it rewards the same old, same old. From an artistic standpoint, the contest is a turnoff." One of the things that some artists decry is the photo-realism that is indicative of most recent winning entries. As another commentator noted, "art that wins is 'photo-realistic' so any of us who would like to enter the contest but don't paint photo-realism know we have 'no' chance to win." For every critic of the artistic aspects of the competition, however, there as many or more fans who find the art beautiful and the process exceedingly fair. Whether more changes to the art contest are in the offing, only time will tell.

THE ARTISTS AND THEIR ART

Behind the art of the duck stamp program are the winning artists. Although they have different backgrounds, skills, and perspectives, each one brings passion to the work, is committed to conservation and believes in the power of art to capture wildlife in all its glory. This small, elite fraternity has left an indelible mark on the history of the program by giving beauty to the stamps and thereby creating effective allies in the cause of migratory waterfowl protection.

The earliest duck stamp artists are among the most famous. Chosen for their already-proven artistic skills, often in areas outside the realm of wildlife art, the honor of creating the duck stamp design could be added proudly to other accolades they had received throughout their careers. Heading the list is Darling who, while not a traditional artist, had already made his mark on American culture through his incisive and insightful political cartoons. Benson, the artist for the 1935 issue, was, at the time, already a renowned artist who belonged to American impressionist school and was also

known as the dean of American etchers. His subjects ranged well beyond wildlife, being best known for his brilliantly lit scenes of women and young children. One of those paintings, The Sisters, depicts his two daughters playing in sun-drenched meadow by the sea. In May 1995, this painting fetched $4,182,500 at auction. He also painted ceiling panels at the Library of Congress depicting the Three Graces and four circular wall panels representing the Four Seasons. Benson's wildlife art reflected a deft hand and an intimate knowledge of his subjects, gained largely from his years as an active hunter, particularly of waterfowl. His selection as the artist for the second duck stamp was especially fitting in light of his active role in conservation, including being one of the founding members of DU. His black and white watercolor wash painting of canvasbacks was extremely simple, almost crude, yet powerful nonetheless. As with many highly skilled artists, he had the ability to capture the essence of an image with seemingly minimal effort.

This pencil and pen sketch of wigeons by A. Lassell Ripley was chosen to appear on the 1942 federal duck stamp. Credit: U.S. Fish and Wildlife Service.

Bob Hines, "Mr. Duck Stamp," did this design of redheads for the 1946 federal duck stamp. Credit: U.S. Fish and Wildlife Service.

Jaques, the artist for the 1940 issue is often called the "Patriarch" of American wildlife artists. Among his most famous and admired works are the many wildlife murals he painted for museums around the country, including the American Museum of Natural History in New York and the Museum of Science in Boston. He also produced and/or illustrated a great variety of books such as Canadian Spring, The Geese Fly High, and Outdoor Life's Gallery of North American Game, and his illustrations graced publications including *Life, The Saturday Evening Post*, and *Field & Stream*. Jaques ink wash painting of black ducks gliding over windswept marsh grass is considered by many educated observers to be the finest of all the duck stamp art in terms of composition, design, simplicity and grace. Another early duck stamp artist of some note was Ripley, whose pen, ink, and pencil drawing of widgeons was the basis for the 1942 stamp. Ripley was well known for his murals and etchings, among them the famous mural of Paul Revere's midnight ride, which hangs in the Post Office in Lexington, Massachusetts. He belonged to numerous prestigious artists' societies, including the American Society of Watercolor Painters and the Guild of Boston Artists, and was elected to the National Academy of Design, a great honor for an American artist. His works are in the collections of many museums including the Chicago Art Institute and the Boston Museum of Fine Arts.

Hines, while not as famous an artist as some of the other early ones, had great success with his art and deserves the accolades of duck stamp lovers everywhere. Often referred to as "Mr. Duck Stamp," Hines drawing of redheads was depicted on the 1946 federal duck stamp. Two years later he was invited to Washington to become an artist-illustrator at the U.S. F&WS, where his first supervisor was Rachel Carson, who would later gain fame as author of nature books, like *The Sea Around Us*, and the environmental treatise, *Silent Spring*. After recommending that the duck stamp competition be open to all entrants, Hines was tapped to run the contest, a position he held until his retirement in 1981. Many improvements in the contest were implemented during his watch. In his long and fruitful career, Hines illustrated more than fifty books, including *Wildlife in America*, by Peter Mathiessen. He also designed the first four stamps in the United States Postal Service's Wildlife Conservation Postage Stamp Series, depicting wild turkey, pronghorn antelope, king salmon and a whooping crane. The latter was chosen by a British philatelic poll as one of the ten best stamps in the world for 1957.

With the advent of open competition for the duck stamp contest, the character of the winning artists shifted. Many were well known, primarily within the field of wildlife art, prior to their win, but for many more the win marked a major turning point in their careers as artists. For some, like Joe Hautman, the financial rewards of winning facilitated the transition from part-time to full-time artist, and gave them the ability to expand their repertoire. As Arthur Anderson put it, "winning really did open doors." But trying to divide duck stamp artists into broad categories is a pursuit doomed to failure. Each one has a unique story that is all their own and invariably fascinating. For example, Clayton B. Seagers, was a longtime employee of the New York State Conservation Department and founder of its official publication, *The Conservationist Magazine*. Jackson Miles Abbott, artist for the 1957 stamp depicting common eiders, had an impressive career in the United States Army, serving in World War II, where he worked on land-mine warfare and designed and erected camouflage. After the war he was decorated

John Ruthven's redhead family appears on the 1960 federal duck stamp. Credit: Wildlife Internationale', Inc.

with a Bronze Star and later served as an intelligence officer and writer of training manuals. Arthur M. Cook, the winner in 1972, was a commercial artist who viewed his painting as an avocation, right along-side lily hybridizing, when he won the contest. Lee LeBlanc's early career involved a duck that was quite different from the Steller's eiders he painted for the 1973 stamp. As an animator for Warner Brothers Merry Melodies and Looney Tunes, LeBlanc helped give life to Daffy Duck, as well as Bugs Bunny and Porky Pig. And Smith, whose first breakthrough in the stamp world came was his win in the 1983 Minnesota Pheasant Stamp contest, has had great success not only in "duck stamp" art, but also a wide variety of dramatic wildlife art focusing on predators and other species. Smith is also the federal duck stamp artist with the best pectoral muscles. A self-described "145-pound weakling" who had developed "love handles" after his first few years as an artist who just sat on his "butt all day", Smith bulked up at the same gym where Hulk Hogan got his start. In one of the Mr. Minnesota contests, Smith grabbed trophies for the best chest and the most muscular.

Just as varied as their backgrounds, are the approaches or steps duck stamp artists take on the way to creating a winning design. While most artists begin with an idea, progress through studies, sketches, and other forms of "rough drafts" on the way to the final piece of art, there is an almost endless variety within each of these stages of the artistic process. And, indeed some artists might skip over one stage or add an unusual variation depending on inclination, inspiration, time, and skill.

In preparing his submissions to the federal contest, Stearns proceeded through five steps. First,

he created small thumbnail sketches, measuring about 1 inch by 1.5 inches, to develop overall patterns and composition for the design including placement of the bird(s) and other elements. One of the reasons for keeping the sketches small, besides saving time, is to avoid getting too detailed at this stage. Having settled on one that he liked the best or felt had the most promise, he would do another series of slightly more detailed and varied thumbnail sketches, keeping in mind the design limitations imposed by the design's ultimate transfer to stamp format, e.g., repetition of the design on a pane or block of stamps. If this approach was not working, Stearns would go back and start again before invest-ing too much more time. If, on the other hand, one of the thumbnails still looked promising, he scaled it up to the full-size of the art as stipulated in the contest rules. Since there are bound to be mistakes at this stage, Stearns used tracing paper so he could trace over problem areas and focus in on the lines that look good. He often went through as many as 10 to 20 sheets before settling a drawing he liked. Stearns then took that drawing and transferred it to the finish support, by use of carbon paper. In the case of his winning design of whistling swans for the 1966 stamp, the finish support was illustration board. Finally, Stearns would render the drawing in the medium he had selected for the final entry. For back-grounds Stearns would rely on his own extensive knowledge of waterfowl as well as photos taken by him or appearing in books. While painting "Whistling Swans" Stearns used his own photo-graphs for the birds, and would pop his head repeat-edly out the door of his studio to check on the back-ground image, which was the marshscape across the creek from his cottage on Kent Island on the Chesapeake Bay.

Murk found inspiration for his winning Ross' geese design on a drive home one late winter's afternoon outside of Kenosha, Wisconsin. Looking to the east out over a wide-open landscape he could see through the falling snow the dark blue sky - "so blue

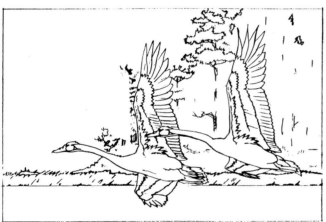

Stearns' whistling swans appeared on the 1966 federal duck stamp. At the top are two of the sketches leading up to the finished design. Credit for the artwork: U.S. Fish and Wildlife Service; Credit for the sketches: Stanley Stearns.

that it was almost black." He always wanted to paint that sky and the snowfall. Adding Ross' geese to the scene seemed particularly appropriate since, as Murk recalls, "the black of the primary feathers of the geese could be contrasted with the snow, creating a nice effect." Murk made seven sketches before doing the final acrylic painting on white paper. By leaving the bottom half of the painting bare, Murk got the snow he was looking for.

The time it takes to create a winner is incredibly variable. Stearns worked methodically for weeks and weeks, nonstop on his entries, always creating new ways to rework and improve the painting. It often got to the point where, for him to finish it would take his wife saying, "you've gone far enough - quit right now!" Steiner is another artist who spends long hours on his entries. Sketching out designs for his winning acrylic painting of a Barrow's goldeneye took a little over a month, during which time he produced 15 iterations each with a slightly different head. Once he settled on what would be the winning design, it took another five weeks, eight hours a day, to complete the painting. At the other end of the spectrum is Ron Jenkins who, commenting on his canvasbacks that appear on 1965 stamp, stated that "it was a last minute idea and I did it on my lap while watching TV one night! In those days more than one entry was allowed and I had already finished two others. This last one was an arrangement of birds that seemed interesting and different from the others." Reece's cinnamon teal's which grace the 1971 stamp took him less than a week to complete, and then, as he recalls, only after "my wife had induced me to take up my watercolors and make a design."

Another variable relating to duck stamp art is the medium chosen by the artist to express their vision. As long as the painting or drawing is done by hand, the artist is free to choose whatever medium they want. And the entries have covered a good cross-section of the artists' palette. Darling's mallards were painted with brush and India ink on illustration board. Richard E. Bishop's Canada geese which are on the 1936 stamp, were done as a dry-point etching. Lynn Bogue Hunt used graphite pencil to give life to his green-winged teal, for the 1939 stamp. John A. Ruthven's redheads, on the 1967 stamp, is a gouache painting (gouache is relatively broad generic term that includes opaque watercolor, tempera, casein, or poster color). The art for the 1970 stamp, which shows Bierly's Ross' geese, was painted in full-color watercolor. The canvasbacks by Maass, for the 1982 stamp, are from an original oil painting. And Scholer's winning art the next year depicted pintails done with acrylic paint.

One of the most interesting mediums employed by winning artists is scratchboard. The neutral pH backing of scratchboard is usually some sort of card-board or hard substance, onto which is applied a

The Evolution of a Duck Stamp

5

6

7

These are the seven sketches that Martin Murk used on the way to painting his winning entry for the 1977 federal duck stamp. Credit for sketches and artwork: Martin Murk; Credit for the 1977 stamp: U.S. Fish and Wildlife Service.

Edward J. Bierly's American mergansers are one of the most unusual of winning designs (1956 federal duck stamp). The spare simplicity and misty-quality give it an oriental feel. Credit: U.S. Fish and Wildlife Service.

layer of gesso, also called China clay. A hardened layer of black India ink is laid down on top of this. Using a sharpened point or scraper, the artist then scratches through the India ink to the white background below, thereby creating the design as white on black. Scratchboard can also be obtained without the India ink layer, enabling the artist to scratch into the white and then lay in the ink afterwards, bringing forth the design. It is not easy working with scratchboard. According to Magee, who used this medium to good effect for his Canada geese, "once you start cutting into the surface there is no way to remove the lines. Scratchboard is very unforgiving. Dropping a tool can really mess things up and you can't fix it by painting over mistakes. You'd be able to see where the repairs were made."

No matter how long it takes artists to complete their drawings or what medium they use, there seems to be an almost immutable law that requires all of them to wait until the very last minute to send their entries to Washington. Deadlines have a way of sharpening one's resolve and forcing a person to wrap up matters, and that is certainly the case for the duck stamp art contest deadline. Stearns remembers sending off one of his entries while it was still wet, in a specially constructed package which he hoped would allow the painting to dry before being opened by contest organizers. That entry failed to win. Perhaps the packaging didn't do such a great job. Arthur Anderson had better luck. His redheads were also sent off wet and they won. Magee finished his scratchboard Canada geese just hours before midnight on the day that the entry was due. The post office nearest to his house was already closed, so he called around and found a central one in Hartford, Connecticut, quite a distance away, that would be open until the magic hour. Magee jumped into his car and got his cancellation with just twenty minutes to spare. He recalls, with a laugh, that he thought he had no chance of winning, so he adhered to the speed limit while driving. "I would have

speeded if I known what was going to happen afterwards!"

Steiner tells what is probably the most interesting story of last-minute maneuverings. On the day the entry was due, he was elated. His acrylic painting of a lone Barrow's goldeneye floating on calmed water was almost complete. The only thing left to do was apply a coat of varnish to give the somewhat flat acrylic a richer look. He reached for his trusty can of varnish, one he had been using for ten years, and just as he was about to spray one of his staff said "you're not going to use that ten-year old can of varnish are you?" The flicker of doubt caused Steiner to put down the can and ask one of his workers to go buy a new one. It was late afternoon by the time the new can arrived, and Steiner was getting nervous. He wanted to make a 5:30 deadline at the local post office because, even though he had until midnight, missing this first deadline would mean driving a great distance to get to another drop-off location. As Steiner remembers,

It was getting late and I got into a rushed state of mind. I picked up the new can and shook it once or twice, when I should have done it twenty or thirty times. The spray came out in fine blobs instead of a fine mist. My heart sank. I thought 'oh my God, I've ruined it.' I called my wife and friends to tell them I ruined it. There was only a half-hour left and I had no idea how to remove the varnish. So I shook the can again and sprayed on more coats of varnish, more than thirty, in the hopes of evening out the rough surface. With all those coats and bumps of varnish, the painting didn't look good at all. It looked nasty. If you looked at the painting from anything expect head-on the glare would allow you to see all the goopy varnish. I decided to send it out anyway. I was totally bummed out and crushed. It was the best entry I had ever painted, and I thought it was ruined.

The time between submitting his entry and the contest was difficult for Steiner, although he had begun to get over his "mistake." He really got over it, though, when he learned that his painting had won. He immediately called up one of his artist friends, with whom he had commiserated earlier. Upon hearing the good news, Steiner's friend said "gee Bob, you've got to tell me where to get that varnish."

Lightning does strike and there are examples of artists entering the duck stamp contest and winning on their first try. Bierly did so with his mergansers in 1956 and Plasschaert with his mallards in 1980. Perhaps even more interesting, both of these artists knew very little about the duck stamp program and virtually nothing about the types of art that had won in previous years. A friend of Bierly's at the U.S. F&WS called him in 1955 and recommended he enter a painting. He got the specifications for the submission, and prepared a gouache painting using his own experience and some books for reference material. "I didn't know anything about the contest or past winning designs until [my friend] called", Bierly remembers. His entry of two mergansers flying past a spit of land with a lone barren tree rising from it is almost oriental in style and stands as one of the most unusual and beautiful of all winning designs. Plasschaert, on the other hand, was more aware than Bierly of the duck stamp program and the fame and fortune that came from winning, but he claims that before entering he "hadn't seen any of the earlier winners." When he sent away for the contest regulations, he made a "conscious effort to not look at" paintings that had won before. "I wanted to avoid doing something that looked like somebody else's work."

The more common story is that of the persistent artist, repeatedly entering the contest, and finally coming home with the prize. For example, Howe entered fourteen times before winning and for Steiner the lucky number was seventeen. Goebel also

entered seventeen times before winning. He was 18 when he entered his first federal contest. Every year from then on he submitted an entry, and they got better and he moved closer to the top. Goebel finally put it all together with his painting of two surf scoters in flight. To give his painting that extra "snap" that would catch the judges' eyes, Goebel placed New Jersey's historic Barnegat Bay Lighthouse in the background. The lighthouse's orange and white echo the colors in the surf scoter drake's bill. Maass began entering the contest in the mid-1950s and has done so every year since then.

Winning artists rarely sit on their laurels and many of them come back again and again, hoping for another win. This, combined with the repeated entries of those who have yet to win, but ultimately do, is why so many familiar names show up in the ranks of top finishers year after year. There are simply an awful lot of extremely talented artists in each contest, and it makes sense that many of the most talented - soon-to-be winners and past winners - come out near the top. After all, practice might not make for perfection, but it sure helps. For example, Goebels came in second in 1990; in 1993, Neal Anderson in third, behind Miller, who himself had placed third in the 1991 contest; and Smith has placed second five times. According to Maass, the federal duck stamp contest "is very frustrating because you know when you are runner up or third, that you are so close that you could have won it." Maass certainly has the experience to support this claim. In addition to his two wins, has come in second five times, and third four times.

Artists whose entries come close one year, often will re-work the same basic design and re-enter another year. In 1995, Steiner's lone Barrow's goldeneye came in third. After the contest, Lesino, Manager of the Federal Duck Stamp Program, recommended that Steiner improve his detailing. When Steiner first took another look at his third

Robert Steiner made some subtle changes to his third place entry in the 1995 contest (left) to create his winning entry for the 1997 contest.   Credit: Robert Steiner.

Above: This graceful pair of canvasbacks set in Pettaquamscutt Cove, Rhode Island, appear on Robert Steiner's winning artwork for that states' 1989 duck stamp. Credit: Robert Steiner. Below: David Maass's winning artwork of wood ducks for the 1974 federal duck stamp. Credit: David Maass and Wild Wings.

place entry he wondered how it could be improved. When he set to work, however, he was very surprised by the changes he was able to make. To the untrained eye, Steiner's third place entry in 1995 looks virtually identical to his winning entry of the same species in 1997. But, according to the artist there are three main differences. "I was able to blend the gradations in the water a lot better so that the ripples and the reflection were a lot more convincing. I did a better job of blending the transitions from dark to light. The chest and head of the third place entry were very out of focus largely because my original reference photo of the goldeneye was out of focus. I took another photo that was much sharper, enabling me to sharpen the chest area. For the head, although I used the out-of-focus reference photo, I was still able to improve the results, making each brush stroke finer, highlighting the details." As a result, the winning entry was more realistic and detailed than its predecessor.

Many artists who win the Federal Duck Stamp Contest also have had great success winning or getting commissions to do other wildlife stamps, including numerous state ducks. The king of the hill in this regard is Steiner. Back in the late 1970s, Steiner, with his recently minted masters degree in fine art printmaking, was part-time teaching and freelancing for magazines and books when he first read about the "million-dollar" federal duck stamp contest. The thing that impressed him most was the thought that a single painting could earn so much money for the artist. He had done some wildlife painting and decided to visit a local pond and paint pintails. Too late to enter the federal, Steiner sent his painting to the competition for the California duck stamp. To his surprise, it came in second. Bolstered by this near-win, he re-entered the California contest the next year and won, with his painting of canvasbacks. Although it would be many years before Steiner's work was chosen tops in the federal contest, the California win opened up a whole new career path for him. The demand for his waterfowl paintings shot up and he began entering other state duck contests and winning, winning, winning. Commissions, too, came his way. Today, Steiner's art can be found on more than 45 state duck stamps, and with his active schedule and great notoriety, that number is sure to rise.

Maass is another prolific stamp artist. In addition to painting the winning designs for the 1974 and 1982 federal duck stamps, he has won or been commissioned to do thirty-one other duck and conservation stamps, including the 1989 Texas duck stamp, the 1979 Minnesota duck stamp, and the 1980 ruffed grouse stamp. Maass has also contributed his talents in other ways to support conservation efforts. For example, his painting, Monarch of the Hardwoods, and prints of it raised over $200,000 for the construction of a research center for the National Wild Turkey Federation.

Maynard Reece - Granddaddy of Federal Duck Stamp Artists

Reece first met Ding Darling in 1938. A friend of Reece's recommended he visit Darling for guidance on his wildlife art. Reece vividly remembers that first encounter.

I was scared to death. He came off as a gruff man but he wasn't at all. I had a bundle of paintings under my arm, and desperately needed help. After explaining that I was trying to learn to paint wildlife, we sat down together and he said 'I can tell you these things you've brought are nice, but that won't help you a bit. Or I can tear them apart and tell you what I don't like. Which do you want?' I told him I wanted help and he said 'fine, let's get to work.' And we did for twenty years. I saw him on many occasions and he would critique my work, all types of wildlife paintings. It came to a point where he felt he couldn't teach me anymore, but he was wrong. He helped me until the day he died.

Maynard Reece's winning design of gadwalls for the 1951 federal duck stamp. Credit Maynard Reece.

Maynard Reece's winning design of white-winged scoters for the 1969 federal duck stamp. Credit: Maynard Reece.

Darling's tutelage helped Reece develop as an artist, and Reece credits Darling with helping to launch his career. It was Darling's knowledge of Reece's talents that led him to ask Reece to submit drawings to be considered during the selection of the art for the 1947 stamp. In the ensuing years, Reece's paintings would grace five federal duck stamps for the years 1948, 1951, 1959, 1969, and 1971, an all-time record. While these wins greatly helped Reece's career, they did not, as is the case for some other winners, make his career. He is one of the best-known wildlife artists in the country. His work is sold through galleries, housed in many public and private collections, and has appeared in numerous books and a great variety of magazines, including *Life, Sports Illustrated, The Saturday Evening Post*, and *Better Homes and Gardens*. Reece has designed over 30 stamps for organizations including DU, Pheasants Forever and Quail Unlimited, and has a number of state duck stamps to his credit. Recently, he was selected as the artist for the 1999 U.S. Senior Open Golf Championship. Although his painting for the event is a golf scene, Reece made sure there was a pond in the foreground so he could "get some ducks into the picture."

One of Reece's most cherished paintings is not of a duck, but of three quail taking flight. A couple of years before Darling died, in 1962, he drew his professional epithet, a cartoon titled "bye now - it's been wonderful knowing you", and left it with his secretary, asking her to have it published upon his death. The drawing shows Darling's spirit leaving in a blur through the door of his office, which is cluttered with many of the things that were important to him in life. Just to the right of the door, next to Darling's outstretched hand and hat, is Reece's painting of the quail. Reece had

given it to Darling in 1950. The first time Reece saw Darling's final cartoon was when it appeared on the front page of the Des Moines Register, on the day Darling died, just as he had wanted. "It shocked me to see it in the cartoon," Reece recalls. "The family was kind enough to return the painting to me, and it is still hanging in my house."

In his long and storied life, Reece has won many honors. But, according to him, "the nicest thing that ever happened to me, and the most meaningful, was the honor of having my name on a marsh in northern Iowa." The 315-acre Maynard Reece Waterfowl Production Area in Kosuth County, Iowa was dedicated on June 20, 1998. The WPA is part of the Union Slough National Wildlife Refuge watershed, one of only six national refuges in Iowa. The Maynard Reece

The 1971 federal duck stamp, featuring Reece's design and marking the fifth time Reece's artwork has appeared on a federal duck stamp. Credit: U.S. Fish and Wildlife Service.

'BYE NOW—IT'S BEEN WONDERFUL KNOWING YOU.

Ding's Farewell

The Des Moines Register—Tuesday, Feb. 13, 1962

Darling's final cartoon which ran in the Des Moines Register on February 13, 1962, the day after he died. To the right of the door is the painting of three quail Reece had given to Darling more than a decade earlier. To the left and slightly above his desk is Darling's sketch for the first federal duck stamp. Credit: J.N. "Ding" Darling Foundation.

WPA will help to protect the water quality for the Union Slough watershed. Commenting on the critical importance of this function, Reece noted that he wants "to implant in people the real value of wetland. This is the best purification system ever in existence. Wetlands help cleanse our water - and if we don't have drinkable water, the results will be deadly." Appropriately enough, federal duck stamp dollars contributed to the purchase of this land. The restoration costs for the WPA are being funded primarily by non-profit organizations, including the Partners Wetland Restoration Project, administered by the National Fish and Wildlife Foundation, DU, the Iowa Natural Heritage Foundation and the South Kossuth Chapter of Pheasants Forever. The U.S. F&WS is also contributing money to this effort. During the dedication, Bruce Mountain, Land Projects Director for the Iowa Natural Heritage Foundation said, "this is a very good prairie pothole restoration site with over 100 acres of water. It is very satisfying to be able to honor one of Iowa's great conservationists this way." Reece has hunted on his namesake marsh, and one can be sure that the hunting was very sweet.

Maynard Reece (right) and Bruce Mountain, Iowa Natural Heritage Foundation Land Projects Director, at the dedication ceremony for the Maynard Reece Marsh, Kossuth County, Iowa. Credit: Iowa Natural Heritage Foundation.

Part of the Hautman clan standing in front of Jim's winning artwork for the 1995 stamp, at an exhibit at the Mall of America. From left to right, Bob, Jim, Dorothy (Jim's wife), Joe, and Elaine. Credit: U.S. Fish and Wildlife Service.

The Hautman Dynasty

The nature versus nurture debate has raging for years, and there's no use looking to the Hautman brothers of Minnesota, Jim, Bob, and Joe, for any help in trying to resolve it. Jim has won the contest three times, and Bob and Joe once each. Of course, they are related, so genetics can be implicated to some extent, but they also grew up in an extremely artistic household, so nurture needs a nod as well. Thus, the Hautman's contribution to the resolution of this debate is a draw. Fortunately, for duck stamp lovers, it really doesn't matter. The Hautman's work speaks for itself.

All three started early with crayons, pencils and paper. Their mother, Elaine Hautman, a commercial artist turned abstract expressionist painter, encouraged the boys' artistic pursuits and is credited by all three as a major influence on their artistic careers. Their father, Tom, now deceased, also had an artistic bent, painting about a dozen duck hunting paintings when he was younger. In addition to giving the boys artistic encouragement, Tom and Elaine Hautman instilled in them a love of the outdoors. Tom was an avid sportsman who greatly enjoyed duck hunting and fishing. He and Elaine often took the boys, along with their four other siblings, on numerous hunting trips (Elaine's duck hunting days ended, however, when she accidentally blew a hole in a canoe with an errant blast from her gun). With this background it is hardly a surprise that when the boys began painting more seriously, wildlife, and ducks in particular, was their subject of choice.

Jim, youngest of the three, was the first to sell his artwork. While still in high school, he started doing pen and ink drawings of waterfowl and birds of prey, which sold for $30 a piece at local art fairs. Soon

Jim Hautman's winning artwork for the 1990 stamp - black-bellied whistling ducks. Credit: Jim Hautman.

thereafter, in 1983, he took to painting birds on sliced logs and driftwood. The inspiration for this work came, in part, from a painting his mom and dad had done years earlier. On a long piece of driftwood, they had painted different types of ducks, listing the species below each image. Looking at this ornithological mural on every trip through the dining room, where it was displayed, helped Jim learn his ducks and also gave him the idea for his new artistic endeavor. Bob soon joined him and the Hautman brothers' "Birds on Boards" became strong sellers.

Jim and Bob spent the mid-1980s entering numerous wildlife stamp contests. In 1983 they both entered the Minnesota pheasant stamp contest, with Jim making it to the semi-finals. Entries to a variety of state duck stamp contests and the federal contest soon followed. Jim, for one, was not particularly confident of his chances. When

he saw Scholer's winning entry for the 1983 federal stamp Jim thought "it was something really special. It was sort of depressing because I realized I couldn't do anything that good." In fact, Jim's first painting for the federal contest never made it to Washington. "I didn't think it had a chance," he recalls. In 1987, however, Jim surprised himself by coming in third in the federal contest, with a painting of two drake buffleheads. The breakthrough for the Hautmans, though, came from Bob. In 1988, his buffleheads took home top honors in the Minnesota duck stamp competition. This first Hautman win buoyed both brothers' confidence levels. Other state wins followed in quick succession, with Jim winning the 1988 duck stamp contests in Delaware and Nevada, and the 1989 Minnesota contest. Bob reached the top in Nevada in 1989 and won another Minnesota title in 1992.

Jim "shocked" himself in 1989, winning the federal contest with a pair of black-bellied whistling ducks in flight. "I had no idea what my chances were," he recalls. "Winning was very intimidating, it turns your whole life upside down."

The night he heard he'd won, friends and family threw a big party. Bleary-eyed and sleepless, Jim flew to Washington, D.C., the next day where he met with President George Bush. Jim found Bush "genuinely interested in the program and the painting."

Joe Hautman's spectacled eider, which is on the 1992 stamp, amazingly was only the fifth duck painting he had ever done. Credit: Joe Hautman.

However exciting Jim's fifteen-minute chat with the President was, it pales in comparison to the importance of another introduction. Dorothy Deas, a young staffer at the U.S. F&WS, was assigned to shuttle Jim around Washington through a flurry of meetings and congratulations. They began a relationship that culminated five years and numerous frequent-flyer miles later, in marriage.

While Jim and Bob were racking up victories in waterfowl art competitions, older brother Joe was doing something that could hardly be more different. In college, Joe had taken a few art classes and enjoyed them. But the pull of science proved a stronger force and he decided become a physicist, ultimately earning a Ph.D. from the University of Michigan and going to work as a researcher at the University of Pennsylvania. Whenever he had some free time, Joe took to the canvas. With the encouragement of his brothers, Joe began entering the federal duck stamp contest in the late 1980s. In 1991, on his fourth try Joe won the federal with a vibrant painting of a spectacled eider gliding over the waves. Amazingly enough, it was only the fifth duck painting Joe had ever done. Joe kept his day job, but continued to paint and enter contests, racking up wins in the South Carolina duck stamp contest in 1994 and New Jersey in 1995. In 1996, Joe decided to trade molecular dynamics calculations for art, leaving the University of Pennsylvania and heading back to Minnesota to pursue painting full time.

In 1994, Jim, Bob, and Joe attended the federal duck stamp contest in Washington. Both Jim and Bob had entered and they watched with increasing anticipation and excitement as their paintings made it through the first and second rounds. Jim's confidence, in particular, was high. "I felt I had a very good chance, it was one of the best paintings I had ever done." In the end it couldn't have been any closer. Bob's Canada goose came in second to Jim's mallards soaring over a lake on an overcast day (which also scored a perfect twenty-five). In announcing the results, former Director of the U.S. F&WS, Mollie Beattie, highlighted this unusual juxtaposition, stating that "Specialists in early childhood artistic development should take note because the first place winner is Mr. Jim Hautman, brother to the second place winner."

In March 1995, Tom Hautman died. During his life he greatly admired and collected federal duck stamps, with specimens going all the way back to the very first one. In fact, it was through their father that the boys first learned about the program. Tom had even thought of entering the contest, but never got around to it. Thus, it was particularly fitting that he had the opportunity to see Jim and Joe take home top honors in Washington. "He was both amused and pleased," Joe says. "He appreciated the strangeness of the occupation, being a duck stamp artist."

For Bob, coming so close in 1994 just intensified the questions he had heard for years. "Jim and Joe have won the federal, what about Bob?" To make matters worse, Bob came in fourth in each of the three previous years. Not one to get down, Bob redoubled his efforts. Having placed second in 1994, he knew his design was strong. Perhaps a few changes would put it over the edge. So he re-painted the goose for his 1996 entry and added some new background features, including a lake and marsh as well as a band on the goose's left leg. It worked. That design is now emblazoned on the 1997 federal duck stamp. Bob attended the judging and thought it was "intense." When he heard his name announced, he remembers, "it was kind of hard to believe. I felt lucky and shocked and have no idea what I said in my acceptance speech." Nobody asks anymore, "what about Bob?"

In 1998 Jim achieved a "three-peat." His greater scaup coming in tight over the white-capped waves of a Minnesota lake topped 336 other entries with his second perfect score of twenty-five. Just like his other federal wins, this one shows two birds, his

Jim Hautman's winning artwork for the 1995 stamp received the first ever perfect score in the judging. Credit: Jim Hautman.

signature light and dark shading and effective use of threatening clouds. It also has a very unique feature. In the background is a boat with hunter and dog. Brother Bob was the model for the hunter. As for the dog, Jim shows his bent for diplomacy. "I have two friends with retrievers. I tell them both the dog in the painting is theirs." At the first day ceremony for the 1999 stamp, Jim reflected on his winning entry. "I was a little concerned that it looked too much like my earlier winning designs, but I really liked it. Many people tell me they like the lighting in my paintings. That is why I decided to have the light break through and hit the thunderheads. I added the hunter and dog because I wanted to make it a real hunting scene, as well as add an extra element that was different from the other two winners. I had some concerns about the hunter, in part because no other winning artwork had ever included a hunter [it should be noted that the 1935 stamp had a hunter in it, however that element is very minor and was not in the original artwork, but added by the BEP engravers later]. I was also concerned about the reproducibility of the hunter on the stamp, but once I looked carefully at what the BEP was capable of, I decided to leave it in. I made that decision on the last day." On the issue of having two birds in all of his winning designs, Jim has an easy answer. "There is no particular reason. For both of my last two wins I

In 1994, Bob Hautmans painting of a Canada goose came in second (above). Two years later he modified the design (top), won the contest, and had the honor of seeing his design on the 1997 stamp. Credit for winning image: Wild Wings; Credit for second place finisher: Sam Houston Duck Company.

wanted to have a flock and, for the last, even painted one version with fifteen or so birds. It just turned out that the most powerful designs had two birds."

The Hautman brothers often find inspiration on their numerous trips to view and hunt wildlife.

Sometimes, ideas come from more unusual places - a roof for example. In 1991, Joe was thinking of painting a red-breasted merganser in the evening sun. Problem was, he didn't have a photograph or image in his mind to work from, so he decided to stage the photo with a stuffed specimen, outside of his house. He couldn't do this at ground level because of the presence of tall pines. Looking skyward, Joe saw the roof was bathed in late day sun. Up he climbed with his props. There was the stuffed bird and a camera, but he also needed a stand on which to place the bird. A coffee table of course! He lugged the table onto the roof and balanced it on the peak. Now he faced a different problem. To get the right shot he needed some black fabric to drape over the table. The only thing that came to mind was his wife's black nightgown. It worked beautifully. "At one point," Joe recalls, "it occurred to me what I must have looked like on the roof. I just hoped my neighbors didn't see me."

Other inspiration has come from the works of great masters. For example, on Jim's living room wall hangs a framed print of Winslow Homer's famous painting, Left and Right, which shows a duck hunting scene on a stormy, windswept day. A hunter who viewed it at its first public showing gave the painting its title, which refers to the act of shooting ducks successively with separate barrels of a shotgun. It is a powerful piece and, according to Jim, "probably the greatest duck painting I have ever seen. I stand in front of it in awe. It was certainly an inspiration for my painting of the greater scaup." That painting's lighting, rough weather and hunter in a boat do, indeed, indicate the influence of Homer's design.

While many federal duck stamp artists achieve fame and fortune, the Hautmans are probably the only ones to have Hollywood credentials. The grisly Academy Award-winning movie, Fargo, centers around Marge Gunderson, a small town police chief in Minnesota, who is investigating a couple of murders that are tied to a kidnapping in Minneapolis. Her husband in the film is a wildlife artist getting ready to enter the duck stamp contest. He laments that "the Hautmans" will be entering the same contest. While Marge tries to buck him up, saying he is better than they are, he is not as optimistic. As might be expected, one of the Hautman's wins, leaving Marge's husband a bit depressed.

Jim Hautman's winning artwork of greater scaup which appears on the 1999 federal duck stamp. Like his entry in 1994, this one scored a perfect 25 in the judging. Credit: Jim Hautman.

Winslow Homer's "Right and Left", painted a year before the artist's death, in 1909. Credit: Gift of the Avalon Foundation, Photograph (c) Board of Trustees, National Gallery of Art, Washington.

"The Hautmans" were childhood friends of the makers of the movie, Joel and Ethan Coen, who lived up the street from the Hautman clan in St. Louis Park, Minnesota. The materials used in the scene of the husband's art studio were borrowed from Jim and Bob, making it a very authentic setting. The Hautmans also receive mention in the film credits. Perhaps the strangest thing about the Fargo connection is a chance meeting at the Bell Museum of Natural History at the University of Minnesota. Jim was there to pick up a painting of his that was in an exhibition and he wandered into the gift store, where a woman was asking the clerk questions about duck stamp art. Jim offered the woman some advice and said he could help her out in her research. She said what she really wanted was to find "the Hautman brothers." Jim smiled and said, "well, I'm one of them." Turns out that the woman was the set decorator for the movie and the Coens had sent her in search of the Hautmans for props.

While some of the other Hautman siblings are quite talented artists, none has expressed any interest in entering the federal duck stamp contest. That might not be much of a relief to other aspiring duck stamp artists, because they still have to contend with Jim, Bob, and Joe, each of whom expects to be entering duck stamp contests for years to come. The Hautmans, dubbed "America's ruling duck stamp dynasty" by *The Washington Post*, do bring some major advantages to these competitions, foremost among them being great painting skill. They also benefit from their extremely close relationship and honesty in critiquing each other's art. There is no doubt that the duck stamp world will be hearing from the Hautmans again. That is a good thing. Not only has their work helped to create some exquisite stamps, but they also have used their celebrity to actively promote the federal duck stamp program and its conservation goals. The program couldn't ask for better spokesmen.

PAINTINGS AND PRINTS

The winning art for the federal duck stamp contest is very valuable in two ways. The paintings or drawings, because of their notoriety can command hefty prices from collectors and wildlife art lovers. That is why winning artists rarely retain their winning artwork. The other value in the artwork comes from its reproduction in print form. Thousands line up each year to add to their collections of framed prints, creating one of the largest and most vibrant markets for collectible art prints in the United States. The demand for original artwork has risen fairly steadily over time, while the demand for prints has fluctuated greatly, rising gradually through the first four decades of the program, taking off in the late 1970s and 1980s, and then coming back down off historic highs thereafter.

There has always been a healthy demand for original artwork, but prices have risen sharply in recent years. Stearns doesn't remember the exact amount, but thinks he didn't get more than $500 for any of his three winning paintings, the last of which was sold in the mid-1960s. When German, the foremost collector of original art, began purchasing paintings in the late 1980s, he was paying between $5,000 and $7,000 per original. Other artists selling at that time recall values in the neighborhood of $10,000. More recent winning artwork has been selling for between $30,000 and $50,000. For example, Steiner's Barrow's goldeneye went for $45,000 in 1998.

According to Russell A. Fink, an art dealer with a great amount of experience selling duck stamp art, some of the prices realized lately are too high. "I think $15,000 is exorbitant for a duck stamp painting. The painting is the winner of a

Walter A. Weber's white-fronted geese landed on the 1944 stamp. Credit: U.S. Fish and Wildlife Service.

design contest. It is meant to catch the eye immediately. It is not fine art. There is no way duck stamp art can compare to a piece of great art by a great artist. It is a collectible as opposed to something that is a real sound investment and the price should reflect that." Another interesting point made by Fink is the value of duck stamp art as related to other art done by the same artist. "Another painting the same size as the duck stamp art would not get nearly as much as the duck stamp piece. It is an anomaly within the artist's own work. It is an anomaly within the art world as well. Being duck stamp art gives it that extra mileage." Sketches done by the artists on the way to a winning piece of artwork are other elements of the original art which are often offered for sale, and can fetch upwards of $1,000 per piece.

The history of federal duck stamp print production and sales is very involved and has plenty of twists and turns. Interestingly enough, Darling was not the first to create a duck stamp print. In 1936, Ed Thomas and Ralph Terrill, working for Abercrombie and Fitch's

Framed print of Richard E. Bishop's Canada geese which appeared on the 1936 federal duck stamp. Credit: Sam Houston Duck Company.

Book and Art Department, decided to follow-up on a request by one of their customers, Dr. Samuel Milbank, to frame the 1936 stamp along with a print of the winning design. Thomas and Terrill contacted Bishop, the artist for the stamp, and asked for an etching. Bishop gladly did it and a limited, unknown number of prints with the corresponding stamp were created and sold. With Terrill's encouragement, and of their own volition, other early artists produced limited-edition prints. By 1944, the series was up to date with the exception of Darling. That year, however, at the continued urging of Terrill, Darling filled the void. In a letter to G. Decker French, of Davenport, Iowa, dated June 10, 1944, Darling reflected on his efforts to create a print and his concern about its potential quality.

I can't promise you much in the way of a classy etching of the original duck stamp, but I've got one on the way. I was never very proud of that job because it was done in such a hurry that I never got a chance to make a finished drawing before it was necessary to send the sketch to the engraving department in Washington ... Just recently Abercrombie and Fitch put in a request [for prints] similar to yours and I promised I would make them an etching. It is now only in the first stages, but ought to be completed and ready to print sometime late in the summer.

Since that time, every winning artist has produced prints. According to William Webster, "in the early years, winning artists published their designs primarily for prestige in the small world of wildlife art; little was realized monetarily and edition sizes were small." Benson produced a scant 100 of what is still the smallest print created, at 3 inches by 5 inches. For many years thereafter, print runs remained relatively low. In 1962, for example, Morris's print numbered fewer than 300. The pace picked up with the introduction of color in 1970, with Bierly increasing the edition size for his Ross'geese to 1,000. The color, plus the increasing popularity of duck stamps, increased demand for prints. In 1974, Maass initiated the practice of taking orders for prints by a date certain and then only creating enough prints to cover the time-limited demand. If a collector called after the deadline, they were too late and would have to try to acquire a print on the secondary market. "I felt strongly about having small editions with any print," recalls Maass, "and I figured that one way to do this with the growing demand for duck stamp prints was to write to dealers, give them a deadline, get the number they wanted and then print that many and no more. At that time artists were quite serious about keeping edition sizes as low as they could." Maass sold 2,700 prints. In contrast, the print run for Maass's 1981 winning design was 22,250. Clearly, he had changed his perspective on the need for small print runs. "I

Framed print of Arthur M. Cook's emperor geese, indicating that this is the 289th print signed out of 950. Credit: Sam Houston Duck Company.

felt more comfortable with the trend towards larger print runs. As long as there was demand, why not do it?" Since Maass initiated the time-limited edition, many of the edition sizes for winning designs have been determined in this manner, while other artists have opted to print a pre-determined number of prints and sell as many as they could. The high water mark for a print run, 31,900, was achieved by the 50th anniversary edition stamp in 1984. More recently, print editions have become smaller, usually between 10,000 to 20,000.

Another interesting feature of duck stamp prints is numbering. This entails placing a number, usually at the bottom of the print. For the prints done prior to the advent of photolithography, which allows for the mass production of identical prints, the number indicated where the print stood in the printing cue for the entire print run. For example, the number 25/400 would mean that the print was the twenty-fifth printed in a run of 400. For prints created photolithographically, the number tells you in which order the artist signed them. While this might be the order in which the prints came off the press, it usually is not. With the exception of Hunt (1939 stamp) and possibly Gromme (1945 stamp), none of the early winning artists numbered their prints. Stearns numbered the print for his whistling swans (1966 stamp), and then beginning with Claremont G. Pritchard (1968 stamp) every subsequent artist has numbered their prints. From the perspective of quality and value, numbering makes the most sense

when the printing process results in variation in print quality as one progresses through the print run. This is the case with printing processes like stone lithography and etching, which were common before the 1970s. Because of wear on the stone or printing plates, the prints of the highest quality and clarity are usually ones done early in the print run. Therefore there is often a premium for low-number prints. With the advent of photolithography in the 1970s, the number on the print became merely an indication of edition size, not quality. This is because with photolithography there is no difference between the first and the last print made - all prints are identical no matter how many are produced. Thus, the value for prints produced by photolithography is the same whether it is the first or the last in a run. Still, numbering is a nice feature and many collectors strive to collect the same number print each year, thereby creating a matched-set of prints.

A more important indicator of a print's desirability than the number printed is the number sold. Publishers are not always willing to share these numbers, but it is clear from what is known that sales of prints has largely mirrored the fluctuations in print runs. A large part of the reason for the dramatic rise and fall in print runs has to do with value. In the 1970s, when the print market took off, prices realizations for the earlier prints soared. Even though many of the early prints were originally purchased for as little as $10 to $15, by the 1970s, some of them were commanding prices in the thou-

President's Edition framed print of Jim Hautman's 1999 stamp. In addition to the print, it includes a 24-karat gold and silver plated bronze medallion featuring a dimensional image of the winning design, two stamps, and an original color remarque. Only 200 of these were produced. Credit: Wild Wings, Inc.

sands. This, combined with the general increased interest in duck stamps caused many to believe that prints were a phenomenal investment, driving demand up even further. The artists and printers, seeing an opportunity, increased print runs to keep pace. They also began creating various versions of the prints. These included the basic framed print with accompanying stamp, and went on from there to, among others, "Medallion Editions," "Executive Editions," and "President's Editions," each with some added element that intended to make the print more desirable and collectible. For example, an "Executive Edition" might include not only a numbered and signed print, but also a remarque, and a gold-plated bronze medallion replicating the design in the stamp. As often happens in a frenzy-like situation, the market became saturated. With such large editions, the appreciation in value for the newer prints was not as great as had been the case for the older ones. Many print collectors who weren't serious in the first place dropped by the wayside. Print runs and sales followed this downward trend. "Like anything that has a run up in value," notes Webster, "it comes back down to seek it own, sustainable level." He adds that, "[t]he heights that surrounded the values of some of the early prints, where small edition numbers made it look like anything purchased would skyrocket in value, were not sustainable. When people started buying multiples and putting them under their bed that is when print prices took a turn towards a more realistic value."

Still, duck stamp prints are highly collectible and valuable. With a dedicated audience of serious collectors that situation is not expected to change. The only potential threats to this situation are if print numbers, as well as the number of different editions, proliferate to the extent that there is no longer something special about purchasing a print. If collectors don't feel that the prints are of value, they won't be and sales will reflect that.

The value of prints is a function of the number printed and the demand by collectors. The most expensive print is the first edition of Jaques' black ducks, which is valued at $13,000. The first edition of Hunt's 1949 green-winged teals is not far behind, at $10,000. In contrast, a print of Ken Michaelsen's 1979 green-winged teals is valued at $425. In valuing prints it is very important to know the edition of the print. For example, the third edition of Jaques' black ducks commands only $4,750, still respectable, but not even close to what you would expect to get for a first edition. Similarly, Smith's snow goose print, collector's edition goes for $150, while the Executive Edition would collect $1,750. (for a complete list of print values, please see appendix titled Federal Duck Stamp Print Values on page 200). There are only two complete collections of all federal prints that include all editions. One is owned by William Webster, the other owner is anonymous. If you loosen the requirements for a complete collection to be one print for each stamp, regardless of which edition it includes for any particular stamp, then the number of complete sets rises to a little over fifty which are in the hands of private collectors and museums.

One particularly practical and responsible way of maintaining print values is to destroy leftover prints after a certain period of time, usually one year after the release date. That way collectors can be assured that only a certain number of prints are in circulation, making it easier to assess value since one doesn't have to worry about the market being flooded at a later date. This is the exact same theory that is behind the U.S. F&WS's destruction of duck stamps not sold after three years. Sometimes, the number of prints destroyed is quite significant. For example, Smith's 1988 duck stamp print run, was 28,500 for all editions, out of which 5,404 were destroyed. Joe Hautmans 1992 print run totaled 12,950, of which 9,018 sold, leaving 3,932 to be destroyed. Of course, for print runs that are based on orders taken through a certain date, the practice of destroying leftovers does not apply.

The methods of making federal duck stamp prints have varied considerably over the years. During the first few decades, there were a number different printing processes employed. With stone lithography, the artist draws a reverse crayon image of the art on a grained block of limestone. Since the limestone surface is pitted, the crayon does not uniformly coat the block; instead, it creates a random set of dots. The stone is then wet with water. The crayon repels the water, while the stone absorbs it. Next, an oil-based paint is applied to the surface. The wetted surface of the stone repels the paint, while the crayon attracts it. Thus, when the prepared stone is pressed onto a piece of paper the artist's image is reproduced exactly. Another technique used was etching. The artist first coats a metal plate, usually copper, with wax, then scratches the design through the wax, exposing the metal. When the plate is immersed in acid the waxed areas remain protected, while the exposed metal is "bitten" by the acid, creating shallow grooves. The number of "stoppings-out" and "bitings" that take place determines the depth and width of the grooves. The finished plate, minus the wax, becomes the template for printing. Ink spread over its surface drops into the etched areas and excess ink is wiped off with a cloth. The inked plate is then put in a press and pressed onto soaked paper which is flexible enough to reach down into the crevices and grooves of the plate and pull the ink out, transferring the design to the paper. This process is repeated for each print. Acquatint is a variation of etching where acid-resistant powder, such as rosin, is sprinkled on the plate's surface and affixed to it through heating. Acquatint is used to create areas of gray-tone. The ink goes only where the acid-resistant powder isn't. The more powder used, the paler the shade of gray. If very little powder is applied, a deep gray results. Drypoint is yet another variation on etching, where the lines are inscribed with a graving tool rather than being created by acid. All of these intaglio processes are very time intensive and require great skill. Because the wear and tear of the printing process can mean that later prints on the same stone or plate are of lesser sharpness and qual-

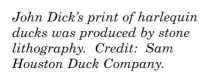

John Dick's print of harlequin ducks was produced by stone lithography. Credit: Sam Houston Duck Company.

A framed print of Albert Earl Gilbert's hooded merganser which appeared on the 1978 federal duck stamp. Gilbert's remarque appears beneath the print. Credit: Sam Houston Duck Company.

ity than the earlier ones, there are cases in which a number of versions of the stone or plate were used to maintain print quality. Sometimes there are worse problems than normal wear and tear. For example, one run of Jaques prints made it only to about thirty before the stone broke. He got another thirty out of the next stone, and then about 200 from the final stone.

Many of the early artists had no experience in printmaking and were forced to learn various printing techniques. Some of them even served as their own printers. Reece's experience, which ranged over more than twenty years, is indicative of the ingenuity employed many of his peers.

When I won in 1948, Abercrombie and Fitch of New York asked me to make prints of the design. I knew nothing about stone lithography, so they told me they had an artist who could copy my design on stone for me. So the first edition of the 1948 was copied from by original. I was so unhappy with the results that I vowed I would learn the technique of stone lithography and do my own prints. I reissued the 1948 design as a second edition in later years as my own lithographs. All the other prints of my duck stamp designs were stone lithographs that I did myself with the printing done by Burr Miller, of George Miller & Son of New York. He furnished me with the stones and taught me to use this fascinating medium. The early prints were sold by Abercrombie and Fitch for $15 with $7.50 to the artist or $6 if they wholesaled to another gallery.

The 1971 print was the last print to be done using stone lithography, which is why it has become so collectible. Because it was in color I drafted my family to help color each print with watercolor. They worked all summer, each of the three doing 300 prints and my doing the balance of the edition. Along the bottom edge are initials of JR for my wife, and MAR and BR for my two boys. This is another reason for the high value of this print. With all the later designs I handled the sales myself, selling to galleries and individual collectors.

Bierly's Ross' geese was the first print to use photolithography, a form of printing in which light sensitive plates, often aluminum, are exposed to a photographic image. The plates are then used to create the print. With the exception of Reece's print the next year, all subsequent federal duck stamp prints have been created using this process.

Federal duck stamp prints are printed and marketed in variety of ways. Many artists, especially earlier ones, did their own printing and marketing. Others have hired a printer and then marketed the prints on their own. Still others have signed on with a full-service marketing outfit that will print and sell the prints. It all depends on the offers the artists receive for the rights to printing and distribution and their desire to maintain control of the process.

Many artists add remarques to their prints. Those images can either closely mirror the design in the print itself, or they can be of the same species but in different poses. They invariably add value to the print and are done in limited editions. Doing remarques is not easy, and for that reason many artists have shied away from doing many or any at all. As Jim Hautman notes, "they can be a real pain sometimes. It's so detailed that it is taxing on your mind and eyes, but collectors really appreciate them." It is hard to imagine anyone having a more difficult time of it that Magee. He decided that his remarques, which he called companion pieces, would be small, original designs done on scratchboard, the same medium used for the original artwork. He limited orders to 1,000 and was almost completely subscribed. Since Magee knew it would take a long time for him to finish all these companion pieces he had the framer leave an opening in the matting into which the scratchboard miniature could be inserted later, when they were completed. Magee used a variety of designs for the companion pieces, some of which took days to complete. For roughly two years, all Magee did was pump out those companion pieces and then ship them off. While Magee didn't seem to mind all this work, his experience did affect other artists that followed. When Plasschaert was asked about whether he did any remarques for his 1980 winning design, he laughed. "I just hated those things with a passion. They are time-consuming and really throw off your

Ron Jenkins created eight remarques on different copies of his 1965 federal duck stamp. The actual stamp is in the lower right hand corner. Credit: Sam Houston Duck Company.

The 1976 federal duck stamp alongside one of the companion pieces painstakingly created by Alderson Magee.

other work. The Magee example was still fresh on everyone's mind, and I wasn't going to go down that path." Some twenty years later, however, Plasschaert did consent to remarque a couple of his federal prints.

In late 1988, Jenkins created a very unusual remarque for Bob Dumaine. Jenkins' painting of three canvasbacks took home winning honors in the 1964 federal contest. Thirty-two was his lucky number. At the time of his winning entry, Jenkins was 32 years old, born in 1932; the stamp was the 32nd duck stamp, and it won in 1964, two times 32. Dumaine asked Jenkins if he would add a duck or two to an original stamp, in effect creating an artist's remarque. Jenkins agreed and as would be expected requested a fee for his services. Instead of just one remarque, Jenkins created eight new stamps by adding birds, subtracting them, and moving them around.

As with the stamps themselves, sometimes error prints are produced. Most errors during the printing process are discarded. Some, however, were sold and are of interest to many print collectors. The two best known of these are the flopped versions of Edwin R. Kalmbach's ruddy ducks for the 1941 stamp and Weber's white-fronted geese for the 1944 stamp. In both cases a small number of reverse image prints (flopped left to right) were made. It is estimated that 100 to 110 of Kalmbach's reverse print were produced, while Weber's reverse run was 100. Bierly's Ross' geese print is the subject of another interesting error. The print was made using four-color photolithography, with each color being printed twice. For part of the run, after each color was printed once, the same sheets were placed back in the press upside down and then printed on again. The resulting prints look like double exposures. According to Fink, all but two of these errors were discarded.

MARKETING THE DUCK STAMP

With the great interest in federal ducks stamps it was only a matter of time before enterprising individuals started thinking about the possibility of placing the duck stamp image on products and marketing them. In 1984, that possibility became a reality, in the form of an amendment to the Migratory Bird Hunting and Conservation Stamp Act of 1934, which authorized the Secretary of the Interior to license productions of the federal duck stamp on products to be manufactured and sold by private sector enterprises. The licensing program, run by the Duck Stamp Office, has dramatically expanded over the years and has been associated with a variety of products, including limited edition shotguns, commemorative knives and plates, and a slew of collectibles such as lapel pins, belt buckles, calendars, decoys, T-shirts, sweatshirts, caps, mugs, wall clocks, computer mouse pads, software screen savers, ice buckets, cotton throws, magnets, tin and porcelain signs, brass ornament replicas, and refrigerator magnets. These products are distributed and sold by major sporting goods stores, Kmart, Wal-Mart, J.C. Penney's, QVC Home Shopping channel, the military exchanges, and NWR visitor centers. Several of the licensees' products are also featured in the Smoky Mountain Knife Works, Bass Pro Shops, DU, and Cabela's catalogs. One hundred percent of the sales-related royalties received from licensed products are deposited into the Migratory Bird Conservation Fund and used by the U.S. F&WS for wetlands acquisition. In 1998, for example, this generated $75,000. With this type of success, the licensing program lives up to its theme - "Partnerships Today, Preserve Wetlands and Waterfowl Tomorrow." The Federal Duck Stamp Licensing Program is always on the lookout for new ventures and new enterprises, and given the beauty of and interest in the federal duck stamp, there is little doubt that new products will join the already substantial lineup.

In 1994 legislation was passed that authorized the licensing and marketing of the Federal Junior Duck Stamp and/or the art design on appropriate products manufactured and/or offered for sale. The reproduction of these handsome designs can be found on T-shirts, caps, Swiss Army knives, patches and long-distance calling cards. The royalties generated from the sale of the Federal Junior Duck Stamps and/or the art design on products are used for awards and scholarships for participants in the junior competition.

A selection of licensed duck stamp products, some of which are no longer offered for sale. Credit: U.S. Fish and Wildlife Service.

The Peabody Ducks

Twice a day, at one of the country's premier luxury hotels, a group of five mallards take a stroll on a red carpet to the booming, military brass beat of John Philip Sousa's King Cotton March. At night, they retire to their $120,000 penthouse marble pagoda "Duck Palace." These VIPs, or Very Important Poultry, are none other than the famous Peabody Orlando Ducks, the most physically appropriate ambassadors the Federal Duck Stamp Program ever had. Since 1997, the ducks have annually "flown" to Washington to be on hand for the judging of the duck stamp art contest, and then made a stop at the Wings 'n Water Festival in Stone Harbor, Cape May, New Jersey, one of the venues where the winning artwork is displayed. When the duck are in Orlando, they not only entertain the guests at the 891-room Peabody Orlando, but they also are very involved in educating people about the Federal Duck Stamp Program and the importance of preserving waterfowl habitats, making trips to elementary schools, rehabilitation centers, and retirement homes.

The tradition of the Peabody Ducks began in the 1930s at the Peabody Memphis in Tennessee. General Manager Frank Schutt and some friends returned from a hunting trip with their "call ducks," live "decoys" used to beckon flying ducks into range. Instead of bringing the ducks to a nearby pond, they placed them in the hotel's ornate fountain. The next morning, a crowd had gathered around the loudly quacking ducks. When hotel management attempted to remove the ducks, the guests howled their disapproval. So, by popular demand, the ducks stayed on and on. Today, the Peabody Ducks march at both Peabody hotels, in Memphis and Orlando.

At the Peabody Orlando, it is Duck Master Mark Hirchert who takes the mallards on their twice-daily promenade, at 11:00 am and 5:00 pm. Prior to their morning performance, Hirchert takes the ducks for their "constitutional" or "duck aerobics" on the tennis courts. During their marches the ducks are usually quite well behaved, but there have been occasions when a stray will wander off to mingle among the guests or, during mating season, a drake might make an unwanted advance on one or more of his female companions.

The Peabody Orlando, the only official hotel sponsor of the Duck Stamp Program, also contributes to the cause of waterfowl preservation by selling federal duck stamps in its gift shops. "The owners, manage-ment and staff of The Peabody Orlando are fully supportive of the aims of the Federal Duck Stamp Program," notes hotel vice president and general manager, Alan C. Villaverde. "And what better mascots could there be for such a program than The Peabody Orlando Ducks."

If there is any doubt that the Peabody Orlando takes ducks seriously, one need only look at the hotel itself to dispel that notion. The walls are awash in duck art and motifs. Guestroom soaps are in the shape of little aquamarine ducks. Some hotel note paper is duck-shaped. The hotel's four-star rated restaurant is called Dux, and on its walls are a specially-commissioned series of duck paintings. Butter patties come to the table in the shape of ducks, and the employee cafeteria is called Quackers. But, if you want to eat duck you've come to the wrong place. There are no duck dishes on the menu.

"J.J." Mallard and the Peabody Orlando duck team in their marble fountain. Credit: The Peabody Orlando.

Alan C. Villaverde, Vice President and General Manager of The Peabody Orlando identified the Federal Duck Stamp art contest as a natural partner for the hotel. He is seen here with a basket of five baby ducks, a new team for The Peabody Orlando's famed marching ducks. Credit: The Peabody Orlando.

Conclusion

The Federal Duck Stamp Program is a work in progress. Although duck stamp revenues have played a critical role in purchasing habitat essential to the survival of migratory waterfowl, the need for additional habitat is clear. While numerous duck, goose, and swan populations are enjoying record highs, many of the same pressures which brought these populations to historic lows in the 1920s and 1930s are still present. Every day, habitat is plowed under and paved over. Each year there remains fewer and fewer acres of land that can be potentially added to the NWRS. The continuation of the Federal Duck Stamp Program will help to ensure that migratory waterfowl and the other wildlife that depend on refuges have a bright future. The U.S. F&WS's five-year effort to increase duck stamp sales will contribute to this goal. If you enjoyed this book and want to help conserve our precious migratory waterfowl populations, then purchase duck stamps. There is no more direct and effective way to benefit the birds.

Credit: U.S. Fish and Wildlife Service.

Stamps & Statistics

The pages that follow present information and statistics on every federal duck stamp. Remember, the date appearing on duck stamps is one year later than the issuance date. For example, the first stamp was issued in 1934, but on the stamp it says "Void after June 30, 1935." Some collectors refer to this issue as the "1934-1935 stamp," since it was valid in both years. We refer to each federal duck stamp issue by both its number in the series (e.g., 1, 2, 3 . . .) and the year of issuance, not the void date.

A number following the artist's name (1) indicates the number of wins as of that date for a multiple winner. The first twelve duck stamps do not have inscriptions on the reverse. Beginning in 1946, inscriptions were added. They have changed over the years. Please see page 52 for a description of these inscriptions. For older issues we have provided information about duck stamp prints. This is because the early print runs were relatively low and of great interest to many collectors. Information on print prices can be found in the price appendix. For most of the art contests up through 1975 we have indicated the number of artists who entered. For some years we were unable to find the data. In 1976, the contest rules changed and each artist was only allowed one entry. Thus, from that point forward, the number of entries is the same as the number of artists. An asterisk (*) following a name indicates that the artist is deceased. Credit for stamp illustrations: U.S. F&WS.

Future Issue No. 67   **Year: 2000**   **Species: Mottled Duck**

Adam Grimm's beautiful oil painting of a mottled duck stretching in the sunlight after a preening session will grace the 2000 federal duck stamp. Grimm, 21, is the youngest winner ever of the Federal Duck Stamp Contest. He placed fourth in the 1996 Junior Federal Duck Stamp Contest. Credit: Adam Grimm.

Issue No. 1   Year: 1934   Species: Mallard

First Day of Sale: Aug. 22, 1934.

No. Sold/Revenue: 635,001/$635,001.

Plates Used: 129199, 129200, 129201, 129202.

Printing Press: flat bed press.

Art Competition/Entries: Honorary invitation/6 entries, 1 artist.

Medium: Brush and ink drawing.

Other Data: Artwork titled "Mallards Dropping In." Darling created the design for the stamp in about one hour, due to a sudden printing deadline. The nickname "Ding" is a contraction of Darling, less the "arl" which he adopted in college to conceal his identity from school officials, which he satirically depicted in the newspaper. Darling won two Pulitzer Prizes for his political cartoons. Multiples of the 1934 stamp, not affixed to a license or Form 3333, were authorized to be sold for the last two weeks the stamp was sold, June 15 through June 30, 1935. This regulation resulted in very few plate blocks and full panes being sold, with less than five panes surviving. Imperforate and partially perforated errors exist from one pane, plate number 129199. The exact number of prints is unknown, but believed to be about 300. The prints are not numbered.

ARTIST: Jay N. "Ding Darling"*

Issue No. 2   Year: 1935   Species: Canvasback

First Day of Sale: July 1, 1935.

No. Sold/Revenue: 448,204/$448,204.

Plates Used: 131980, 131981, 131982, 131983.

Printing Press: flat bed press.

Art Competition/Entries: Honorary invitation/1–3 entries, 1 artist.

Medium: Black and white wash painting.

Other Data: The 1935 issue is the rarest duck stamp with only 448,204 sold. Note the boat, blind, and hunters in the background.. This was the first year to require a signature across the face of the stamp. The artist was known as the "dean" of duck etchers, and was personally selected by Darling for the artwork. Only 100 unnumbered prints were issued, and their size was the smallest of any federal print at 3 inches x 5 inches. Since the original artwork did not contain the boat, blind or hunters, they are not on the prints. It has been claimed that slightly larger imitation prints, of foreign origin, were made.

ARTIST: Frank W. Benson*

Issue No. 3   Year: 1936   Species: Canada Goose

First Day of Sale: July 1, 1936.

No. Sold/Revenue: 603,623/$603,623.

Plates Used: 134317, 134318.

Printing Press: flat bed press.

Art Competition/Entries: Honorary invitation/1–3 entries, 1 artist.

Medium: Etching.

Other Data: Artwork titled "Coming In." Notice the bird in the center of the design is banded. By these bands, biologist can trace migration routes of birds. This is the first duck stamp not to use the word "dollar" in the stamp design. An unknown number of prints exist, as Bishop did not keep precise printing records. Specialists estimate about 400-600 unnumbered prints were produced on various type papers. Some fakes are believed to exist.

ARTIST: Richard E. Bishop*

Issue No. 4   Year: 1937   Species: Greater Scaup

First Day of Sale: July 1, 1937.
No. Sold/Revenue: 783,039/$783,039.
Plates Used: 136267.
Printing Press: flat bed press.
Art Competition/Entries: Honorary invitation/1–3 entries, 1 artist.
Medium: Black and white wash painting.
Other Data: Joseph D. Knap, although handicapped his entire life, participated in many sports such a golf, tennis, and sailing, but duck hunting was his favorite. Real estate was his profession, and he always considered art his hobby. Interesting that it was this "hobby" which was to bring him immortality in the art world. Approximately 260 unnumbered first–edition prints are believed to exist; later printings are unknown. Notice the ducks landing with the wind direction, a possible technical flaw. Mr. Knap had a stroke in later life, so his signatures exist in both scroll and block printing.

ARTIST: Joseph D. Knap*

Issue No. 5   Year: 1938   Species: Pintails

First Day of Sale: July 1, 1938.
No. Sold/Revenue: 1,002,715/$1,002,715.
Plates Used: 138602.
Printing Press: flat bed press.
Art Competition/Entries: Honorary invitation/1–3 entries, 1 artist.
Medium: Etching.
Other Data: The first issue to sell more than one million stamps. Although the official color is listed as purple, most specialists feel the color is red violet. Shades of light and dark red violet examples exist. Some variations with very weak color may be the result of ultraviolet bleaching. Well-centered stamps are exceptionally difficult to locate on this issue, and the artist seldom signed stamps. The number of prints is believed to be 300, and later edition printings are unknown. The prints are not numbered.

ARTIST: Roland Clark*

Issue No. 6   Year: 1939   Species: Green-winged Teal

First Day of Sale: July 1, 1939.
No. Sold/Revenue: 1,111,561/$1,111,561.
Plates Used: 141428.
Printing Press: flat bed press
Art Competition/Entries: Honorary invitation/1–3 entries, 1 artist.
Medium: Pencil Drawing.
Other Data: The first stamp issued by the Department of the Interior. A Presidential order on July 1, 1939, transferred the Bureau of Biological Survey to the Department of the Interior along with the stamp. The following year the Bureau of Biological survey was renamed the Fish and Wildlife Service. July 1, 1939 was a Saturday, so it is likely sales did not begin until Monday, July 3, 1939. The prints had two editions, each of approximately 100 pieces. The prints are marked 1st E and 2nd E, they are both from the same plate, which was slightly retouched. This was an original print, and some specialists feel since it was hand-drawn, it may have been done by another artist.

ARTIST: Lynn B. Hunt*

Issue No. 7   Year: 1940   Species: Black Duck

First Day of Sale: July 1, 1940.
No. Sold/Revenue: 1,260,810/$1,260,810.
Plates Used: 143743, 143776.
Printing Press: flat bed press.
Art Competition/Entries: Honorary invitation/1–3 entries, 1 artist.
Medium: Black and white wash painting.
Other Data: Artist chosen by honorary limited competition. This was the first stamp to be sold by the Philatelic Sales Division which catered to collector's wishes for well-centered stamps, plate number singles, and plate blocks. As today, most sales were made via mail order. Three editions of the print exist, first edition about 30; second 30, and third about 200.

ARTIST: Francis L. Jaques*

Issue No. 8   Year: 1941   Species: Ruddy Duck

First Day of Sale: July 1, 1941
No. Sold/Revenue: 1,439,967/$1,439,967.
Plates Used: 146271, 146282.
Printing Press: flat bed press.
Art Competition/Entries: Honorary invitation/1–3 entries, 1 artist.
Medium: Black and white wash, tempera painting.
Other Data: First issue to depict ducklings, first to show swimming ducks, and first that did not depict birds in flight. Kalmbach hoped featuring the ducklings would illustrate the purpose for which duck stamp funds are used: the perpetuation of the species. The first edition print was flopped (reversed), with ducks moving right to left. Approximately 100 prints are believed to exist. The second edition corrected the problem, and an estimated 100 prints exist, although this is an unconfirmed estimate.

ARTIST: Edwin R. Kalmbach*

Issue No. 9   Year: 1942   Species: Wigeon

First Day of Sale: July 1, 1942.
No. Sold/Revenue: 1,383,629/$1,383,629.
Plates Used: 149599, 149600.
Printing Press: flat bed press.
Art Competition/Entries: Honorary invitation/1–3 entries, 1 artist.
Medium: Pen and ink drawing.
Other Data: Besides the first issue, this stamp was the first to show a decline in sales from the prior year, perhaps due to WWII. Only one edition of the print exists, and the number of prints is unknown. Ripley's wife signed a number of prints and they generally are worth about half of those signed by Ripley himself. The artist was elected to the National Academy of Design, considered one of the highest honors an artist in this country can attain.

ARTIST: A. Lassell Ripley*

Issue No. 10   Year: 1943   Species: Wood Duck

First Day of Sale: July 1, 1943.
No. Sold/Revenue: 1,169,352/$1,169,352.
Plates Used: 152826, 152827.
Printing Press: flat bed press.
Art Competition/Entries: Honorary invitation/1–3 entries, 1 artist.
Medium: Dry point etching on copper.
Other Data: Stamp sales plummeted by 214,277, about 18% from the prior year in all probability due to the effect of WWII. Well-centered examples are difficult to locate, and these stamps were of a poorer quality paper, often plagued by carbon specks, and large gum skips. Two editions of the print exist, 290 impressions on the first, and an unknown number of second editions. Walter Bohl began painting in 1930 when recovering from a serious illness. He also illustrated and published several books.

*ARTIST: Walter E. Bohl**

Issue No. 11   Year: 1944   Species: White-fronted Goose

First Day of Sale: July 1, 1944.
No. Sold/Revenue: 1,487,029/$1,487,029.
Plates Used: 155590, 155603.
Printing Press: flat bed press.
Art Competition/Entries: Honorary invitation/1–3 entries, 1 artist.
Medium: Black and white wash painting.
Other Data: Stamp sales recovered to their 1941 level with this issue. Weber was a scientist and curator of birds in the National Museum, Washington, D.C. July 1, 1944 was a Saturday, so it is likely no sales occurred until Monday, July 3, 1944. Three editions of the prints exist. The first is flopped (reversed) of which 100 exist; the second 200, and the third edition 90.

*ARTIST: Walter A. Weber**(1)*

Issue No. 12   Year: 1945   Species: Shoveler

First Day of Sale: July 1, 1945.
No. Sold/Revenue: 1,725,505/$1,725,505.
Plates Used: 157248, 157249.
Printing Press: flat bed press.
Art Competition/Entries: Honorary invitation/1–3 entries, 1 artist.
Medium: Black and white wash painting
Other Data: Stamp sales gained more than 238,000 from the prior year, a positive sign that duck hunting was alive and well. July 1, 1945 was a Sunday, so it is likely no sales occurred until Monday, July 2, 1945. The artist was an accomplished author, and Curator Emeritus of the Milwaukee Public Museum in addition to numerous wildlife advisory roles including the Encyclopedia Britannica. Only one edition of 250 of the print exists, plus ten artist's proofs.

*ARTIST: Owen J. Gromme**

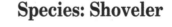

Issue No. 13   Year: 1946   Species: Redhead

*ARTIST: Robert W. Hines**

First Day of Sale: July 1, 1946.
No. Sold/Revenue: 2,016,841/$2,016,841.
Plates Used: 158448, 158449, 158456, 158457; back-offset 47510.
Printing Press: flat bed press.
Art Competition/Entries: Honorary invitation/1–3 entries, 1 artist.
Medium: Pen and ink and wash drawing.
Other Data: First issue to sell more than two million stamps, first with a back inscription and offset plate number, and the first without straight edges.   Offset plate number 47510 is position 24 of the upper right pane only and continued through the 1951 issue. The plate number appears on the upper right pane, position 24, for all six years. Only one back plate number exists for each 112 stamps. A major color error of rose red exists. Mr. Hines was employed as a U. S. Fish and Wildlife artist, and also designed the voluntary purchase and rare 1960 Duck Stamp Certificate. Hines also served as Administrator of the Duck Stamp Contest for more than 30 years. He has also illustrated many wildlife books, and four United States postage wildlife stamps. Two editions of the "Redheads" print exists, 300 of the first, and 385 second editions.

Issue No. 14   Year: 1947   Species: Snow Goose

*ARTIST: Jack Murray**

First Day of Sale: July 1, 1947.
No. Sold/Revenue: 1,772,677/$1,772,677.
Plates Used: 159461, 159462, 159463, 159464; back-offset 47510.
Printing Press: flat bed press.
Art Competition/Entries: Honorary invitation/multiple entries, at least two artists.
Medium: Black and white wash drawing.
Other Data: Artist Jack Murray was an illustrator for the American Museum of Natural History, Outdoors Magazine, and numerous other national magazines. Only one edition of 300 of the print, titled "From Beyond the North Wind" was issued. Mr. Murray had a stroke later in life and his signature was modified to printing. He also had the habit of signing his stamps in red ink whenever possible.

Issue No. 15   Year: 1948   Species: Bufflehead

ARTIST: Maynard Reece(1)

First Day of Sale: July 1, 1948.
No. Sold/Revenue: 2,127,603/$2,127,603.
Plates Used: 160099, 160100, 160101, 160102; back-offset 47510.
Printing Press: flat bed press.
Art Competition/Entries: Honorary invitation and unsolicited submissions/multiple entries, at least two artists.
Medium: Wash and tempera painting.
Other Data: Last $1 issue, face value of the first 15 issues. This was to be the first of five winning designs by artist Maynard Reece. There were four editions of the print "Buffleheads Aloft," as follows: 200 plus 15 artist's proofs, 150 plus 25 artist's proofs, 400, 350, the latter printed in offset color.

Issue No. 16   Year: 1949   Species: Common Goldeneye

First Day of Sale: September 1, 1949.

No. Sold/Revenue: 1,954,734/$3,909,468.

Plates Used: 160790, 160791, 160792, 160793; back-offset 47510.

Printing Press: flat bed press.

Art Competition/Entries: Honorary invitation and unsolicited submissions/multiple entries, 8 artists.

Medium: Black and white wash drawing.

Other Data: First $2 duck stamp, first to raise more than $3 million and latest issued, dated September 1, 1949, due to delays caused by congressional deliberations raising the price from $1 to $2. At 26, he was the youngest artist to have ever submitted a winning design (later eclipsed by Jim Hautman in 1990 and Adam Grimm in 2000). One edition of 250 prints was produced.

ARTIST: Roger E. Preuss

Issue No. 17   Year: 1950   Species: Trumpeter Swan

First Day of Sale: July 1, 1950.

No. Sold/Revenue: 1,903,644/$3,807,288.

Plates Used: 161533, 161534, 161535, 151536; back-offset 47510.

Printing Press: flat bed press.

Art Competition/Entries: Open Competition/88 entries, 65 artists.

Medium: Black and white wash and gouache drawing.

Other Data: This was the first year to have an open national design contest and the first issue to feature a repeat artist. Weber also designed the 1944 stamp. July 1, 1950 was a Saturday, so the likely first sale took place on Monday, July 3, 1950. Although some references feel the back inscription was trimmed, examples do exist with partial plate numbers. This is also the first to depict a protected waterfowl species. The run for the first edition print is 500, and the second edition, 300.

ARTIST: Walter A. Weber* (2)

Issue No. 18   Year: 1951   Species: Gadwall

First Day of Sale: July 1, 1951.

No. Sold/Revenue: 2,167,767/$4,335,534.

Plates Used: 162125, 162126, 162127, 162128; back-offset 47510.

Printing Press: flat bed press.

Art Competition/Entries: Open competition/74 entries by 51 artists.

Medium: Black and white wash and tempera drawing.

Other Data: First to raise more than $4 million and also the second win for Reece. As with the prior year, offset back plate number examples do exist, but with partial number showing. Such examples are extremely scarce. July 1, 1951 fell on a Sunday, so the actual first day of sale was likely Monday, July 2, 1951. Two-hundred and fifty of the first edition print were issued and 400 of the second edition.

ARTIST: Maynard Reece(2)

Issue No. 19   Year: 1952   Species: Harlequin Duck

ARTIST: *John H. Dick**

First Day of Sale: July 1, 1952.

No. Sold/Revenue: 2,296,628/$4,593,256.

Plates Used: 162602, 162603, 162604, 162605; back-offset 47510.

Printing Press: flat bed press.

Art Competition/Entries: Open competition/70 entries by 49 artists.

Medium: Black and white wash drawing.

Other Data: First to depict name of waterfowl on the stamp, a format continued on all later issues. While back offset plate numbers were used, no examples have been reported. Only issue to use "United States" rather than "U.S." for Department of the Interior. The print, titled "Harlequin Ducks," was issued by a dealer, and the exact number is unknown, but believed to be about 250 for the first and 300 for the second editions. Prints are titled and signed in blue ink. Judy Ellen Wines, a 12-year-old, received "honorable mention."

Issue No. 20   Year: 1953   Species: Blue-winged Teal

ARTIST: *Clayton B. Seagers**

First Day of Sale: July 1, 1953

No. Sold/Revenue: 2,268,446/$4,536,892.

Plates Used: 163622, 163623, 163624, 163625; back offset 47510.

Printing Press: flat bed press.

Art Competition/Entries: Open competition/92 entries, 53 artists.

Medium: India ink wash drawing.

Other Data: The last issue printed with the back inscription under the gum. This issue also utilized the offset plate number 47510 for the back inscription, but no examples have been reported, having been trimmed off in production. The artist used a pair of hand-raised teal and several action sketches as models for this design. The action sketches were originally drawn by Seagers in 1934 and were based on a drake he had collected on the same day he purchased his first duck stamp, Darling's mallards. Prints were done by a dealer who ran off 250 copies for the first edition and 1,500 for the second.

Issue No. 21   Year: 1954   Species: Ring-necked Duck

ARTIST: *Harvey D. Sandstrom*

First Day of Sale: July 1, 1954.

No. Sold/Revenue: 2,184,550/$4,369,100.

Plates Used: 164744, 164745, 164746, 164747.

Printing Press: flat bed press.

Art Competition/Entries: Open competition/114 entries, 87 artists.

Medium: Black and white watercolor.

Other Data: First to use the dry pre-gummed printing method and first to place reverse inscriptions on top of the gum. A different plate was used for the back inscription, #52412, but trimmed off on this and all subsequent issues. The only issue that lists the VOID AFTER date twice, possibly done to balance the stamp's letter engraving. The title of the original art was "Ring-necked Ducks," and two print editions were issued, the first of 250 and second of 400 prints.

Issue No. 22   Year: 1955   Species: Blue Goose

First Day of Sale: July 1, 1955.
No. Sold/Revenue: 2,369,940/$4,739,880.00.
Plates Used: 165282, 165283, 165284, 165285.
Printing Press: flat bed press.
Art Competition/Entries: Open competition/93, 66 artists.
Medium: Ink and pencil drawing on scratchboard.
Other Data: This was the first of three wins by Stearns. The highest number of stamps sold for the first 36 issues was achieved with this issue. This was the first issue using a scratchboard medium. There are 250 copies of the first edition of the print. The second edition, of 100 with 16 artist's proofs, was issued in 1967.

ARTIST: Stanley Stearns(1)

Issue No. 23   Year: 1956   Species: Common Merganser

First Day of Sale: July 1, 1956.
No. Sold/Revenue: 2,332,014/$4,664,028.
Plates Used: 165826, 165827, 165829, 165860.
Printing Press: flat bed press.
Art Competition/Entries: Open competition/64 entries, 42 artists.
Medium: Black and white watercolor painting.
Other Data: The first of three wins for Bierly, and the first time a pane was autographed by the Postmaster General and presented to the artist. Each successive winner receives a signed pane of their stamp, and it is the only compensation the artist receives from the federal government. July 1, 1956 was a Sunday, so likely first day of sale was Monday, July 2, 1956. One print edition of 450.

ARTIST: Edward J. Bierly(1)

Issue No. 24   Year: 1957   Species: Common Eider

First Day of Sale: July 1, 1957.
No. Sold/Revenue: 2,355,190/$4,710,380.
Plates Used: 166256, 166257, 166258, 166259.
Printing Press: flat bed press.
Art Competition/Entries: Open competition/106 entries, 60 artists.
Medium: Black and white watercolor.
Other Data: With this issue, rules state no species is to be considered if used for the previous five designs. Artists were allowed to submit more than one entry, and this year Abbott finished first and second. Some examples of this issue exist with an inverted reverse inscription. There are three print editions. The first run was 250, the second 500, and the third 1,500. The last edition was done in four-color offset lithography.

*ARTIST: Jackson M. Abbott**

Issue No. 25 Year: 1958 Species: Canada Goose

First Day of Sale: July 1, 1958.
No. Sold/Revenue: 2,176,425/$4,352,850.
Plates Used: 166753, 166754, 166755, 166756.
Printing Press: flat bed press.
Art Competition/Entries: Open competition/96 entries, 55 artists.
Medium: Black and white wash drawing.
Other Data: First issue to repeat a species. Canada Geese were also featured on the third stamp, the 1936 issue. This was the last of the $2 stamps, a series which lasted ten years. This design is the only $2 issue to depict standing waterfowl as the main theme. This was also the first of two wins for artist Les Kouba.

ARTIST: Les Kouba*(1)

Issue No. 26 Year: 1959 Species: Mallard

First Day of Sale: July 1, 1959.
No. Sold/Revenue: 1,626,115/$4,878,345.
Plates Used: 167109, 167120.
Printing Press: sheet fed, Giori rotary press.
Art Competition/Entries: Open competition/110 entries, 64 artists.
Medium: Black and white wash and tempera drawing.
Other Data: First $3 stamp, first multicolor, first prepared on the rotary press, first to feature a subject other than waterfowl, first pane of 30 stamps and plate block of four, first to feature a theme, "RETREIVERS SAVE GAME," and first three-time winner, Maynard Reece. Because of the shift to the rotary press and relocation of the plate number, plate blocks of four were collected rather than six on the flat bed press on the first 25 issues. The 1959 stamp was the first of a series of five stamps designed to conserve game during this drought period. The next two years also

ARTIST: Maynard Reece(3)

have messages on the face of the stamps. A souvenir card was also offered to enhance sales, but was a failure. There were eleven ducks on the original artwork, but only seven made it to the stamp. The retriever on the stamp is King Buck, a national champion owned by John Olin of Winchester. An error exists with the reverse writing inverted. Only one example known at this time.

Issue No. 27 Year: 1960 Species: Redheads

First Day of Sale: July 1, 1960.
No. Sold/Revenue: 1,725634/$5,176,902.
Plates Used: 167498, 167503.
Printing Press: sheet fed, Giori rotary press.
Art Competition/Entries: Open competition/unknown.
Medium: Black and white watercolor drawing.
Other Data: First to raise more than $5 million. The theme for this year was "WILDLIFE NEEDS WATER *PRESERVE WETLANDS*," printed in the upper left of the stamp. Another souvenir card was offered to stimulate sales, but again failed. The drought and conservation message continued, and artists were required to build designs around the theme "Wildlife Needs Water: Preserve Potholes." The brood of ducklings and hen and drake portray the essence of potholes for waterfowl survival. Redheads were also depicted on the 1946 issue.

ARTIST: John A. Ruthven

Issue No. 28   Year: 1961   Species: Mallards

First Day of Sale: July 1, 1961.
No. Sold/Revenue: 1,334,236/$4,002,708.
Plates Used: 167768, 167772.
Printing Press: sheet fed, Giori rotary press.
Art Competition/Entries: Open competition/100
Medium: Black and white watercolor painting.
Other Data: Theme "HABITAT PRODUCES DUCKS" printed at bottom. A nesting bird or a duck and her brood were necessary for the design to emphasize importance of waterfowl aspects of marshes. This was the first of two wins for artist Edward A. Morris, the only artist to win in two consecutive years. July 1, 1961 was a Saturday, so likely first day of sale was Monday, July 3, 1961.

ARTIST: Edward A. Morris(1)

Issue No. 29   Year: 1962   Species: Pintails

First Day of Sale: July 1, 1962.
No. Sold/Revenue: 1,147,212/$3,441,636.
Plates Used: 168073.
Printing Press: sheet fed, Giori rotary press.
Art Competition/Entries: Open competition/124
Medium: Black and white wash drawing.
Other Data: First and only time an artist won in back-to-back years. Only stamp to feature two species, pintails and scaup decoys. The theme, although not printed on the stamp, was "Know Your Ducks, Let Them Come In Close, and Be Sure before You Shoot" to encourage hunters to select drakes. A blind and boat are also clearly visible for only the second time, the other being on the 1935 issue. Because of the drought, revenues dropped back to $3.4 million, the lowest since 1948. July 1, 1962 was a Sunday, so likely first day of sale was Monday, July 2, 1962.

ARTIST: Edward A. Morris(2)

Issue No. 30   Year: 1963   Species: American Brant

First Day of Sale: July 1, 1963.
No. Sold/Revenue: 1,448,191/$4,344,573.
Plates Used: 168269, 168273.
Printing Press: sheet fed, Giori rotary press.
Art Competition/Entries: Open competition/161 Entries, 87 Artists
Medium: Black and white watercolor drawing.
Other Data: First issue to feature a lighthouse, Bodie Island. This was the second of three wins for Bierly. The theme for this year was "Ducks For Recreation."

ARTIST: Edward J. Bierly(2)

Issue No. 31   Year: 1964   Species: Nene Goose

First Day of Sale: July 1, 1964.
No. Sold/Revenue: 1,573,155/$4,719,465.
Plates Used: 168629, 168630.
Printing Press: sheet fed, Giori rotary press.
Art Competition/Entries: Open competition/158 Entries, 87 Artists.
Medium: Black and white watercolor drawing.
Other Data: Although a rotary press printing, placement of the plate number on the second stamp's selvage rather than first, requires this issue's plate block to be collected as six instead of four stamps. Note: Nene Geese are native to the Hawaiian Islands and are a protected species. This was the second of three wins for Stearns.

ARTIST: Stanley Stearns(2)

Issue No. 32   Year: 1965   Species: Canvasback

First Day of Sale: July 1, 1965.
No. Sold/Revenue: 1,558,197/$4,674,591.
Plates Used: 168790, 168791.
Printing Press: sheet fed, Giori rotary press.
Art Competition/Entries: Open competition/138 Entries, 85 Artists.
Medium: Black and white wash drawing.
Other Data: The artist has many magazine covers and illustrations to his credit, including National Geographic magazine. This was the second stamp to feature canvasbacks, the other being the 1935 issue. This was the first duck stamp to be issued without a defined border.

ARTIST: Ron Jenkins

Issue No. 33   Year: 1966   Species: Whistling Swan

First Day of Sale: July 1, 1966.
No. Sold/Revenue: 1,805,341/$5,414,349.
Plates Used: 169058, 169063.
Printing Press: sheet fed, Giori rotary press.
Art Competition/Entries: Open competition/181 Entries, 105 Artists
Medium: Black and white tempera drawing.
Other Data: Third win for Stearns (he also won in 1955 and 1964). Stamp revenues bounced back to the $5.4 million level, the highest to this time, and the only year to top $5 million since 1960. The drought was over and the hunters returned in droves.

ARTIST: Stanley Stearns(3)

Issue No. 34   Year: 1967   Species: Oldsquaw Duck

First Day of Sale: July 1, 1967.
No. Sold/Revenue: 1,934,697/$5,804,091.
Plates Used: 169457, 169487.
Printing Press: sheet fed, Giori rotary press.
Art Competition/Entries: Open competition/170 entries.
Medium: Wash and tempera drawing.
Other Data: Kouba's second contest winner, the first was 1958.
He had placed second three times and third twice prior to this win.
The stamps produced were of high quality, but centering was often
poor. Exceptionally well-centered examples bring a premium price.
July 1, 1967 was a Sunday, so likely the first day of sale was
Monday, July 2, 1967.

ARTIST: Les Kouba*(2)

Issue No. 35   Year: 1968   Species: Hooded Merganser

First Day of Sale: July 1, 1968.
No. Sold/Revenue: 1,837,139/$5,511;417.
Plates Used: 170436, 170443.
Printing Press: sheet fed, Giori rotary press.
Art Competition/Entries: Open competition/184 entries.
Medium: Black and white wash drawing.
Other Data: C. G. Pritchard was an artist with the Nebraska
Game and Parks Commission at the time he won. He died shortly
after winning the contest.

ARTIST: Claremont G. Pritchard*

Issue No. 36   Year: 1969   Species: White-winged Scoter

First Day of Sale: July 1, 1969.
No. Sold/Revenue: 2,072,108/$6,216,324.
Plates Used: 170765, 170767.
Printing Press: sheet fed, Giori rotary press.
Art Competition/Entries: Open competition/218 entries.
Medium: Black and white wash drawing.
Other Data: Reece's art is depicted on the duck stamp for the
fourth time! This issue was the first to raise more than $6 million.

ARTIST: Maynard Reece(4)

Issue No. 37   Year: 1970   Species: Ross' Goose

First Day of Sale: July 1, 1970.
No. Sold/Revenue: 2,420,244/$7,260,732.
Plates Used: 171165, 171169..
Printing Press: sheet fed, Giori rotary press.
Art Competition/Entries: Open competition/148 entries.
Medium: watercolor painting.
Other Data: Bierly's third win, having 1956 and 1963 also to his credit. First stamp to have the art print produced in full color, and first time that the Fish and Wildlife Service allowed the art to be submitted in other than black and white. From this date forward, all stamps have been in color except the 1976 issue. First stamp to breach the $7 million mark in revenues.

ARTIST: Edward J. Bierly(3)

Issue No. 38   Year: 1971   Species: Cinnamon Teal

First Day of Sale: July 1, 1971.
No. Sold/Revenue: 2,445,977/$7,337,931.
Plates Used: 171586, 171587.
Printing Press: sheet fed, Giori rotary press.
Art Competition/Entries: Open competition/191 entries.
Medium: Wash.
Other Data: Reece's incredible fifth win. His work also appeared as stamps in 1948, 1951, 1959 and 1969. The last of the thirteen $3 duck stamps issued; raised record revenues, and sold the most stamps ever, totaling 2,445,000.

ARTIST: Maynard Reece(5)

Issue No. 39   Year: 1972   Species: Emperor Goose

First Day of Sale: July 1, 1972
No. Sold/Revenue: 2,183,981/$10,921,715.
Plates Used: 171862, 171864.
Printing Press: sheet fed, Giori rotary press.
Art Competition/Entries: Open competition/213 entries.
Medium: Watercolor painting.
Other Data: First $5 duck stamp, and while sales were less than the previous year, raised, more than $10 million due to the price increase. July 1, 1972 was a Saturday, so likely first day of sale was Monday, July 3, 1972.

ARTIST: Arthur M. Cook*

Issue No. 40   Year: 1973   Species: Steller's Eider

First Day of Sale: July 1, 1973.
No. Sold/Revenue: 2,094,414/$10,472,070.
Plates Used: 172101, 172102.
Printing Press: sheet fed, Giori rotary press.
Art Competition/Entries: Open competition/249 entries.
Medium: Opaque watercolor.
Other Data: LeBlanc's initial art endeavors included painting cartoon characters such as Bugs Bunny, Daffy Duck and Porky Pig. July 1, 1973 was a Sunday, so likely first day of sale was Monday, July 2, 1973.

ARTIST: Lee LeBlanc*

Issue No. 41   Year: 1974   Species: Wood Duck

First Day of Sale: July 1, 1974.
No. Sold/Revenue: 2,214,056/$11,070,280.
Plates Used: 172500, 172505.
Printing Press: sheet fed, Giori rotary press.
Art Competition/Entries: Open competition/291 entries.
Medium: Oil painting
Other Data: The first of two contest wins for artist Maass. He also finished in the top three positions four times prior to this win.

ARTIST: David Maass(1)

Issue No. 42   Year: 1975   Species: Canvasback (decoy)

First Day of Sale: July 1, 1975.
No. Sold/Revenue: 2,237,126/$11,185,630.
Plates Used: 172775, 172777.
Printing Press: sheet fed, Giori rotary press.
Art Competition/Entries: Open competition/268 entries.
Medium: Watercolor.
Other Data: The only stamp to depict a decoy. After this design was selected, contest rules were changed requiring living water-fowl to be featured. This design, along with the black Labrador depicted on the 1959 issue are each one of a kind to date, and were both the subject of considerable controversy. First stamp to raise more than $11 million for wetlands.

ARTIST: James P. Fisher*

Issue No. 43

Year: 1976

Species: Canada Goose

First Day of Sale: July 1, 1976.
No. Sold/Revenue: 2,170,194/$10,850,970.
Plates Used: 173029, 173030.
Printing Press: sheet fed, Giori rotary press.
Art Competition/Entries: Open competition/263 entries.
Medium: India ink scratchboard drawing.
Other Data: Second scratchboard medium to win the contest, and first black and white artwork selected since 1970. Instead of remarques, Magee produced nearly 1,000 "companion" miniature scratchboard drawings to go along with the special edition print run. He required two years to complete the miniature scratchboards.

ARTIST: Alderson "Sandy" Magee

Issue No. 44

Year: 1977

Species: Ross' Goose

First Day of Sale: July 1, 1977.
No. Sold/Revenue: 2,196,774/$10,983,870.
Plates Used: 173205, 173206.
Printing Press: sheet fed, Giori rotary press.
Art Competition/Entries: Open competition/271 entries.
Medium: Acrylic painting.
Other Data: The name of the stamp changed to "United States Migratory Bird Hunting and Conservation Stamp" to better reflect the full impact of the duck stamp program and to encourage non-hunters to purchase stamps.

ARTIST: Martin Murk

Issue No. 45

Year: 1978

Species: Hooded Merganser

First Day of Sale: July 1, 1978.
No. Sold/Revenue: 2,216,421/$11,082,105.
Plates Used: 173331, 173333.
Printing Press: sheet fed, Giori rotary press.
Art Competition/Entries: Open competition/295 entries.
Medium: Watercolor painting.
Other Data: First issue to depict a single bird. Last of the $5 duck stamps issued, of which there were seven. July 1, 1978 was a Saturday, so the likely first day of sale was Monday, July 3, 1978.

ARTIST: Albert Gilbert

Issue No. 46　　Year: 1979　　Species: Green-winged Teal

First Day of Sale: July 1, 1979.
No. Sold/Revenue: 2,090,155/$15,676,162.
Plates Used: 173422, 173423.
Printing Press: sheet fed, Giori rotary press.
Art Competition/Entries: Open competition/373 entries.
Medium: A gouache painting.
Other Data: First $7.50 stamp, and the first to raise more than $16 million for wetlands. This is the second time green-winged teal have appeared on a duck stamp; the other was in 1939. July 1, 1979 was a Sunday, so likely first day of sale was Monday, July 2, 1979.

ARTIST: Ken Michaelsen

Issue No. 47　　Year: 1980　　Species: Mallard

First Day of Sale: July 1, 1980.
No. Sold/Revenue: 2,045,114/$15,338,355.
Plates Used: 173492, 173493.
Printing Press: sheet fed, Giori rotary press.
Art Competition/Entries: Open competition/1,362 entries.
Medium: Acrylic painting
Other Data: First print to sell more than 7,000 copies, 12,950. All three finishers in the contest were from Minnesota at the time of the judging. The contest was widely advertised in art circles and drew a record number of entries, beating previous years by many times.

ARTIST: Richard Plasschaert

Issue No. 48　　Year: 1981　　Species: Ruddy Duck

First Day of Sale: July 1, 1981.
No. Sold/Revenue: 1,907,120/$14,303,400.
Plates Used: 173572, 173573.
Printing Press: sheet fed, Giori rotary press.
Art Competition/Entries: Open competition/1,507 entries
Medium: Gouache painting.
Other Data: Another year of a record number of contest entries. Ann D. Dohoney is the first woman to place in the top three finishers.

ARTIST: John S. Wilson

Issue No. 49   Year: 1982   Species: Canvasback

First Day of Sale: July 1, 1982.
No. Sold/Revenue: 1,926,253/$14,446,897.50
Plates Used: 173669, 173672.
Printing Press: sheet fed, Giori rotary press.
Art Competition/Entries: Open competition/2,099 entries
Medium: Oil painting.
Other Data: Maass' second win, the first occurring in 1974. Largest number of entrants in the Federal Contest of any date thus far, making this an incredible win. The second time the top three finishers in contest were from Minnesota at the time of the judging. Printing errors exist missing the orange and purple colors on the stamp.

ARTIST: David Maass(2)

Issue No. 50   Year: 1983   Species: Pintail

First Day of Sale: July 1, 1983.
No. Sold/Revenue: 1,867,998/$14,009,985.
Plates Used: 173765, 173767.
Printing Press: sheet fed, Giori rotary press.
Art Competition/Entries: Open competition/1,564 entries.
Medium: Acrylic painting.
Other Data: This was the 50th stamp issued, although not the 50th anniversary issue since the first year of issue 1934 plus 50 years is 1984, the next year's stamp. This was the first year that a $20 contest entry fee was put into effect.

ARTIST: Phil Scholer

Issue No. 51   Year: 1984   Species: American Wigeon

First Day of Sale: July 2, 1984.
No. Sold/Revenue: 1,913,861/$14,353,957.50.
Plates Used: 173871, 173872, 173873, 173874.
Printing Press: sheet fed, Giori rotary press.
Art Competition/Entries: Open competition/1,582 entries.
Medium: Watercolor painting.
Other Data: A Special Printing 50th Anniversary Issue, of 15 uncut, fully perforated sheets of 120 stamps was also printed and auctioned by an Act of Congress. Vertical and horizontal gutters exist between panes, and "50th Anniversary" is printed in gold on the selvage. Single stamps from this printing are identical to the normal stamps, so all such stamps must be accompanied by a certificate of authenticity. A record number of prints, 33,940 were published for the anniversary. The primary feathers were omitted from the original artwork due to the artist's photo reference being taken from a zoo. The stamp was revised to add the feathers. President Ronald Reagan proclaimed National Duck Stamp Week on July 3, 1984.

ARTIST: William C. Morris

Issue No. 52   Year: 1985   Species: Cinnamon Teal

First Day of Sale: July 1, 1985.
No. Sold/Revenue: 1, 780, 636/$13,354,770.
Plates Used: 174343,174350.
Printing Press: sheet fed, Giori rotary press.
Art Competition/Entries: Open competition/1,515 entries.
Medium: Watercolor painting.
Other Data: Error examples exist missing the blue color. This particular error was created by a paper splice, and only one pane with five stamps is known. This pane is in the collection of Jeanette Cantrell Rudy, and will be donated to the National Postal Museum.

ARTIST: Gerald Mobley

Issue No. 53   Year: 1986   Species: Fulvous Whistling Duck

First Day of Sale: July 1, 1986.
No. Sold/Revenue: 1,794,484/$13,458,630.
Plates Used: 176844, 176845.
Printing Press: sheet fed, Giori rotary press.
Art Competition/Entries: Open competition/1,242 entries
Medium: Acrylic painting.
Other Data: In addition to his painting, Moore is also an accomplished parachutist, diver, and avid collector of Civil War firearms. Last of the eight $7.50 stamps issued. Error examples exist missing the black engraved printing. Approximately 70 examples are believed to exist.

ARTIST: Burton E. Moore

Issue No. 54   Year: 1987   Species: Redheads

First Day of Sale: July 1, 1987.
No. Sold/Revenue: 1,663,470/$16,634,700.
Plates Used: 178171.
Printing Press: offset/intaglio D press.
Art Competition/Entries: Open competition/798 entries.
Medium: Acrylic painting.
Other Data: First $10 stamp issued. Only duck stamp to incorrectly name the Department of the Interior as "Department of Interior." First time an artist's hometown event was held, which took place in Onalaska, Wisconsin. First year BEP souvenir cards issued for federal duck stamps. BEP cards are in full color and come numbered, canceled, and mint.

ARTIST: Arthur Anderson

Issue No. 55   Year: 1988   Species: Snow Goose

First Day of Sale: July 3, 1988.
No. Sold/Revenue: 1,403,005/$14,030,050.
Plates Used: 180059.
Printing Press: offset/intaglio D press
Art Competition/Entries: Open competition/884 entries.
Medium: Acrylic painting.
Other Data: Last $10 stamp issued, which lasted only two years.
This duck stamp set the pace for the future of using airbrush techniques, and raised the bar considerably on the artwork quality needed to compete. The snow goose species has made one other appearance on a duck stamp, the 1947 issue. This was the last year artists were allowed to choose from an open field of species. Smith also won honors in the Mr. Minnesota body building contest, an interesting hobby for such a skilled artist.

ARTIST: Daniel Smith

Issue No. 56   Year: 1989   Species: Lesser Scaup

First Day of Sale: June 30, 1989.
No. Sold/Revenue: 1,415,882/$17,698,525.
Plates Used: 182531.
Printing Press: offset/intaglio D press.
Art Competition/Entries: Open competition/682.
Medium: Gouache painting.
Other Data: First $12.50 stamp. First win for Anderson who entered the contest five previous times, finishing second and third in two instances. Anderson now had the technique, and was destined to repeat in 1994. The first year only five species were eligible as entrants for the contest. They were black-bellied whistling duck, lesser scaup, spectacled eider, Barrow's goldeneye, and red-breasted merganser. According to the Fish and Wildlife Service, these were among several species which had never appeared on a federal duck stamp. This was an attempt to be certain all North American species were depicted by 2003. First stamp to raise more than $17 million.

ARTIST: Neal Anderson(1)

Issue No. 57   Year: 1990   Species: Black-Bellied Whistling Duck

First Day of Sale: June 30, 1990.
No. Sold/Revenue: 1,408,373/$17,604,662.50
Plates Used: 186307.
Printing Press: offset/intaglio D press.
Art Competition/Entries: Open competition/603 entries
Medium: Acrylic painting.
Other Data: At age 25, artist Jim Hautman became the youngest winner of the Federal Duck Stamp Contest to date. This was the fifth time he entered. He placed third in the 1987 contest. This win was to mark the beginning of the Hautman "dynasty", with either Jim, or brothers Joe or Bob winning four more times through 1999. Errors exist missing the back inscription. Errors must have full gum, since the writing is printed on top of the gum, and will disappear when washed off. Last $12.50 issue.

ARTIST: Jim Hautman(1)

Issue No. 58   Year: 1991   Species: King Eiders

First Day of Sale: June 30, 1991.
No. Sold/Revenue: 1,423,374/$21,350,610.
Plates Used: 188404.
Printing Press: offset/intaglio D press.
Art Competition/Entries: Open competition/626 entries
Medium: Acrylic painting.

Other Data: First and only woman to win the Federal Duck Stamp Contest. Howe is not only an artist, but also a sheep farmer and a model for the Orvis Company's catalogs. She had previously entered the contest about thirteen times without winning. There was a three-way tie for first place, and the judges decided on Howe's painting as the winner. This was the first $15 stamp, and first stamp to raise more than $21 million for wetlands conservation. Error stamps exist missing black engraved color. All known examples were discovered in the San Francisco, California area and approximately 6-10 stamps are believed to exist.

ARTIST: Nancy Howe

Issue No. 59   Year: 1992   Species: Spectacled Eiders

First Day of Sale: June 30, 1992.
No. Sold/Revenue: 1,347,393/$20,210,895.
Plates Used: 190493.
Printing Press: offset/intaglio D press.
Art Competition/Entries: Open competition/585 entries
Medium: Acrylic painting.

Other Data: First time a brother of a former winner won the contest. Joe is the older brother of Jim Hautman, winner in 1990. Joe also has a doctorate in physics and was a full-time post-doctoral researcher at the time of this win. The proceeds from winning helped him change careers from scientist to a full-time artist.

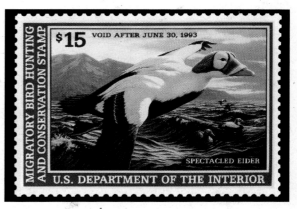

ARTIST: Joe Hautman

Issue No. 60   Year: 1993   Species: Canvasback

First Day of Sale: June 30, 1993.
No. Sold/Revenue: 1,402,569/$21,038,535.
Plates Used: 191659.
Printing Press: offset/intaglio D press.
Art Competition/Entries: Open competition/629 entries
Medium: Acrylic painting

Other Data: Fifth time a canvasback has been depicted on the stamp, the species most frequently featured on the federal duck stamp as of this date. Error examples exist missing black engraved printing. Approximately 150 examples are believed to exist, but 90 of these are in full panes of 30, or transition, which shows the gradual loss of the black engraved color. Bob Dumaine, co-author of this book served as one of the five judges for this contest.

ARTIST: Bruce Miller

Issue No. 61

Year: 1994

Species: Red-Breasted Mergansers

First Day of Sale: June 30, 1994.
No. Sold/Revenue: 1,466,366/$21,995,490.
Plates Used: 193700.
Printing Press: offset/intaglio D press.
Art Competition/Entries: Open competition/434 entries.
Medium: Gouache painting.
Other Data: Anderson's second win, a painting his children fondly refer to as "Punk Ducks" for the wild hairdo of the mergansers. The artist had first attempted to paint another species, and decided at the last minute to change to the red-breasted mergansers. Anderson, a Nebraska native, was also the sole artist for that state's duck stamps from 1991 through 1995.

ARTIST: Neal Anderson(2)

Issue No. 62

Year: 1995

Species: Mallards

First Day of Sale: July 1, 1995.
No. Sold/Revenue: 1,527,341/$22,910,115.
Plates Used: 195213.
Printing Press: offset/intaglio D press.
Art Competition/Entries: Open competition/585 entries.
Medium: Acrylic painting.
Other Data: Second win for Jim Hautman. The first time the winning painting receives a perfect score from the judges. Jim's brother Bob Hautman finished second in this same contest. This winning entry of mallards is the fourth time this species is featured on a duck stamp. First stamp to raise more than $22 million for wetlands.

ARTIST: Jim Hautman(2)

Issue No. 63

Year: 1996

Species: Surf Scoters

First Day of Sale: July 1, 1996.
No. Sold/Revenue: 1,559,926/$23,398,890.
Plates Used: 195744.
Printing Press: offset/intaglio D press.
Art Competition/Entries: Open competition/435 entries.
Medium: Oil painting.
Other Data: Features the Barnegat Lighthouse, only the second duck stamp to depict a lighthouse, the other was on the 1963 issue. First stamp to raise more than $23 million for wetlands.

ARTIST: Wilhelm Goebel

Issue No. 64

Year: 1997

Species: Canada Goose

First Day of Sale: June 21, 1997.
No. Sold/Revenue: 1,696,610/$25,449,150.*
Plates Used: 196441.
Printing Press: offset/intaglio F press.
Art Competition/Entries: Open competition/477 entries.
Medium: Acrylic painting.
Other Data: First time the third of three brothers won; Jim in 1990 and 1995, Joe in 1992.

First stamp to raise more than $25 million, but complete sales data is not available as of this date. The artist submitted a similar entry for the 1995 stamp, and finished second. For this entry, he added the marshland in the background, and it proved to be the difference.

*(Data through May 1999; on sale until June 30, 2000)

ARTIST: Robert Hautman

Issue No. 65

Year: 1998

Species: Barrow's Goldeneye

First Day of Sale: July 1, 1998.
No. Sold/Revenue:1,627,521/$24,412,815.*
Plates Used: 197573.
Printing Press: offset/intaglio F press.
Art Competition/Entries: Open competition/380 entries.
Medium: Acrylic painting.
Other Data: First year to issue a self-adhesive stamp in addition to the conventional gummed version. The artist finished second with a similar entry for the 1996 stamp, so he revised the artwork slightly. The artist accidentally sprayed too much protective varnish on the painting just prior to the mailing deadline, but it proved to be a good omen, and perhaps just the finishing touch the artwork needed to win.

*(Data through May 1999; on sale until June 30, 2001)

ARTIST: Robert Steiner

Issue No. 66

Year: 1999

Species: Greater Scaup

First Day of Sale: July 1, 1999.
No. Sold/Revenue:
Plates Used: 198654.
Printing Press: F press.
Art Competition/Entries: Open competition/337 entries
Medium: Acrylic painting
Other Data: The third win for Jim Hautman in ten years. Considering artists must wait until the fourth year after a win to re-enter, this is quite a feat. A boat, hunter and dog are shown in the artwork. The hunter is his brother Robert, who was winner of the preceding year's contest. Only the second time an entry has won with a perfect score, the other being Hautman in 1995.

ARTIST: Jim Hautman(3)

Duck Stamp Errors and Varieties

Printing mistakes seldom occur on federal duck stamps because of the low quantity printed and extra care taken by the BEP in their production. However, in any printing process mistakes can happen and we have tried to list some major and interesting anomalies. The following is not intended to be a complete list of all errors and varieties, but those of more value, popular with collectors, and known to the authors. Major errors differ from varieties by the gravity of the flaw. Imperforate and partially perforated stamps, wrong color, missing color, or inverted writing are all considered major errors. They can be identified by the letters "a" or "b" after the issue number. Varieties are identified by the letters "var" after the issue number.

Year	Issue	Description	Value In U.S. Dollars (Estimate)
1934	1a	Imperforate Pair, vertical examples	35,000
1934	1b	Imperforate Pair, lacking horizontal perforations only	35,000
1935	2var	Diagonally perforated plate block of 12, plate #131983, only example recorded	15,000
1936	3var	Paper Fold on bottom pns #134317, created crazy perforations in selvage	2,500
1940	7var	Paper Fold, wide pre-printing crease caused large unprinted section on stamp	2,500
1944	11var	Paper Fold, pre-printing crease created large diagonal unprinted section on stamp, possibly unique	3,000
1946	13a	Rose Red Error, normal color red brown, certificate of authenticity recommended, beware of fakes	20,000
1948	15var	Gutter Snipe, upper left corner block of four	750
1951	18var	Paper Fold, affects four stamps from plate #161228, lower left	2,000
1952	19var	Misperfed diagonally, full pane of 28, perforations diagonal through stamps. One pane believed to exist	3,000
1957	24a	Inverted back inscription, six examples known thus far; writing should be upright as face of stamp	5,000
1959	26a	Inverted back inscription, one known thus far, writing should be upright as face of stamp; valued accordingly	25,000
1967	34var	Plate number single, corner folded over during printing, portion of blank, probably unique	3,500
1970	37var	Color Shift, red color shift creates double feet, legs, beaks of ducks, fairly common	95
1972	39var	Faulty Plate, probably warped, causes vertical streaks of missing color creating the appearance of a rainstorm	125
1973	40var	Full Offset Image in Reverse on gum, small quantity believed to exist, image is complete and clear	500
1975	42var	Color Misregistration, lead duck has solid black head, cause unknown, very scarce	600
1977	44var	Full Offset in Reverse on gum, very clear, approximately 15 examples believed to exist	500
1980	47var	Color Shift, 3 to 4mm multicolor shift causes kaleidoscope of color, less than five believed to have survived	500

| 1981 | 48var | Color Shift downward, missing "void after June 30, 1982," all four known artist signed . . . . .750 |

| 1982 | 49a | Missing violet and orange color; less than ten examples believed to exist, beware of faked or altered stamps, must have certificate of authenticity . . . . .750 |

| 1982 | 49var | Color Shift, 5mm radical black shift, complete doubling of some areas, spectacular, four examples believed to exist . . . . .7500 |

| 1984 | 51var | Special Commemorative Issue authorized by Congress for the 50th Anniversary, only 1,800 stamps printed in 15 sheets of 120. Each sheet has four panes with vertical and horizontal gutters and a center gutter block. Sheet #15 resides in the National Postal Museum in Washington D.C. A Philatelic Foundation Certificate should accompany all singles certifying it as a special commemorative issue, with the plating position in pencil on reverse, as affixed by the Philatelic Foundation. |

Mint, NH single (1,800 possible) 350
Plate Block of 6 (60 possible) 3,800
Vertical Pair, Horizontal Gutter (120 possible) 950
Horizontal Pair, Vertical Gutter, (150 possible) 750
Center Gutter Block of four (15 possible) 6,000
Full Sheet of 4 panes (15 possible; 3 believed still intact) 45,000

| 1985 | 52a | Blue Color Omitted, Created as a result of sheet splice, which prompted a color shutoff, one pane exists, top row of five without blue; in National Postal Museum . . .65,000 |

| 1985 | 52var | Roller Flaw, foreign matter on felt creates ink starvation area which forms a 3mm tan circle with red dot, termed 'Shot Duck' variety . . . . .125 |

| 1985 | 52var | Color Shift, red orange color shifted down; duck appears to be floating on a 'Pool of Blood' . . . . 75 |

| 1986 | 53a | Missing Black Engraved, writing, denomination, eye of duck, and some feathers missing, 60-70 believed to exist . . . . .4,000 |

| 1986 | 53var | Color Shift, called 'Blind Duck' black shifted upward and other features 2 to 3mm moving eye out of socket . . . . .95 |

| 1987 | 54var | Severe Color Shift, causes collage of color and duplicate images . . . . .350 |

| 1988 | 55var | Color Shade, yellow to tan color; a contrasting color shade is deep rose color, possibly caused by ink distribution variation . . . . .50 |

| 1990 | 57a | Reverse Inscription Missing, back writing placed on top of gum omitted, 300 to 400 examples believed to exist gum . . . . .400 |

| 1990 | 57var | Color Shades, dull bluish gray shade and a contrasting deep lavender shade, possibly caused by ink distribution variation . . . . .50 |

| 1991 | 58a | Missing Black Engraved, highlight feathers on breast of both ducks missing black engraved (raised ink), six to eight examples believed to exist . . . . .12,500 |

| 1993 | 60a | Missing Black Engraved; ducks missing black engraved highlights, discovered in Hastings, Nebraska, 150 believed to exist . . . . .3,500 |

| 1993 | 60var | Roller Flaw, creates appearance of bug above hen's beak, hence termed 'firefly' variety; caused by roller dirt blocking color application . . . . .50 |

| 1993 | 60var | Color Shades, bright reddish brown shade and contrasting deep brown shade, caused by ink distribution . . . . .50 |

| 1995 | 62v2 | Color Shades, light greenish shade, and contrasting deep purple shade possibly caused by ink distribution variation . . . . .50 |

| 1996 | 63var | Frame Line Broken or Missing, caused by improper plate pressure wipe, common, many exist . . . . .35 |

| 1996 | 63var | Roller Flaw, extraneous object blocks color application, causing distinct 'Floating Bottle' shape in water . . . . .95 |

| 1997 | 64var | Plate Flaw, double breast feathers, possibly caused by plate deterioration. Examples exist with the flaw extending into the lake and bring a premium . . . . .125 |

Federal Duck Stamp Values (Values In U.S. Dollars)

| Issue Year | Species | Mint, NH Singles | | | | | Used & Artist Signed Singles | | |
		Fine +	VF	XF	Hinged F-VF	Plate Block	Unsigned No Gum	Artist Signed	Hunter Signed
1934	Mallards	450	750	1,200	275	12,500	150	3,000	110
1935	Canvasback	395	675	1,050	275	10,000	175	3,000	125
1936	Canada Geese	165	295	425	175	3,000	110	2,000	65
1937	Greater Scaup	125	250	350	85	2,250	85	2,000	50
1938	Pintails	125	325	850	150	2,500	85	2,500	50
1939	Green-winged Teal	115	195	295	85	2,000	60	2,500	40
1940	Black Ducks	115	195	295	85	1,750	65	2,500	40
1941	Ruddy Ducks	115	195	295	85	1,750	65	2,000	40
1942	Wigeon	115	195	295	85	1,750	65	2,000	40
1943	Wood Ducks	45	75	125	35	600	45	500	35
1944	White-fronted Geese	45	85	150	35	625	25	1,600	20
1945	Shovelers	39	65	95	30	425	28	550	15
1946	Redheads	39	45	75	30	300	22	250	13
1947	Snow Geese	29	45	75	30	275	22	1,750	13
1948	Buffleheads	29	50	85	25	350	20	125	13
1949	American Goldeneyes	35	60	95	30	375	22	125	13
1950	Trumpeter Swans	49	75	125	35	475	25	1,500	10
1951	Gadwalls	49	75	125	35	475	25	125	10
1952	Harlequins	49	75	125	35	475	25	350	10
1953	Blue-winged Teal	49	75	150	35	475	25	1,500	12
1954	Ring-necked Ducks	49	75	125	35	475	25	125	8
1955	Blue Geese	49	75	125	35	475	25	125	8
1956	American Mergansers	49	75	125	35	475	25	125	8
1957	American Eider	49	75	125	35	475	25	450	8
1958	Canada Geese	49	75	125	35	475	20	125	8
1959	Black Lab w/Mallard	65	95	150	50	450	35	150	8
1960	Redheads	59	85	110	45	395	30	125	8
1961	Mallards	59	85	110	45	425	30	150	8
1962	Pintails	69	95	125	55	450	40	150	8
1963	American Brant	69	90	110	50	450	40	150	8
1964	Nene Geese	69	95	150	50	2,000	40	150	8
1965	Canvasback	69	95	125	50	450	40	150	8
1966	Whistling Swans	69	95	125	50	450	40	150	8
1967	Oldsquaws	69	95	150	50	450	40	350	8
1968	Hooded Mergansers	45	55	75	35	275	25	2,500	8
1969	White-winged Scoters	45	55	75	30	250	20	110	5
1970	Ross' Geese	45	60	75	30	285	20	110	5
1971	Cinnamon Teal	29	40	55	20	195	20	75	6
1972	Emperor Geese	13	22	25	12	100	10	350	6
1973	Steller's Eiders	13	20	25	12	95	10	250	5
1974	Wood Ducks	13	18	25	12	85	8	50	5
1975	Canvasback / Decoy	9	15	20	9	60	7	225	5
1976	Canada Geese	9	15	22	8	50	7	30	5
1977	Ross' Geese	9	15	22	8	60	7	30	5
1978	Hooded Mergansers	9	12	18	8	50	7	25	5
1979	Green-winged Teal	10	12	18	8	50	7	25	5
1980	Mallards	12	15	18	8	50	7	25	5

Issue Year	Species	Mint, NH Singles					Used & Artist Signed Singles		
		Fine +	VF	XF	Hinged F-VF	Plate Block	Unsigned No Gum	Artist Signed	Hunter Signed
1981	Ruddy Ducks	12	15	18	8	50	7	25	5
1982	Canvasbacks	12	15	18	8	50	7	25	5
1983	Pintails	12	15	18	8	50	7	25	5
1984	Wigeon	12	15	18	8	50	7	50	5
1985	Cinnamon Teal	12	15	20	8	50	7	25	5
1986	Fulvous Whistling Duck	12	15	20	8	50	7	25	5
1987	Redheads	14	15	20	11	50	10	25	7
1988	Snow Goose	14	15	20	11	50	10	25	7
1989	Lesser Scaup	15	18	20	12	65	12	25	7
1990	Black-bellied Whistling Duck	14	16	20	9	75	12	25	7
1991	King Eiders	18	22	30	15	85	14	30	7
1992	Spectacled Eiders	18	22	25	15	85	14	30	7
1993	Canvasbacks	18	22	25	15	85	14	30	9
1994	Red-breasted Merganser	18	20	22	15	85	14	30	9
1995	Mallards	18	20	22	15	85	14	30	9
1996	Surf Scoter	18	20	22	15	85	14	30	9
1997	Canada Goose	18	20	22	15	85	14	30	9
1998	Barrow's Goldeneye	18	20	22	15	85	14	30	9
	Self-adhesive	18	20	20	15	85	14	30	9
1999	Greater Scaup	18	20	22	15	85	14	30	9
	Self-adhesive	18	20	20	15	85	14	30	9
	Totals:	3,607	5,739	8,977	2,731	53,325	1,994	36,760	1,059

The total reflects what a collector should expect to spend
to aquire one specimen of each stamp of a given condition.

Federal Duck Stamp Print Values _(Values In U.S. Dollars)_

Year	1st Ed.	1st Ed. Remq.	2nd Ed.	2nd Ed. Remq.	3rd Ed.	
1934	6,000					
1935	9,000					
1936	1,000					
1937	2,200					
1938	3,200					
1939	10,000		7,250			
1940	13,000		8,000		4,750	
1941	4,000		1,700			
1942	1,750		850			
1943	1,500		550			
1944	2,750		1,300			
1945	7,500					
1946	1,750		225			
1947	2,450					
1948	1,600		1,000		600	
1949	2,400	3,250	300			
1950	1,550		500			
1951	1,150		700			
1952	2,250		300			
1953	2,000		250			
1954	1,500		300	425		
1955	1,300		550			
1956	1,050		950			
1957	1,300		300		175	
1958	1,150		800		300	
1959	5,500		3,000		2,800	
1960	875		600		500	
1961	1,500					
1962	1,500					
1963	1,100		900			
1964	1,100		800			
1965	800		500		250	
1966	1,200		500			
1967	1,200		1,200			
1968	1,000					
1969	1,000					
1970	2,150	2,750	500			
1971	3,500					
1972	1,850	3,000	250			
1973	2,100	2,400	225			
1974	1,100					
1975	1,100	1,500				
1976	750		1,300			
1977	400	550				
1978	425	750				
1979	425		425			
1980	350					
1981	175					
1982	250					
1983	250					
1984	135					
1985	200		425			
1986	135					
1987	150					
1988	150					
1989	175					
1990	175					
1991	200					
1992	135					
1993	135					
1994	135					
1995	175					
1996	135					
1997	135					
1998	175					
1999	179					

3rd Ed. Remq.	4th Ed.	Medallion	Executive	Canvas Transfer	Presidential
	500				
	500 (b&w)	1,000 (color)			
500					
		700			
		250			
		225			
		175			
		200			
		250	1,750		
		250	800		
		250	650		
		275	625		
		250	650		
		275	650		
		250	650		
		225	650		
		275	650	500	
		275	750		
		275	750		1,000
		329	950		1,200

Bibliography

Allen, Frederick Lewis, *Only Yesterday,* (New York: Bantam Books, 1946).

Amick, George, *Linn's U.S. Stamp Yearbook 1997,* (Sidney, Ohio: Amos Press, 1998)

Amick, George, *Linn's U.S. Stamp Yearbook 1992,* (Sidney, Ohio: Amos Press, 1993)

Amick, George, *Linn's U.S. Stamp Yearbook 1995,* (Sidney, Ohio: Amos Press, 1996).

Amick, George, *Linn's U.S. Stamp Yearbook 1990,* (Sidney, Ohio: Amos Press, 1991)

Amick, George, *Ding and the Ducks,* Scotts Stamp Monthly, Vol. 2, No. 7, 8 (May 1984).

Bean, Michael J., *The Evolution of National Wildlife Law,* (New York: Praeger, 1983).

Castenholz, Bill J., *An Introduction to Revenue Stamps,* (Pacific Palisades: Castenholz & Sons, 1994).

Chadwick, Douglas H., *Sanctuary, U.S. National Wildlife Refuges,* National Geographic, Vol. 190, No. 4 (October 1996):2-35.

Cleveland, Grover, *Fishing and Shooting Sketches,* (New York: The Outing Publishing Co., 1906).

Cotton, Ira W., *The Duck Stamp Phenomenon,* The Congress Book 1995, Sixty-First American Philatelic Congress (August 25, 1995).

Cronon, William, *Changes in the Land,* (New York: Hill and Wang, 1983).

Dague, William E., *Duck Stamps: Helping to Save America,* The American Philatelist (December 1984):1203-1204.

Darling, J.N. Ding, *The Story of the Wildlife Refuge Program,* National Parks Magazine (January-March 1954):6-10, 43-46.

Darling, J.N. Ding, *The Story of the Wildlife Refuge Program, Part II,* National Parks Magazine (April-June, 1954):53-56, 86-91.

Day, Albert M., *North American Waterfowl* (New York: Stackpole and Heck, Inc., 1949).

Dickson, Jim, *Duck Art Dynasty,* The Minnesota Volunteer (July-August, 1997):18-25.

Doherty, Jim, *Sleek painted ducks lay golden eggs for wild-life artists,* Smithsonian, Vol. 13 (June 1982):67-73.

Dolin, Eric Jay, *Environmental Issues.* The American Philatelist, Vol. 112, No. 12 (December 1998):1122-1126.

Dolin, Eric Jay, *Bucks for Ducks,* American Philatelist, Vol. 111, No. 8 (August 1997):728-740.

Dolin, Eric Jay, *The U.S. Fish and Wildlife Service,* (New York: Chelsea House Publishers, 1989).

Drabelle, Dennis, *The National Wildlife Refuge System,* in Amos Eno, ed., Audubon Wildlife Report, 1985 (New York: National Audubon Society, 1985).

Duck Tracks (1994-1999), published by the National Duck Stamp Collectors Society, Delaware.

Dumaine, Bob, *Linn's Stamp News,* numerous Duck Stamp columns from 1989-1999.

Eno, Amos S., Roger L. Di Silvestro, and William J. Chandler, *Audubon Wildlife Report 1986,* (New York: The National Audubon Society, 1986).

Faiad, Andrea and Cathy Clauson, *The Luck of the Duck,* U.S. Art (August 1994).

Fox, Stephen R., *The American Conservation Movement,* (Madison, Wisconsin: University of Wisconsin Press, 1985).

Gabrielson, Ira N., *Wildlife Refuges,* (New York: The Macmillan Company, 1943):12.

Gillespie, Nancy, *Answering the Call of the Wild,* Art of the West (September/October 1996):42-48.

Gilmore, Jene C., *Art for Conservation, The Federal Duck Stamps,* (Barre: Barre Publishers, 1971):10.

Hazelton, William C., *Lake Koshkonong – Historical and Sporting,* in William C. Hazelton, ed., Wildfowling Tales From the Great Ducking Resorts of the Continent, (Chicago: William C. Hazelton, 1921).

Hawkins, A.S., R.C. Hanson, H.K. Nelson, and H.M. Reeves, editors, *Flyways: Pioneering Waterfowl Management in North America,* (Washington, D.C.: U.S. Department of Interior and the Fish and Wildlife Service, 1984).

Holland, Linda, *A Golden Anniversary,* Field & Stream (March 1984).

Holland, Ray P., *Bulletin of the American Game Protective Association,* in Field & Stream (July 1920).

Holland, Ray P., *A Law At Last!,* Field & Stream (May, 1934): 28-29, 66.

Hollingsworth, John and Karen, *Seasons of the Wild,* (Bellvue, Colorado: Worm Press, 1994).

Iker, Sam, *The World's Richest Art Competition,* National Wildlife Magazine (December/January 1979):41-43.

Johnson, Laurence F., *Federal Duck Stamp Story: Fifty Years of Excellence,* (Davenport, Iowa: Alexander & Company, 1984).

Judge, Gillian, *Understanding the basics on collecting stamp prints, with expert Russell Fink,* U.S. Art (May/June 1991):70-73, 84.

Lendt, David L., *Ding,* (Iowa: Iowa University Press, 1989).

Mathiessen, Peter, *Wildlife in America,* (New York: Viking, 1987):303.

McCaddin, Joe, *Duck Stamps and Prints: The Complete Federal and State Editions,* (City: Park Lane, 1988).

McBride, David P., *The Federal Duck Stamps,* (Piscataway, NJ: Winchester Press, 1984).

Missouri v. Holland, Supreme Court of the United States (collected cases, pp. 433-435).

National Gallery of Art, *National Gallery of Art, Washington* (London: Thames and Hudson, 1995).

Price, Jennifer, *Flight Maps,* (New York: Basic Books, 1999).

Quarles, E.A., *Bulletin of the American Game Protective Association,* Forest and Stream (May 1919).

Reiger, George, *The Wings of Dawn: The Complete Book of North American Waterfowling,* (New York: Stein and Day, 1980).

Richard, Paul, *Magee: Artistic Success on the Wings of a Duck,* The Washington Post (October 31, 1975):B7.

Richoux, Howard, *Fish, Game, Nature, and Society Catalog,* (February 1997 – hard copy and CD ROM).

Ruscoe, Michael, *American Waterfowl,* (New York: Hugh Lauter Levin Associates, Inc., 1989).

Sam Houston Duck Company, *A Specialized Duck Stamp Catalogue,* (Houston, Texas, 1997, 1998).

Shoemaker, Carl D., *The Stories Behind the Organization of the National Wildlife Federation and its Early Struggles for Survival,* (Washington D.C.: Carl D. Shoemaker, 1960).

Stearns, Jean Pride and Russell A. Fink, *A Catalog of the Duck Stamp Prints with Biographies of the Artists,* (privately published, 1985).

The Duck Report (1992-1999), published by Sam Houston Duck Company, Houston, Texas.

Thoreau, Henry David, *Thoreau on Birds,* Notes on New England Birds from the Journals of Henry David Thoreau, introduction by John Hay (Boston, Massachusetts: Beacon Press, 1993).

Tonelli, Donna, *Portrait of a Master,* Ducks Unlimited (January/February 1999):16.

Torre, David R., *1999 Specialized Catalog of U.S. Non-Pictorial Waterfowl Stamps,* (Santa Rosa, California: David R. Torre, 1998).

Torre, David R., *The fish and game stamps of Marion County, Kansas,* The American Revenuer, Vol. 47, No. 6 (June 1993):152-172.

Trefethen, James B., *An American Crusade for Wildlife,* (New York: Winchester Press and the Boone and Crockett Club, 1975).

Turbak, Gary, *Those Million-Dollar Ducks,* American Legion Magazine (January 1988):36-37.

Udall, Stewart, *The Quiet Crisis,* (New York: Avon Books, 1963).

U.S. Census Bureau, *Statistical Abstracts of the United States,* (September 16, 1998).

U.S. Postal Service, *The Postal Service Guide to U.S. Stamps (1996 Stamp Values),* (Washington, D.C.: U.S. Postal Service, 1995).

U.S. Fish and Wildlife Service, Office of Migratory Bird Management, Harvest Survey (May 1999).

U.S. Fish and Wildlife Service, The Duck Stamp Image Library (www.fws.gov/r9dso/rw1.html)

Weed, Clarence M., and Ned Dearborn, *Birds in Their Relation to Man,* (Philadelphia: J.B. Lippincott Company, 1903).

Weidensaul, Scott, *Duck Stamps, Art in the Service of Conservation,* (New York: Gallery Books, 1989).

Williams, L.N., *Fundamentals of Philately,* (State College: American Philatelic Society, 1990).

Williams, Ted, *Miss America Contest of Wildlife Art,* Audubon: (July 1990) 22,24,26,28-29.

Williamson, Lonnie, *50 Years of Duck Stamps,* Outdoor Life (July 1984):53, 62-66.

Worster, Donald, *Dust Bowl, The Southern Plains in the 1930s,* (New York: Oxford University Press, 1979).

Wunderly, Kathleen. *What Is This Word Philately?,* American Philatelist (June 1999).

Index

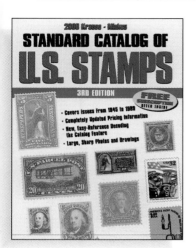
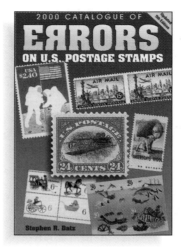
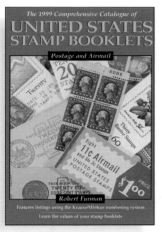

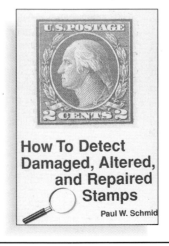

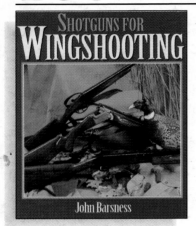